HAWKER
HURRICANE

1935 onwards (all marks)

COVER CUTAWAY: Hawker Hurricane Mk I. *Mike Badrocke*

First published in August 2010

A catalogue record for this book is available from the British Library

ISBN 978 1 84425 955 7

Library of Congress control no. 2010924918

Published by Haynes Publishing, Sparkford, Yeovil, Somerset BA22 7JJ, UK
Tel: 01963 442030 Fax: 01963 440001
Int. tel: +44 1963 442030 Int. fax: +44 1963 440001
E-mail: sales@haynes.co.uk
Website: www.haynes.co.uk

Haynes North America Inc.
861 Lawrence Drive, Newbury Park,
California 91320, USA

Printed and bound in the USA

Acknowledgements

The assistance of several pilots and owners in the Hawker Hurricane preservation and historical research world was of great help in compiling this book. Appreciation is particularly made to the members of the Battle of Britain Memorial Flight (BBMF) at RAF Coningsby, Lincolnshire, who are responsible for keeping two historic Hurricanes in airworthy condition in Britain. These aircraft form the main focus of this book. A specific vote of thanks is made to two pilots from the BBMF who are very well acquainted with the Hurricane – the current Officer Commanding BBMF, Squadron Leader Ian Smith, and Squadron Leader (Retd) Clive Rowley, for their observations on piloting the Hurricane. Thanks are similarly given to private owners of airworthy Hurricanes, including Peter Vacher and Guy Black, and to the owner of an on-going Hurricane restoration project, Tony Dyer. Professionals in the aircraft restoration business were also of great assistance, particularly Tony Ditheridge of Hawker Restorations Limited, who is very much in the front-line of the high standards of workmanship that are to be seen in several currently airworthy Hurricanes, and to Clive Denny of Vintage Fabrics. A number of historians in Britain and elsewhere in the world were of great assistance with information and rare photographs, including Nikolay Baranov, John Batchelor, David Harvey, Alexey Goss, John Levesley (of the Friends of the New Forest Airfields Association – FONFA), Lucy Maynard, Jim Smith, Andy Sweet, Didier Waelkens (of IPMS Belgium), and Peter Walter. Particular thanks to Jim Douthwaite, and Classic Aero Limited, for many detail photographs and images of Hurricane restoration in progress. Grateful thanks are also expressed to Richard Paver and Keith Wilson for the superb air-to-air photographs of preserved Hurricanes that grace this book. Assistance with photographic material was additionally provided by the RAF Museum (London), at Hendon, in particular by Andrew Renwick, Curator of Photographs, and his staff. Last but by no means least, Louise Blackah and Victor Lowe worked with great enthusiasm behind the scenes on the preparation of this book and in checking text and proofs. Thank you from the co-authors to all these contributors.

HAWKER HURRICANE

1935 onwards (all marks)

Owners' Workshop Manual

An insight into owning, flying and maintaining
the RAF's classic single-seat fighter

Paul Blackah, Malcolm V. Lowe and Louise Blackah

Contents

6 Introduction

34 The Hurricane Story

Hurricane: Variations on a theme –
  Hurricane Mk I, II, IIa, IIb, IIc, IId, IIe, III, IV, V 39
Canadian-built Hurricanes 46
Sea Hurricane – Mk Ia, Ib, Ic, IIc, XIIa 46
Two-seat Hurricanes 50
Other Hurricane versions and projects 52
Foreign employment and manufacture 54
Hurricane facts and figures 65
Hurricane weaponry 66
Hurricane aces 71
Power for the Hurricane 74

78 Restore to Flight

How do refurbished Hurricanes differ
  from their original state? 80
Restoring a Hurricane – Tony Ditheridge 81
Aspects of restoration 83
Fabric covering – Clive Denny 84

86 Anatomy of the Hurricane

120 The BBMF's Hurricanes

Hurricane Mk IIc, LF363 122
Hurricane Mk IIc, PZ865 125
Power for the BBMF's Hurricanes 128

130 The Owners' Views

Acquiring a Hurricane 132
Case History 1
  Peter Vacher and Hurricane Mk I, R4118 132
Case History 2
  Guy Black and Hurricane Mk XII, Z5140 135
Case History 3
  Tony Dyer: Build and own your
  own Hurricane 137

142 The Pilots' Views

Displaying the BBMF's Hurricanes –
  Squadron Leader Ian Smith,
  Officer Commanding, BBMF 144
Flying and displaying the Hurricane –
  Squadron Leader Clive Rowley 147
The RAF's point of view in 1938 –
  Squadron Leader J.W. Gillan 151

158 The Engineer's View

Thoughts of a Hurricane ground engineer –
  Paul Blackah MBE 160
Safety first 160
Tools and working facilities 161
Recommended lubricants and fluids 161
Servicing the Hurricane 161
Keeping records 165

166 Appendices

Appendix I Airworthy Hurricanes 166
Appendix II Glossary of Terms and
      Abbreviations 170
Appendix III Useful Contacts 172

174 Index

OPPOSITE Canadian-built Hawker Hurricane Mk XII, Z5140, is owned and operated by the Historic Aircraft Collection, Duxford. *(Keith Wilson/SFB Photographic)*

Introduction

The Hawker Hurricane was one of Britain's finest and most successful fighter aircraft of the Second World War. It was one of Britain's principal fighter and ground-attack aircraft and a worthy adversary to its Axis opponents. A contemporary of the legendary Supermarine Spitfire, the Hurricane fought alongside the Spitfire in the Battle of Britain and was one of the few high-performance front-line aircraft to remain in service for the entire war.

OPPOSITE Sleek and streamlined when compared to the biplanes that preceded it, the Hurricane was a major step forward in Britain's rearmament in the late-1930s. The original prototype, K5083, shows a mixture of prototype and production features in this 1937 view, including the early-style radio mast behind the cockpit and landing and navigation lights in the wings, plus the production layout for the under-fuselage radiator fairing. *(RAF Museum/Charles E. Brown Collection)*

The Hawker Hurricane is an aircraft with a quintessential British aviation pedigree. Designed and built by one of the country's celebrated aircraft manufacturers, Hawker Aircraft Limited, of Kingston upon Thames, it was heir to an outstanding tradition of aviation design and construction that can be traced back to the superlative Sopwith Camel fighter of the First World War. The inter-war period saw Hawker become one of the world's most important producers of high-performance, state-of-the-art, biplane combat aircraft, culminating in the magnificent Hawker Fury, which is held by many to be the finest expression of the fighter biplane. As a continuation of that great tradition, the Hurricane proved to be a worthy successor, and established a combat record for itself in the Second World War which included its crucial role during that most significant of all aerial conflicts, the Battle of Britain in 1940.

A rugged and dependable workhorse, the Hurricane gained many battle honours for its various users, and fought in virtually every battleground of the Second World War. Yet fame has come at a price for the Hurricane, and it has often been – both at the time and subsequently – overshadowed by that most famous of all piston-engined fighters, the Supermarine Spitfire. Nevertheless, the Hurricane thoroughly deserves its place in aviation's hall of fame, and the popularity of the type today as a 'warbird', and the affection with which it is held by many, is a rightful testimony to the aircraft's significant place in British military history.

The Hurricane was destined from the start to become one of Britain's great fighter aircraft, and it was thanks to the willingness of the far-sighted designers at Hawker to press ahead with continuing design improvements – which had begun with their excellent biplanes of the late 1920s and early 1930s – that the Hurricane came about. Hawker Aircraft Limited was created in 1933 out of the former H. G. Hawker Engineering Co. Ltd, which in itself could trace a direct link to the Sopwith Aviation Company that had become famous in the First World War for such important aircraft as

Why the Hurricane Mk IIc version was chosen for this book

The Mk IIc version of the Hurricane series was chosen as the focus of this manual for a number of reasons: first and foremost, the Mk IIc model is the mark of Hurricane that is flown by the RAF's Battle of Britain Memorial Flight. The two Hurricanes of this unit, serial numbers LF363 and PZ865, are among the best-known and most-loved by the public of the currently airworthy Hurricanes anywhere in the world. These two aircraft are genuine Hawker-built Hurricanes, with PZ865 being the very last Hurricane that was manufactured. LF363 saw important RAF service, while PZ865 fulfilled a number of roles for the manufacturer and also had a spell post-Second World War as a racing aircraft. Both are extremely valuable historic aircraft, which always draw much interest and admiration from those who see them performing at air shows. Indeed, both aircraft have been well-known participants at air shows and commemorative events throughout Britain for many years, and a great deal of the affection shown to these aircraft stems from them being authentic, priceless and irreplaceable reminders of the great aerial victory achieved by the RAF during the Battle of Britain in 1940. For these reasons alone they are worthy of being the focus of this book. The Mk IIc is also a well-documented version of the Hurricane, for which a large amount of information and background material exists. It is arguably one of the most important versions of the fighter, and was built in larger numbers than any other sub-variant. As a result, much of the documentation and photography in this manual concentrates specifically on this particularly remarkable version and its history and engineering.

Keeping the two Hurricane Mk IIc aircraft of the Battle of Britain Memorial Flight in the air is made possible by a dedicated team of ground crew and pilots. It is very much a labour of love, but they also perform a professional role that demands skill, knowledge and experience. The representation of that effort on the following pages is a testament to their devoted work, and another good reason why these aircraft are the subject matter of much of what is to be found in this volume. One of the co-authors, Paul Blackah, works on these Hurricanes on a daily basis, giving him a unique position from which to describe many of the technical aspects.

the Pup, Triplane and Camel – the latter, in particular, being a significant contributor to the eventual Allied victory. In 1920 Thomas Sopwith had closed the business through voluntary liquidation and created the new H. G. Hawker company (named after one of his test pilots and co-founder of the new enterprise) in the same year. Through the 1920s and into the 1930s, H. G. Hawker grew to become one of the main suppliers of combat aircraft to the RAF, due in part to the hiring of several talented designers, the chief of whom was Sydney Camm. Responsible with the increasingly able Hawker design team for biplanes such as the Hart light bomber, Nimrod sea-going fleet fighter and the beautiful Fury, Camm became one of the most important aircraft designers in Britain. The original Fury (initially named Hornet) first flew in May 1929, and the type entered service with the RAF's No 43 Squadron at Tangmere, Sussex, during May 1931. It was the RAF's first fighter capable of exceeding 200mph in level flight.

The creation of Hawker Aircraft Limited in 1933 saw the new company taking over much of the facilities of the former H. G. Hawker, including design and prototype construction shops at Canbury Park Road, Kingston upon Thames, and the airfield at Brooklands, near Weybridge, Surrey. Brooklands was becoming increasingly important not only as a company airfield, but as a car-racing circuit as well, with its distinctive, partly banked motor-racing track being famous worldwide.

During this period a number of Air Ministry Specifications were issued in Britain which, although intending to push forward the frontiers of what was achievable with fighter design, were unable to produce a fighter that was sufficiently advanced to compete with the combat aircraft that ominously were beginning to take shape in Germany. Hawker was one of the main companies involved in trying to meet these new specifications, with the holy grail of a maximum speed of 250mph being a major, but difficult objective to achieve. The Hurricane is often traced back to the issue of Specification F.7/30, which called for an interceptor fighter with a top speed of 250mph at 10,000ft, an armament probably of four guns, out of reach of the pilot (then a novel idea), and an in-service

date of 1934. In the event, these Air Ministry requirements were never fully addressed, but as an interim, and by a long drawn-out process, the Gloster Gladiator radial-engined biplane fighter emerged later in the 1930s as the RAF's first 250mph fighter and met some of these early criteria.

Fighter design in those days was starting to draw in many new ideas, and forward-looking designers were quick to take up some of the new concepts, including the enclosed cockpit, retractable undercarriage, and all-metal construction and skinning. The most important concept of all was the idea of the sleek, streamlined, low-wing monoplane, rather than the now long-in-the-tooth braced biplane layout. Both Hawker and Supermarine readily embraced these new concepts, probably much more readily than some other companies. Good designer as he was, Camm was continually looking at ways to advance the art of fighter design, and even as the Fury was entering service he was examining ways to improve on the design and incorporate the new thinking that was to be expressed in his future projects.

It is interesting to note that the design

evolution at Hawker that was to lead on to the creation of the Hurricane was taking place at about the same time that designers at Vickers Supermarine, notably the celebrated R. J. Mitchell, were working virtually from a blank sheet of paper to come up with the Spitfire. Supermarine had no long-standing pedigree of production RAF fighter designs, unlike Hawker, but did have the superbly streamlined and successful Schneider Trophy monoplane seaplane layout to draw from. On the other hand, Hawker designers had little experience of working with the low-wing monoplane layout, being instead more familiar with the biplane. In essence, both the Hurricane and the Spitfire were to owe much of their subsequent success, and indeed their beautifully streamlined fuselage profiles, to the development work that was being undertaken by aero-engine manufacturer Rolls-Royce. Drawing, like Hawker, on years of experience in design and evolution, in the early 1930s Rolls-Royce developed the engine layout that was to mature into the Merlin. This engine type went on to power all production Hurricanes and many Spitfires (in addition to other types) and was a war-winner in its own right.

Rolls-Royce's own engine evolution dated back to the First World War, with inline engine development in the post-war period drawing on the success of the Eagle, among others. This evolutionary process had gained particular stimulus as a result of the Schneider Trophy races of the 1920s and early 1930s. To power Britain's seaplanes created by Supermarine for the final three of these races, Rolls-Royce devised special, high-performance, inline racing engines that achieved great results. At the same time, Sydney Camm was developing a close relationship with Rolls-Royce, and the beautifully streamlined Hawker Fury was powered by an engine type closely linked to Rolls-Royce's advances in inline engine design and manufacture: the Kestrel inline engine, formerly known as the F.XI. The use of the Kestrel in the Fury successfully broke the RAF's tendency to operate radial-engined fighters, and paved the way for Hawker's future fighters to be powered by the best available Rolls-Royce inline engine.

There were, therefore, two developing lines of excellence in Britain in the early 1930s – one in engine design and the other in fighter aircraft design – which were to culminate in the creation of the Hurricane and Spitfire. These two aircraft evolved in very different ways: in the case of the Hurricane it was a gradual evolution from biplane to monoplane; with the Spitfire it was basically a new aircraft layout without the pedigree of a string of already successful front-line aircraft behind it. Camm and his design colleagues at Hawker continued to refine their fighter design activities to follow on from the successful Fury, spurred on by contact with members of the Air Ministry and RAF (both of which had a far greater sense of the urgent need for rearmament than the politicians of the day), and helped by official Specifications. Important among these was Specification F.5/34, which was devised largely to cover developments that both companies were achieving on paper, although it must

BELOW The Hurricane prototype, K5083, is seen here at Brooklands in a very early form prior to its first flight. Noteworthy are the early-style cockpit canopy, lack of radio mast, additional hinged doors for main wheel covers, and a small bracing strut beneath the vertical tail. (Hawker Aircraft Ltd)

be stressed that Supermarine and Hawker did not liaise – there was too much at stake commercially for each business.

Specification F.5/34 included the need for a six-gun armament, and also referred in general terms for the first time to a maximum speed of approximately 300mph. This was potentially the new Holy Grail, and one that was looking more likely due to developments at Rolls-Royce, where the new PV.12 inline engine was showing much promise. Indeed, a specially converted Hawker Hart was used in some of the development flying for the PV.12, which eventually evolved into the immortal Merlin engine. Hawker's approach to the creation of the new fighter for the RAF, which effectively would be a Fury successor, was all about bringing the monoplane layout to fruition. Nevertheless, the evolving design on the Hawker drawing boards still drew on some of the aspects that had been important in the established series of Hawker biplanes, including a fabric covering over a metal framework. The fuselage of the new monoplane fighter looked at the time – and still does – remarkably like that of the Fury, and the tail surfaces are similar. At first Hawker internally referred to the new design as the Fury Monoplane, later the Interceptor Monoplane, and detailed information was submitted to the Air Ministry in August 1934. That month a new Specification, F.36/34,

was drawn up around Hawker's ambitious but very acceptable proposals, and detailed design work led to manufacturing drawings reaching the Hawker experimental department for construction of a prototype to begin in November 1934, Hawker's detailed proposals having been formally tendered to the Air Ministry in the September.

On 6 November 1935, at Brooklands, the prototype Hurricane made its first flight. This was four months before the maiden flight of the Supermarine Spitfire, which took place at Eastleigh on 5 March 1936. That Britain had these two excellent aircraft available for front-line service by the start of the Second World War, in September 1939, is unquestionably a major factor in the country's survival of the German aerial onslaught in 1940; without these fighters and the brave pilots who flew them the outcome could have been very different.

The test pilot for the Hurricane's first flight was Hawker's P. W. S. 'George' Bulman. All went well with the initial testing. Official trials with the Aeroplane and Armament Experimental Establishment (A&AEE) at Martlesham Heath, in Suffolk, revealed a maximum speed of 315mph at 15,000ft, making the Hurricane the first RAF fighter to reach the almost mythical 300mph barrier. Power for the prototype was provided by a Merlin 'C' engine, the PV.12 having now taken on the Merlin name with which it was to

become famous. The new aircraft looked sleek and advanced, but with some of the traditional features still present, such as the fabric-covered outer wing sections and fabric-covered rear fuselage over wooden stringers – all of which had the appearance of early 1930's technology. Nevertheless, the strong construction that lay beneath the fabric was to prove useful in later years, when the Hurricane was shown to be rugged and capable of surviving a considerable mauling in combat. It also turned out to be comparatively easy to repair, compared to the Spitfire's more advanced, but less easily patched-up, all-metal monocoque fuselage construction. Later production Hurricanes were

fitted with all-metal wings, which were also retrofitted to some surviving early production examples that originally had fabric-covered outer wings.

The name Hurricane was officially approved for Hawker's new fighter by the Air Ministry in June 1936. A considerable amount of deliberation at the highest levels went into the allocation of funds for the production go-ahead of the new fighter, and indeed, as an interim measure, a further batch of Hawker Fury biplane fighters was ordered. Known as the Fury II, these had a more powerful Kestrel engine and other minor refinements. The Hurricane and Spitfire came to play a large part in the expansion schemes of the British armed forces as the 1930s wore on, despite the now-notorious lack of reality among many politicians and members of the public in the face of the growing threat from Nazi Germany.

An initial production batch of 600 Hurricane Mk I aircraft was ordered from Hawker in June 1936 – it was to be the first of many substantial orders. Hawker had successfully proven the possibility for the installation of four machine-guns in each wing, making the Hurricane the first true eight-gun fighter

ABOVE The Hurricane prototype underwent a considerable amount of detail change during its flight-testing and initial military evaluation. Evident in this view is the altered cockpit canopy and developing shape of the under-fuselage radiator housing and intake, the latter taking some time to perfect. *(RAF Museum)*

RIGHT The metal framework with wood stringers construction of the rear fuselage is well illustrated in this view of early Mk I Hurricanes. The fabric covering would be attached over the rear fuselage, a facet of Hurricane construction that remained constant throughout the production life of the type. These L-series serial number Hurricanes are being built at the Hawker factory at Canbury Park Road in Kingston upon Thames during 1938. *(Hawker Aircraft Ltd)*

LEFT The initial and early production standard of the Hurricane Mk I is evident in this view of K5083 in a late stage of its development flying in 1937 at Martlesham Heath. Also particularly evident are the aircraft's fabric-covered rear fuselage and wing surfaces, the latter now featuring the shape of gun-bay cover used on the early production aircraft which also had fabric-covered outer-wing panels. *(RAF Museum/Charles E. Brown Collection)*

LEFT K5083 at A&AEE Martlesham Heath in 1937. The trials that the prototype undertook here were significant for the Hurricane's eventual assimilation into RAF service. By this time the prototype had been almost fully developed to the initial Hurricane production standard. *(RAF Museum/Charles E. Brown Collection)*

LEFT With war clouds gathering, a major aviation exhibition was held in Brussels, Belgium, on 8 to 23 July 1939. Pictured is a part of the Royal Air Force stand at the exhibition, with a Hurricane at left (with Watts two-bladed wooden propeller), a Vickers Wellington behind, and a very glossy Supermarine Spitfire exhibit at right. It would not be long before all these types were involved in the largest conflict the world has ever known. *(RAF Museum)*

CENTRE No 111 Squadron was the first RAF squadron to fly the Hurricane in December 1937 and was based at RAF Acklington in Northumberland during the early part of the war. It was involved in some of the first combats involving Hurricanes. By this point the unit was still flying the Mk I Hurricane (coded 'JU', as in the background here), but most of the squadron's aircraft were of the later Mk I production standard with Rotol three-bladed propellers. The squadron was also very active, further south, during the Battle of Britain. *(RAF Museum)*

BELOW A formation of early Hurricane Mk Is assigned to No 111 Squadron. At this time the squadron was based at RAF Northolt. The success of this unit in converting onto the monoplane Hurricane was an important step forward in the RAF's rapid modernisation programme of the period, paving the way for the widespread service introduction of the type. *(RAF Museum/Charles E. Brown Collection)*

and the heaviest armed fighter monoplane in existence. The first production Hurricane Mk I (there was only the one prototype) was flown on 12 October 1937. By then many refinements had already been incorporated in the design as a result of successful flight-testing with the single prototype. The power plant for the first production aircraft was the Merlin II. Subsequently, a number of further detail refinements were incorporated as production increased and the versatility of the Hurricane became apparent (see Chapter 1).

No 111 Squadron, based at Northolt, became the first operational RAF squadron to convert to the Hurricane, receiving its initial deliveries in December 1937. The RAF's Fighter Command had been created a year earlier and the Hurricane was to become the new command's most numerous and important fighter in the coming final period of peace and in the opening stages of conflict. By the outbreak of war in September 1939 there were 16 fully operational Hurricane squadrons in the RAF's inventory, with two others either almost converted or involved with the Hurricane in other ways. In comparison, ten squadrons were flying Spitfires. There were some 280 Hurricanes operational with the RAF at that time.

The Hurricane can truly be said to have been involved in the Second World War from start to finish. In the opening days of the war, four RAF Hurricane squadrons moved to France to cover British forces that were rapidly deployed to French soil. Two of these, Nos 1 and 73, were soon transferred to the Advanced Air Striking Force (AASF) to escort the increasingly beleaguered Fairey Battles, and the war that Sydney Camm and other far-sighted people in Britain had foreseen coming years before began in earnest. The Hurricane's first aerial victory over the Continent took place on 30 October 1939 when Pilot Officer P. W. O. 'Boy' Mould of No 1 Squadron shot down a high-flying Dornier Do17P reconnaissance aircraft near the German border. Several days earlier, on 21 October, Hurricanes of No 46 Squadron based at North Coates in Lincolnshire had achieved the first aerial victories for the Hurricane when several of the squadron's pilots shot down four Heinkel He115 seaplanes performing an anti-shipping operation off the English coast.

In addition to deliveries to the RAF, the Hurricane had also found favour with several foreign air arms and fared well as an export fighter. Both Belgium and Yugoslavia indulged in licence production until overrun by German forces. In British service, the Hurricane went on to operate in virtually every theatre, as the Second World War gradually engulfed the world. In the first half of 1940, Hurricanes briefly participated in the ill-fated operations over Norway, with No 46 Squadron again being involved in the fighting. The real battle for the Hurricane began when the Germans invaded the Low Countries and France beginning on 10 May 1940. This ended the so-called 'Phoney War', and from then on the Hurricane played a vital role as one of Britain's principal combat aircraft. The RAF's fighter contribution in the Battle of France principally comprised the Hurricane, with many Spitfires kept in reserve for home defence. It was, however, a losing battle, even though the Hurricane force, often temporarily bolstered by home-based Hurricanes and Spitfires, provided the first real fighter opposition the Luftwaffe had encountered. As retreat followed retreat, Hurricanes and Spitfires became involved in air battles over the evacuation of British and French forces from Dunkirk in Operation 'Dynamo'.

After the defeat of France, the real battle

BELOW Hurricane Mk I, coded PO-C, of No 46 Squadron, is carefully hoisted aboard ship for transport to Norway in May 1940. The Hurricanes of this unit flew a short and ultimately fruitless campaign during the fighting in Norway. *(RAF Museum)*

for survival was thrust upon the British Isles. Numerically, the main fighter type available to RAF's Fighter Command during the Battle of Britain that summer and autumn was the Hurricane, with some 32 operational squadrons employing the type by the latter stages, compared to 19 Spitfire squadrons available when the battle commenced. The Battle of Britain took place between July and October 1940 (some writers start the period on 10 July and end it in the first week of October, while others claim 1 July to the end of October), during which the Hurricane, in concert with Spitfires and other less significant types, won the greatest and arguably most important air battle ever to take place. The Hurricanes were flown not only by British pilots, but also by those from several other nationalities who had joined the RAF, and the aircraft eventually outscored in the battle all other RAF types put together. The Hurricane Mk I production aircraft bore the brunt of this fighting, the later production Mk I having been further improved, compared to the rather austere early aircraft, with the installation of the more powerful Merlin III and the use – at last – of a fully variable-pitch (constant speed) propeller, which considerably added to the aircraft's performance.

The principal adversary of the Hurricane was the legendary Messerschmitt Bf109 single-engined fighter in its Bf109E version, but the Germans also committed their much-vaunted – and by the end of the battle virtually completely defeated – twin-engined Messerschmitt Bf110 heavy fighter and destroyer. The Bf109E was more than a match for the Hurricane, but a well-flown Hurricane could take on anything that the Luftwaffe had to offer, including the Bf109E, particularly at lower levels and if allowed the advantage of beginning and ending the fight, especially with initial height advantage. It has often been claimed that the Hurricanes were left to take on the German bombers – mainly Heinkel He111 and Junkers Ju88 medium bombers, but also Ju87 'Stuka' dive-bombers, all of which the Hurricane could cope with – while the faster and more nimble Spitfires dealt with their Bf109 escorts, with which they were more on a par. This is, in fact, a myth: in the heat of battle RAF pilots had to be ready to take on any of the Luftwaffe's combat aircraft

and many Hurricane pilots shot down Bf109Es. It was a pilot of No 249 Squadron, Flight Lieutenant James Nicolson, who was to give the Hurricane a particular fame. On 16 August, at the height of the battle, Nicolson continued to attack a Bf110 while his Hurricane burned, having itself been fired on by a Bf109. While recovering from his injuries, Nicolson was awarded Britain's highest military gallantry award, the Victoria Cross. It was the only such honour ever bestowed on a pilot of Fighter Command.

Britain's victory in the Battle of Britain was achieved as a result of extraordinary teamwork between the various elements of the air defences, including the important ground-based radar stations that gave sufficient early warning of many Luftwaffe raids to allow the defending Hurricanes and Spitfires time to get airborne and ready with a height advantage. Many Hurricane pilots achieved impressive scores of aerial victories during the frantic summer months of 1940, but the cost was high for Fighter Command. Without doubt, the foreign volunteers in the RAF played a vital role in the overall picture, with several pilots from Poland achieving impressive tallies. The highest scoring RAF airman of all in the Battle of Britain was a Hurricane pilot, and he was from Czechoslovakia. Sergeant Josef František, who flew with the Polish-manned No 303 Squadron, achieved 17 aerial victories during September 1940.

It is interesting to note that there was a certain amount of what has come to be referred to as 'Spitfire snobbery' among the Luftwaffe aircrews who fought in the Battle of Britain. Germans who were shot down preferred to claim that they were targeted by a Spitfire rather than a Hurricane, which they tended to hold in lower esteem than the Supermarine fighter. Similarly, German fighter pilots returning to their bases in Occupied France following combat with British fighters often preferred to claim that it was a Spitfire they had shot down rather than a Hurricane. This explains some of the Luftwaffe's over-claiming during this period in relation to Spitfires rather than Hurricanes, but there is no doubt that Hurricanes did bring down a significant number of Bf109E fighters despite the conflicting claims.

The Hurricane had proved itself to be a vital part of Britain's defences in 1940, and as the war progressed and the country went on to the offensive, so the number of roles the Hurricane performed continued to grow. By late 1940, production of the Spitfire had increased so that all home-based fighter squadrons could be progressively equipped with them. Nevertheless, production of the Hurricane also continued to grow as new roles were found, and continuing development and experimentation by Hawker led to the most numerous Hurricane series, the Mk II. Several versions of the Mk II series were produced, with different armament layouts, more powerful versions of the Merlin engine, and overall improved capabilities compared to the Mk I series, which bore the brunt of the fighting during the Battle of Britain. These later Hurricanes became associated with ground-attack and intruder air-to-ground operations, at which the Hurricane was found to excel.

As production increased, so further manufacturing facilities were required to fulfil the ever growing need for new Hurricanes. In 1934/5 the Gloster Aircraft Company had been brought by Thomas Sopwith into the group that included Hawker, under a new Hawker Siddeley Group umbrella, and it was therefore natural that Gloster would also build Hurricanes. The Gloster factory at Brockworth (Hucclecote), near Gloucester, was thus introduced into

Hurricane manufacture, with the first Gloster-built Hurricane Mk I flying in October 1939. A little later, the Austin Motor Company at Longbridge, Birmingham, was brought into Hurricane construction, building Mk IIb and Mk IIc Hurricanes between February 1941 and October 1942. In addition, the Hawker Aircraft Ltd's own production facilities at Brooklands and Kingston upon Thames were considerably expanded, with the addition to Hurricane production from 1939 of the Hawker factory at Langley, in Buckinghamshire. It was here in the summer of 1944 that the final Hurricanes to roll off the production lines were completed.

Hurricanes were also built at several other locations around the world. Two of the overseas buyers of the Hurricane, Yugoslavia and Belgium, were able to build some Hurricanes before their defeat, but the most important source of overseas production of the Hurricane was Canada. With its potentially extensive aircraft production facilities and established aviation heritage, Canada was an excellent location for additional manufacture. It was far enough from Nazi Germany to be well away from any threat of attack, and was on Britain's side as a Commonwealth country. The Canadian Car & Foundry Company Ltd, based in Montreal (but with additional works at Fort William, Ontario), was brought into Hurricane production at a comparatively early stage, and eventually

ABOVE A formation of No 601 Squadron Hurricanes, including UF-W, UF-O, UF-Y and UF-P, during 1941. Several of these are twelve-gun Hurricane Mk IIb fighters. The introduction of the Mk IIb gave the Hurricane a comparatively heavy 'punch', although some pilots did not prefer the rifle-calibre 0.303in machine guns of all the early Hurricanes, which often needed a large number of hits to be achieved before an enemy aircraft was successfully brought down. No 601 Squadron was one of the Hurricane squadrons fully involved in Battle of Britain operations. *(RAF Museum)*

more than 1,400 Hurricanes were produced in Canada. Many of these were subsequently shipped across the Atlantic for use in Britain and elsewhere, but a significant number stayed in Canada where they were used for training and local defence – the latter including readiness to intercept Japanese incendiary balloons coming in over the west coast of Canada. Canadian Hurricanes started as Mk I aircraft, but the designation was soon changed to begin with the Mk X onwards, and Canadian production also introduced a new and important ingredient into Hurricane operation, the use of the Packard-built Merlin engine, produced in the US under licence from Rolls-Royce.

Although the first Mk II-series Hurricanes entered service in September and October 1940 primarily in the fighter role, it was as a fighter-bomber and intruder that the Hurricane was to find its true vocation in the mid-war period. From 1941 onwards the RAF began to operate over Occupied France and Belgium, seeking out German ground targets and battling with the Luftwaffe in what was effectively a new aerial front. The Hurricane was at once fully involved in this new phase of the war, and it was quickly found that the Mk II-series Hurricanes, with their more powerful Merlin XX-series engines (compared to the Merlin II and III of the Mk I Hurricanes), were ideal as daytime and night-time intruder and ground-attack aircraft. With the tempo of German attacks, particularly against RAF installations, dropping off as the Battle of Britain began to slide into history, many in the RAF from the top downwards were keen to take the fight across the English Channel against the Germans in occupied Europe – and thus reverse the trend solely of defensive operations that had preoccupied Fighter Command for so long, and provide a much needed morale boost for the British people and their Allies. In the event, the ensuing offensive operations eventually widened in scope and turned out to be a very important part of the war in the following years, as the Germans were increasingly harried in their occupied areas and needed to tie up forces there that were often required elsewhere.

To begin with, the main instrument in taking the fight to the enemy was the Hurricane, aided by types such as the Bristol Blenheim light bomber, and a variety of different operations were undertaken. For the Hurricane, these included fighter sweeps of various kinds, as well as escorting the light bombers and harrying German shipping wherever it could be found. Best-known of these operations were 'Rhubarbs', which were comparatively small-scale but often effective tactical operations, generally flown by around four aircraft, often in bad weather, against targets of opportunity. There were many targets in occupied northern France that were suitable for attack, including German road transport, railways, airfields and the whole range of small-scale German military installations and individual targets that were spread across Normandy and beyond. Other operations were the larger-scale 'Rodeo' attacks, similar to the 'Rhubarbs', but sometimes carried out at squadron strength, and the 'Circus' and 'Ramrod' missions specifically aimed at escorting light bombers. Also flown were anti-shipping 'Roadstead' operations along the French coastline, but these eventually widened to include a larger campaign known as 'Channel Stop', which aimed to prevent German ships running the blockade created in the English Channel by the 'Roadstead' and other operations. Unfortunately, these had largely run down by the time of the 'Channel Dash' by several German capital ships in February 1942 for which the Hurricanes could have been more effective than the brave, but token, British operation using Fairey Swordfish.

Many Hurricane squadrons were involved in these offensive operations, including the long-standing Nos 249 and 257, as well as relative newcomers such as the American-manned No 71 Squadron, one of eventually three Eagle squadrons that later in the war formed the nucleus of the 4th Fighter Group of the US Army Air Force, which gained so much success flying the Merlin-engined P-51 Mustang. In addition, Hurricanes also flew convoy patrols over the Thames estuary, and 'Kipper' patrols over the North Sea to protect British fishing vessels.

All of these operations were carried out by day, but the Hurricane was to prove its worth at night as well. As mentioned in Chapter 6, the Hurricane was generally well-liked by its pilots, being straightforward to fly even at night. This latter trait proved useful from 1940 onwards, when the number of roles this capable aircraft could carry out was added to with that of night-fighter. During 1940 some Hurricanes were specifically delegated to fly night-time patrols, supplementing early Bristol Blenheims configured as night-fighters. To begin with this was on a simple, almost ad hoc basis. As the need for greater night defence became necessary, with the Luftwaffe increasingly using the cover of darkness to launch major bombing raids, so the necessity for a more organised night defence became obvious. This became especially true as the Germans began to rely on night-time blitz from the autumn of 1940 onwards. Probably one of the best-known RAF squadrons to operate in this role was No 87 Squadron. Blooded in the frantic aerial fighting over France in May 1940, No 87 Squadron was eventually re-allocated as a night-fighter/intruder squadron, and flew Hurricanes in the home defence night-fighter role in the mid-war years. Some Hurricanes also served in North Africa and India for local night defence.

The Hurricane was particularly suitable for night flying, with its uncomplicated handling

ABOVE With power supplied by the ever-present RAF starter trolley, Hurricane Mk IIa, Z2487, FC-T, of the Station Flight at RAF Northolt prepares for take-off during 1941. Northolt had a long and important association with the Hurricane, being the airfield where the first operational RAF Hurricanes were received for No 111 Squadron in late 1937. *(RAF Museum)*

BELOW A beautiful in-flight view of night-fighter/intruder Hurricane Mk IIc, BE500, coded LK-A, of No 87 Squadron in 1942. Named *Cawnpore I*, this was the aircraft of the unit's commanding officer, Squadron Leader D.G. Smallwood. During the Second World War Hurricanes were used for night-fighting duties to some effect. *(RAF Museum/Charles E. Brown Collection)*

and wide-track main undercarriage – the latter allowing for safer landings at night. The Spitfire, in contrast, was not so well suited to night operations, and its narrow-track undercarriage made it a challenge to land in darkness, particularly on grass – although this was not impossible in the hands of a good pilot. Generally, the home-defence night-fighter Hurricanes were not equipped with radar. Their success at night depended on the exceptional flying skills of the pilot and the relevant information on the position of German aircraft relayed to him from the ground – and more than a little help from ground-based searchlights. Indeed, the only modification that was made to some Hurricanes to turn them into night-fighters was the installation of a crude but effective external projecting metal plate ahead of the windscreen on each side of the upper fuselage to prevent the glare from the aircraft's exhaust dazzling the pilot.

Efforts were made during 1941 and 1942 to give the night-fighter Hurricanes more chance of finding and destroying German aircraft in darkness, including the curious and potentially dangerous concept (for those involved) of the Turbinlite experiment. A number of twin-engined Douglas Havoc light day-bombers were converted for night-fighting with the addition of airborne interception radar (AI Mk IV), and the installation of a large searchlight in the nose. In theory the Turbinlite aircraft was supposed to find a German bomber with its radar having been vectored into the general area by ground radar, and then illuminate it with the searchlight so that accompanying Hurricanes could move in and shoot down the intruder. This meant that the accompanying Hurricanes (often one, but sometimes two) had to fly in close proximity to the Turbinlite aircraft at night – a hazardous principle that was much disliked by those Hurricane pilots who were caught up in the experiment. In practice it did not work, although one German night-raider is believed to have been shot down by a Hurricane from one of the units that had been delegated to this task. Fortunately, the coming into service of high-performance, radar-equipped night-fighters, such as the de Havilland Mosquito, nullified the need for the Turbinlite concept (and indeed the need for night-fighter Hurricanes), which was abandoned early in 1943. Instead, the highly capable Mosquito was able to detect and then shoot down its target by itself. As a footnote, it must be stated that during 1941 AI Mk V radar was tried out for operational Hurricanes, mounted in an under-wing fairing.

The continuing development of the Hurricane that led to the type becoming an exceptional daytime ground-attack aircraft – particularly with the four-cannon armament of the Mk IIc version – also had a positive effect for night operations. Increasingly, Hurricanes came to be used for night-intruder sorties over occupied Europe, in which they excelled. It was another of the roles undertaken by the Hurricane for which the type is little known, and yet proved to be very successful. Beginning in earnest during 1941, several home-based squadrons took the fight

BELOW A nice line-up of Hurricane Mk IIs (FT-L, FT-H and others) of No 43 Squadron at RAF Tangmere in August 1942. At that time the Hurricane was one of the RAF's principal ground-attack aircraft types and was fully utilised taking the war to the Germans over Occupied France and along the Channel coast. *(RAF Museum)*

to the enemy literally in his own back yard, at night, over occupied France. This ground-attack work was safer than similar daylight operations, and had the added benefit of potentially denying night-time flying and movement on the ground to the enemy. One of the greatest exponents of this type of warfare was a Czechoslovak pilot, Flight Lieutenant Karel Kuttelwascher. Already a seasoned Hurricane pilot from his experiences in previous months on daylight operations, Kuttelwascher achieved a string of night-intruder victories against night-flying German aircraft over occupied France between April and July 1942 while with No 1 Squadron, and finished the war with a score of 18 victories in Hurricanes, 15 of these at night.

In addition to service in north-west Europe, as the Second World War progressed Hurricanes were increasingly used on operations worldwide with British and Commonwealth forces. Their crews fought bravely against German and Italian forces in the Middle East, the Mediterranean, the Balkans, and in various parts of Africa. The Hurricane's chief adversary, the Messerschmitt Bf109E, was present in most of these areas, as were a mixed bag of Italian fighters. Hurricanes coped easily with the Italian biplane Fiat CR.42 fighters, and were generally able to tackle the radial-engined Fiat G.50 monoplane with little trouble, these being two of the chief Italian front-line fighters that Hurricanes came up against. Similarly, most of the Italian bombers were comparatively easy to deal with. RAF-operated Hurricanes also flew briefly from Russian airfields

in defence of northern Russian ports into which British supply convoys sailed, while Hurricanes were also employed against the Japanese in the Far East, especially in the difficult early phase of operations in Singapore, Sumatra and Burma, where Allied forces were in almost constant retreat. In all these areas, with the exception of the northern Russian operations, the Hurricane acted as a fighter and a fighter-bomber, increasingly taking on the latter task as it was replaced by newer Allied types in the pure fighter role.

In general, Hurricanes were increasingly outclassed as newer marks of Axis fighters came into service. In particular, the appearance from late 1940 onwards of the Messerschmitt Bf109F (successor to the Battle of Britain era Bf109E) and the very potent radial-engined Focke-Wulf Fw190 from the late summer of 1941 onwards spelled great danger for Hurricane pilots. It was in the Mediterranean and North Africa that the Hurricane really came

ABOVE Hurricanes played an important role for the RAF and Indian forces in the Burmese and Indian theatres where the type proved to be invaluable in the ground-attack and reconnaissance roles. In this view a 'Hurribomber' attacks a Japanese target in Burma. *(Malcolm V. Lowe Collection)*

LEFT The Hurricane played a vitally important role in the fighting in North Africa where it became one of the RAF's most valuable assets. This Hurricane Mk I (V7544, TP-S) of No 73 Squadron is pictured having made a wheels-up landing at El Adem on 14 February 1941, in typically featureless desert. It has a 'tropical' Vokes filter installation beneath its nose, and reveals the prominent lower rear fuselage 'keel' and rudder base extension that was introduced into Hurricane Mk I production. *(RAF Museum)*

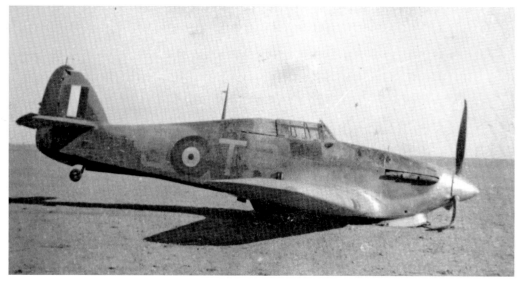

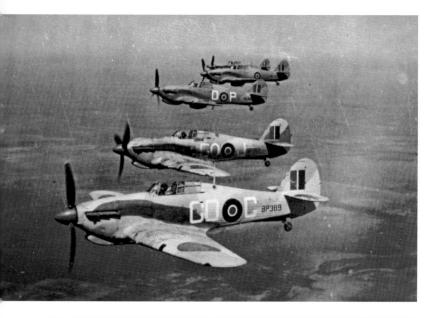

LEFT Hurricanes played an important part in all the battlegrounds where they participated, from the Battles of France and Britain in 1940 to the hard-won victories in North Africa and the Far East later in the war. These battered but still very effective 'tropicalised' Hurricane Mk IIcs are from No 94 Squadron in North Africa during 1942, and include BP389 (GO-G), BP387 (GO-J), HL85? (O-P), and HL735, with the machines in the foreground exhibiting very prominent exhaust staining. *(RAF Museum)*

CENTRE This Hurricane Mk I, Z4172, 'G', from No 260 Squadron, operated in the Middle East where it was photographed in 1941. Hurricanes literally operated world-wide, the only theatre in the Second World War where the type was not used in numbers was the Pacific. *(RAF Museum)*

BELOW An eight-gun RAF Hurricane Mk IIa 'Hurribomber' awaits its running pilot at Hal Far, Malta, during the autumn of 1942. The Hurricane was vital for the defence of the besieged and strategically important island of Malta, but by the time this photograph was taken the Allies were increasingly using the island as a base for offensive operations against Axis forces in North Africa, Sicily and the Italian mainland. *(Malcolm V. Lowe Collection)*

into its own in the period after the Battle of Britain. Virtually from the first, Hurricanes were engaged against Italian forces in North Africa after Italy's entry into the Second World War in mid-1940. From then onwards, until victory was achieved in the Middle East well into 1943, Hurricanes played a vital role as fighters and increasingly as fighter-bombers. This was the true home of the 'Hurribomber' and, as with the Battle of Britain, it is difficult to imagine what the eventual outcome would have been without the Hurricane being available in numbers to take the fight to the Germans.

For operations in the Mediterranean area, getting the Hurricanes into the right place was a logistical problem. In the early war period, some aircraft had been ferried there via France, but following the defeat of France in June 1940 this became impossible. One solution involved sending Hurricanes by sea in crates from Britain to West Africa, where the aircraft were put ashore in Sierra Leone, assembled, test flown and ferried in stages from Takoradi across Africa to Egypt, from where they could be allocated to operational units. The problem of supplying Hurricanes and Spitfires to the strategic island of Malta was overcome by transporting them on aircraft carriers from which they were flown when Malta came within range. The latter method was highly dangerous and some of the most epic sea and air battles of the war raged as the possession of Malta was contested during 1941 and 1942.

For the defence of Malta, which became a vital strategic consideration following Italy's entry into the war, Hurricanes were rapidly sent to reinforce the locally based RAF Gloster Gladiator biplanes, the two types initially forming the complement of No 261 Squadron. As with the general situation in North Africa, British forces began by holding the line well against the Italians, but with the arrival of German air assets from December 1940 onwards the situation became rapidly more serious. Malta subsequently became the focus of much aerial activity, with the Hurricane being the main line of defence for some time until supplies of Spitfires (and more Hurricanes, plus other types) also started to arrive in numbers.

Similarly, the role of the Hurricane in North Africa cannot be underestimated. Hurricanes quickly became the best Allied fighter and fighter-bomber available to hold the line, and soon had to face the full force of the Luftwaffe after the German intervention gained momentum in early 1941 to save the increasingly beleaguered local Italian forces. Operating with the RAF's Desert Air Force, a succession of Hurricane squadrons took on the combined German and Italian forces, reinforced by various types of light bombers, as well as Curtiss Tomahawk and Kittyhawk fighters from the US. Hurricanes operating in this theatre had the tropical modifications of so-called dust filters, which were particularly necessary for the carburettor air intake beneath the aircrafts'

ABOVE By the later stages of 1944 some Hurricanes had already become redundant. This partly silver-coloured Hurricane Mk IId, with 'tropical' filter beneath its nose, was apparently unarmed but carried drop tanks beneath its wings and appeared to be in use as a 'hack' transport. It was photographed at Naples, Italy, in September 1944.
(RAF Museum)

RIGHT A salvage
convoy of Hurricanes
near Cairo, circa
1942. The repair and
recycling of damaged
but repairable
Hurricanes was highly
important wherever
they were operated,
with many hundreds
returned to active duty
during the war. The
nearest aircraft, Z4967,
was a Hurricane Mk
IIa/Trop of No 229
Squadron wearing
that squadron's codes,
'HB'. (RAF Museum)

centre section, resulting in the prominent 'chin'
fairing under the nose of Hurricanes with this
modification. At least 15 RAF squadrons served
with the Hurricane in North Africa and its related
areas, bolstered by foreign-manned units,
including three Hurricane squadrons of the
South African Air Force.

In North Africa some Hurricanes served as
impromptu night-fighters, while others operated
in the reconnaissance role, another of the tasks
for which the Hurricane is little known. The
comparatively small number of reconnaissance
Hurricanes were specially made conversions,
some of which were achieved in the field. In
Egypt, several Hurricane Mk Is were converted
for this role, starting in early 1941. A few aircraft
carried a pair of F.24 cameras with 8in focal-

length lenses, or a less common combination
of a vertical and two oblique F.24 cameras with
14in focal-length lenses mounted in the rear
fuselage, near to the trailing edge of the wing. A
distinguishing fairing was installed over the lenses
aft of the prominent lower fuselage radiator
housing. Two more Hurricanes are known to
have been converted on Malta during April
1941. Later in 1941, approximately 18 Hurricane
Mk IIs were converted to PR Mk II standard,
and a final batch, thought to be of 12 aircraft,
was converted in late 1941. These aircraft
were intended primarily for long-range strategic
reconnaissance, and it is widely claimed that in
clean conditions they could reach 38,000ft.

For lower-level armed tactical
reconnaissance, some Hurricanes were

RIGHT The Hurricane
came into its own in
the mid-stages of the
Second World War
as a ground-attack
aircraft, one of the
important marks
involved in this work
being the hard-hitting
20mm-armed Mk IIc.
In this image, several
No 3 Squadron Mk IIc
(Z3464 QO-Z, BD868
QO-P, Z3069 QO-F,
Z3092 QO-T, Z3894
QO-R, and BD867
QO-Y) fly in formation.
(RAF Museum)

converted into tactical reconnaissance (TacR) aircraft. An additional radio was fitted for liaison with ground forces and some aircraft also had a vertically mounted camera located in the rear fuselage. This added weight and affected the aircraft's centre of gravity, so to compensate one or two Brownings (if the aircraft was machine-gun-armed) or two cannons (if it was originally a Mk IIc) would be omitted. Externally, these aircraft were only distinguishable by the missing armament. This was, however, a role in which the Hurricane was not widely used, the Allison-engined North American Mustang proving to be a far better possibility for such work.

Alongside these land-based developments, the Hurricane also found a new and exacting career as a ship-borne naval fighter. In the early months of the Second World War, the Royal Navy's Fleet Air Arm was in dire need of a modern sea-going fighter. The existing single-engine, two-seat, Blackburn Skua monoplane fleet fighter was hopelessly outclassed by the German Bf109E, as proved by operations over Norway in 1940, even though a Skua had achieved Britain's first aerial victory of the Second World War in the opening days of the conflict. Continuing the eight-wing-gun philosophy, which was manifest also in the earliest production Hurricanes and Spitfires, the Royal Navy had the Fairey Fulmar naval fighter to fall back on, but clearly this two-seater

with a redundant rear gunner was not going to fit the bill in the air war either. In the event, both the Hurricane and the Spitfire ended up going to sea to fill the gap, the former as the Sea Hurricane and the latter as the Seafire. The Hurricane was better suited for operations aboard aircraft carriers than the Spitfire, the latter's narrow-track main undercarriage in particular being a major disadvantage. In contrast, the rugged Hurricane with its wide-track main undercarriage and comparatively docile handling was a perfect aircraft for carrier operations, and the type subsequently became an important fighter for the Fleet Air Arm. In addition, RAF-operated Hurricanes could also be transported by aircraft carriers to a war zone and then flown off to their intended land bases,

ABOVE This rare colour photograph is of a Hurricane Mk I of No 806 Squadron, Fleet Air Arm, at Sidi Hanish, Western Desert, in 1942. Some of the Royal Navy's fighters were land-based in the North African campaign, apparently including this aircraft. The keel below the rear fuselage has been removed while the aircraft is being worked on, making it difficult to determine if this aircraft was fitted with a tail hook. *(RAF Museum)*

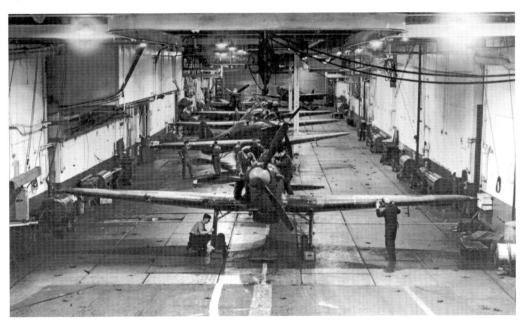

LEFT The Hurricane in its Sea Hurricane derivative went to sea aboard aircraft carriers and proved to be very suitable for carrier operations. In this view several Sea Hurricane Mk Ibs of No 768 Squadron are housed on the hangar deck of the aircraft carrier HMS *Argus*, in August 1943. This squadron acted as a deck landing training school. *(RAF Museum)*

ABOVE A Sea Hurricane Mk Ib, coded M2K, of No 768 Squadron, is seen just after take-off from HMS *Argus* in August 1943, during a training embarkation aboard the ship. The Sea Hurricanes of this squadron played an important role in training naval pilots in the art of aircraft carrier deck landing, a task at which the Hurricane was excellent with its comparatively vice-less handling and wide-track main undercarriage. *(RAF Museum)*

BELOW Landing onboard an aircraft carrier is a difficult task even in good weather and favourable wind, but even so accidents can happen. Here, Sea Hurricane Mk Ib, P2886, M2H, of No 768 Squadron, has ended up on the edge of the deck of HMS *Argus* after crashing in August 1943. *(RAF Museum)*

thus solving the problem of how to deliver much-needed fighters to distant areas of conflict.

The first naval Hurricanes were simply Mk Is, which were delegated to the Royal Navy in 1940. They were austere naval fighters, without a tail hook or catapult equipment for carrier operations, but they were very useful as land-based trainers for naval pilots. They were followed by a succession of dedicated naval versions, equipped for catapult take-offs and later examples were also fitted with a tail hook for deck-landings aboard aircraft carriers. Many of these were converted from existing land-based Hurricanes, and some of them were included among the Hurricane production in Canada.

There was a particular quirk in Hurricane naval operations that gave the type a unique place in Britain's naval aviation history: the use of specially converted Sea Hurricanes based aboard merchant ships for convoy protection. So-called 'Hurricats', they were expendable fighters that were fired from specially installed catapult equipment aboard merchant ships when danger was thought to be present. However, with no landing deck to return to, the pilot of the Hurricane had to either ditch in the sea near to the ships that he was protecting, or bale out nearby, or (the preferred option) head for the nearest friendly land if it was in Allied hands. This was a stop-gap solution to the large problem of protecting Allied shipping from enemy air attack, and was only used until there were sufficient aircraft carriers available to do the job properly. The concept did, however, work quite effectively, and particularly on the supply convoys from Britain to the Soviet Union – into the Arctic Circle and around the North Cape – Hurricats were successful in driving away several significant German air attacks.

Initial conversions of ships into suitable Hurricane catapult carriers included a modified seaplane tender, but two specific types were later standardised for the catapult Hurricanes: the Fighter Catapult Ships, crewed exclusively by Royal Navy personnel, and the Catapult Aircraft Merchantmen (CAM ships), crewed by merchant seamen with the aircraft flown and maintained by RAF personnel. The operating unit for the catapult Hurricanes

LEFT Hurricanes and Sea Hurricanes were vitally important to the concept of basing aircraft on converted merchant ships for convoy protection on the high seas. In this role they proved to be of great value, until aircraft carriers were available in sufficient numbers to fill the gap more suitably. Here, a Hurricane or Sea Hurricane, is installed and ready for launch from the catapult of a CAM (Catapult Aircraft (or Armed) Merchantman) ship, in this case the SS *Empire Franklin*. *(RAF Museum)*

was the Merchant Ship Fighter Unit (MSFU), headquartered at RAF Speke near Liverpool. The first success for a Hurricat was achieved by Australian pilot Robert Everett, flying from the Fighter Catapult Ship HMS *Maplin* (which had two Sea Hurricanes aboard) on 2 August 1941, when he shot down a four-engined Focke-Wulf Fw 200 Condor while defending a convoy inbound from Sierra Leone. Thereafter the Hurricats enjoyed a moderate amount of success in shooting down German aircraft, but their greatest contribution was to disrupt

German attacks on convoys, and make them less willing to attack in the first place, thus saving many ships and their valuable cargoes. Hurricats persisted in service well into 1943, with the last actions for Sea Hurricanes of the MSFU being in July of that year.

The Hurricats did not need arrestor hooks as they had no deck to land on, but subsequent Sea Hurricanes were all hooked and served comparatively widely on Royal Navy aircraft carriers from the early mid-war period onwards. Perhaps the greatest moments for the aircraft-

LEFT An extremely rare colour photograph of a Hurricane on the catapult of a CAM ship. The use of Hurricanes in this way for convoy protection was a stop-gap solution to the problem of German attacks on convoys that were beyond the range of land-based Coastal Command aircraft. It proved to be generally effective and became another battle honour for the Hurricane. *(RAF Museum/Michael Lyne Collection)*

LEFT A number of Fleet Air Arm Sea Hurricane squadrons were involved in the Operation *Torch* landings in North Africa in November 1942, with their aircraft temporarily painted in US national insignia to avoid confusion with (and by) the newly-arrived Americans. This twelve-gun Canadian-built Sea Hurricane Mk XIIb with Mk IIb wings, JS327, of No 800 Squadron (some sources claim No 804 Squadron), was lost near Oran on 8 November 1942, possibly after combat with Vichy French Dewoitine D.520 fighters. *(Malcolm V. Lowe Collection)*

LEFT Hurricanes saw service in many countries during the war. This Hurricane Mk IIc/Trop, HV817, FT-C, of No 43 Squadron, is pictured at Maison Blanche, Algeria, during November 1942 in support of the Operation *Torch* landings. The bulges on the upper wing surface in this version are due to the installation of the 20mm cannons. *(RAF Museum)*

BELOW Many early Sea Hurricanes were eventually used for training in second-line Fleet Air Arm units such as No 762 Naval Air Squadron. In this formation, Sea Hurricane Mk Ib, Z4039, of No 762 Squadron, flies in company with Supermarine Seafire Mk IIcs, MB217 and MB264, of the operational No 894 Squadron in 1943. *(RAF Museum/Charles E. Brown Collection)*

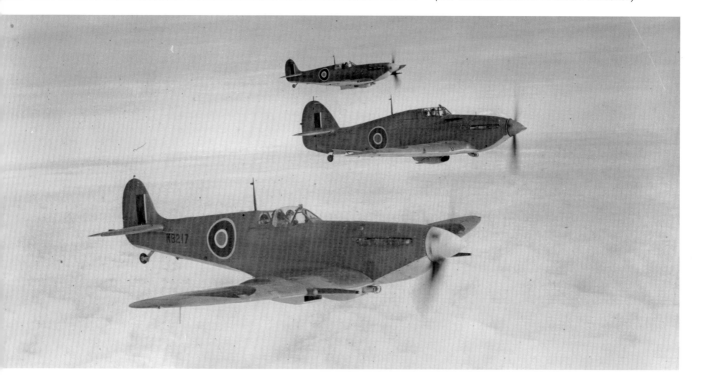

RIGHT Sea Hurricanes were among the last Hurricanes of any type to remain in front-line operational use during the Second World War. This aerial view of HMS *Nairana* shows Sea Hurricanes ranged on the forward deck when the carrier was operating in North Russian waters in the latter stages of the war. Sea Hurricane Mk IIcs of No 835 Squadron, Fleet Air Arm, achieved what are generally regarded as the final Hurricane air-to-air victories, in May 1944. *(RAF Museum)*

carrier-based Sea Hurricanes were the air battles to defend the Malta Convoy 'Pedestal', in August 1942, and the Operation 'Torch' landings in North Africa, in November 1942. Thereafter, the Sea Hurricanes were gradually replaced by more modern types such as the Vought Corsair, Grumman Hellcat and Grumman Martlet (Wildcat), and later marks of Supermarine Seafire, although the vital role of convoy escort in home waters was handled by carrier-based Sea Hurricanes until well into 1944. The type continued in naval service in Britain until the end of the war, mainly in training roles.

The final aerial victories credited to the Hurricane line were achieved by Sea Hurricanes in May 1944. Indeed, the Sea Hurricane continued as a pure day-fighter long after the land-based RAF Hurricanes had finished with this role and gone over to fighter-bomber work. The final air-to-air kills by the Hurricane line are now recognised as having been achieved by Sea Hurricanes operating from the aircraft carrier HMS *Nairana* on 26 May 1944, when two Sea Hurricane Mk IIcs of No 835 Squadron, Fleet Air Arm, shot down two Junkers Ju 290

RIGHT Continuing development of the Hurricane family led to what many regard as the ultimate Hurricane version, the Mk IV. Fitted with a so-called 'universal' wing, this derivative was considerably versatile in being able to carry a variety of offensive loads for ground-attack work, and was the last major production model of the Hurricane. This Mk IV, KX877, is fitted with a stores rack beneath the wing and was used for development work related to the Mk IV version, being temporarily known as a Mk V. *(RAF Museum)*

LEFT Hurricanes found their way into all types of role. This aircraft, Mk IIa Z2487, FC-T, was assigned to the Station Flight at RAF Northolt in 1941. *(RAF Museum)*

CENTRE Made in Canada, but broken in England. Hurricane Mk I (actually a Mk X), AF998, PA-62, of No 55 Operational Training Unit, is seen here after crashing in a railway cutting during May 1942. Accidents were a frequent occurrence during aircrew training, but this Hurricane has been demolished particularly effectively. *(RAF Museum)*

BELOW One of the last tasks of land-based Hurricanes in the Second World War was to carry letters and other important documents between Britain and Continental Europe. The unit that was involved was the Air Dispatch Letter Service (ADLS). This ADLS Hurricane has had a mishap on the Continent but still forms the backdrop for a group photograph. *(RAF Museum/Charles E. Brown Collection)*

maritime reconnaissance and convoy surveillance aircraft.

By that time the Hurricane had been almost completely removed from front-line status, having been progressively replaced even in the ground-attack role by newer types such as – in north-west Europe – the massive Hawker Typhoon. Some RAF squadrons, however, continued to operate the type, notably No 309 (Polish) Squadron on shipping protection duties alongside North American Mustangs, and No 26 Squadron, which specialised in reconnaissance and artillery spotting. Some Hurricanes soldiered on in second-line duties to the end of the war, including meteorological flying, liaison work (a particularly important air link existed between Brussels and London following the liberation of Belgium) and training. Hurricanes had been used by some training units, mainly for advanced training, for a number of years, with an early user, No 5 OTU, at Aston Down, in Gloucestershire, flying Hurricanes from February 1940. The Air Dispatch Letter Service (ADLS) exclusively used Hurricanes (mainly of the IIc variety) to fly important papers between Britain and the Continent (and vice versa) following D-Day in June 1944, and also to carry important press releases. The paperwork was usually carried in modified (and presumably cleaned out) underwing fuel tanks.

It was unfortunate for the Hurricane that there were few of the aircraft visibly in service when the Second World War ended, for this undoubtedly allowed the type to slip into history almost unnoticed. Despite the undoubted success and usefulness of the Hurricane from the start of the Second World War onwards, it very often found itself in the shadow of the Spitfire, with the Spitfire often grabbing the limelight and the headlines. Very few Hurricanes remained operational after the end of the Second World War in any quantity, except in a number of countries such as Portugal. In RAF front-line service, only No 6 Squadron soldiered on with the Hurricane in the post-war period, finally converting on to Spitfires in Palestine in late 1945/early 1946. Other Hurricanes continued in RAF service in small numbers for a short time post-war in second-line duties such as meteorological flying. This was in complete contrast to the Spitfire, which

TOP Hurricanes served in a wide range of different units. Here, Hurricane Mk IIc, LF579, 6H-P, of No 1688 Bomber Defence Training Flight, is readied for take-off. This unit was a gunnery training flight which also operated Spitfires. It is believed that this photograph was taken at RAF Wyton, one of the bases used by this unit. *(RAF Museum)*

continued in its later marks in British service in a variety of roles well into the 1950s – and also persisted in front-line service in other countries elsewhere in the world. On the contrary, surplus Hurricanes were scrapped in their hundreds in the months after the end of the war, and the type slowly disappeared into history, largely but not totally forgotten. A few Hurricanes went on display in museums around the world in the post-war period, but it was the Spitfire that tended to stay foremost in the public's mind. Indeed, a number of airworthy examples of the Spitfire continued to persist, but thankfully a small quantity of Hurricanes also remained in flying condition, too, mainly due to private interest and partly through the actions of the Hawker company, which kept one Hurricane, PZ865 (the last Hurricane built), in its own flying museum. At least one airworthy Hurricane was

ABOVE This Canadian-built Hurricane Mk XII, JS290, wears the code letters 'WN' of No 527 Squadron and was used for radar calibration duties while at RAF Digby during 1944–45. It had been used in the Turbinlite experimental night-fighter concept earlier in the war. *(RAF Museum)*

also maintained for official purposes by the RAF, particularly for special events like those to commemorate the Battle of Britain.

Overall, and in addition to the Hurricane, a small number of historic airworthy aircraft remained extant in Britain in the decades after the Second World War, thanks largely to individual efforts and the actions of various companies. This situation dramatically improved from the late 1960s, due in no small part to the making of a motion picture, which was to raise the status of the Hurricane in the minds of the public. The *Battle of Britain* brought together a most unusual collection of what were then coming to be called 'warbirds' – airworthy Second World War veterans, owned and operated by private individuals or companies outside any sort of official or military ownership. Under the energetic direction of retired RAF Group Captain Hamish Mahaddie, a strange mix of RAF and 'Luftwaffe' aircraft was brought together in 1967 and 1968 for the making of the film, which loosely told the story of the Battle of Britain in 1940. The movie included spectacular aerial sequences – mainly filmed from a specially converted North American B-25 Mitchell – that really caught the public's imagination. The RAF aircraft were genuine, comprising a mix of Spitfires and the less numerous Hawker Hurricanes, although many of the Spitfires were of later marks than those that fought in the real Battle of Britain. The 'Luftwaffe' aircraft were represented by a mix of Spanish-built Hispano HA-1112-M1L Buchón

fighters and CASA-built Heinkel He111 bomber lookalikes. The Buchóns were Spanish-built developments of the Bf109G, powered by Rolls-Royce Merlin engines, ironically the same engine type that powered the Hurricane and Spitfire – albeit a different version of the Merlin.

In total, five Hurricanes were available for use in the movie, drawn together from a number of sources. The filming of the aerial sequences began in Spain with the Spanish aircraft, but later 17 of the Buchóns were flown via France to Duxford, Cambridgeshire. During the summer of 1968, a number of the Buchóns and CASA-built Heinkel He111 lookalikes, and several of the Spitfires and Hurricanes, were flown by specially commissioned pilots in aerial sequences above the East Anglian and southern England countryside. Special areas were reserved over the Midlands specifically for the shooting of some of the mock dog-fights, which were quite superb and were probably the best aerial sequences that had been seen in any film up to that time. The Hurricanes performed admirably in this role, but in at least one aerial sequence their number had to be bolstered by some of the Buchóns, which were painted in RAF colours and markings for the occasion, but kept to the back of the Hurricane formations so that they could not be so easily spotted.

On its release in 1969, the film was an instant success, but its real stars were the aircraft. There can be no doubt that historic aircraft preservation, and particularly the desire to retain in flyable condition aircraft such as the

RIGHT Having played such an important role in the real Battle of Britain in 1940, it was fitting that Hurricanes should be prominent in the famous movie, the *Battle of Britain*, which was made in the late 1960s. Several airworthy Hurricanes as well as static replicas appeared in the film, including the opening sequences that showed Hurricanes in action during the Battle of France.

Hurricane and Spitfire, received a real shot in the arm as a result of this one single event. In the years following the release of the movie, aircraft restoration in general and the fate of the Hurricane in particular were changed forever. This was a very positive development, and we continue to reap the benefits of this change in outlook and fortune.

There is, interestingly, a footnote to this particular part of the Hurricane's story. The film *Battle of Britain* was by no means the only movie in which Hurricanes have starred. Indeed, right from the start the Hurricane has been a film star. During 1937, when the Hurricane prototype K5083 was nearing the end of its service and manufacturer's evaluation, it was used in flying sequences for a movie entitled *Test Pilot*. Starring Clark Gable, the film was a showcase for the beautifully sleek, silver prototype, with many of the scenes featuring the aircraft shot at Martlesham Heath, in Suffolk, where service evaluation had taken place. Two decades later, Hurricanes starred in the movie *Angels One Five*, including PZ865, which is currently with the Battle of Britain Memorial Flight.

In more recent times, the opening up of the former Soviet Union at the end of the Cold War has resulted in a number of interesting Second World War airframes being rescued from their crash sites. This has led to at least one viable Hurricane restoration, and a small trickle of others have, over the years, started to reach airworthy condition, albeit thanks to private initiative and the expenditure of large sums of money. The fact that, at the time of writing, there are about a dozen airworthy Hurricanes around the world is an incredible achievement, for which their owners, restorers and pilots should be justifiably proud. The aircraft restoration movement is now big business, involving a number of wealthy individuals, together with many talented craftsmen who carry out the necessary work to keep these historic aircraft alive.

Nevertheless, just how genuine some of these airworthy aircraft really are, bearing in mind that virtually everything has had to be replaced and new components manufactured to enable them to fly, is open to debate. There are some people who would prefer ground-up restorations of this type to be called 'replicas containing some original parts', rather than

The importance of classic aircraft preservation

Without doubt there remains a great fascination for all things aviation, especially historic aviation, and both modern and historic aircraft draw their own supporters at the many air shows and museums across Britain and elsewhere in the world.

From the beginning of aviation history little thought has been given to the preservation of the aircraft that have preceded the newer, more effective models. Each generation has tended to look ahead, rather than preserving the past for future generations to learn from and enjoy.

Nowadays, the populace is more interested in history; in tracing their forebears and in understanding the historical background of the era. The historical significance of classic aircraft has grown in more recent times, and with it has come the desire and the responsibility to preserve the few examples that we still have of our aviation history.

Whether it's a biplane, a rugged and effective monoplane such as the Hurricane, or a large four-engined bomber, the aircraft reflect the development and the engineering of the days that gave them birth. If they are flying, they ensure that the grace of their aerial performance is kept alive for future generations.

being considered as genuine restored historic aircraft. A few of the existing Hurricanes, including the two belonging to the RAF Battle of Britain Memorial Flight, can trace their histories back to the Second World War and have not required the type of ground-up restoration that others have needed, having been well looked after throughout their lives.

The warbird movement is very strong today, as is the more widespread interest in preserving historic aircraft for restoration and museum display, and the Hurricane is a fortunate beneficiary of this now well-established and on-going desire to preserve aviation's rich and internationally important heritage. While around 12 Hurricanes of various different marks remain airworthy, with several others potentially airworthy, an important number also exist as non-flying exhibits in museums around the world. Among the best-known of the airworthy Hurricanes are the two examples maintained by the Battle of Britain Memorial Flight at RAF Coningsby, which are rightly regarded in Britain as national treasures, being reminders of the RAF's defeat of Germany's Luftwaffe in 1940.

Chapter One

The Hurricane Story

The Hurricane was a true workhorse of RAF operations in the Second World War. Conceived in the 1930s during a period of great change in fighter design and construction, the Hurricane drew on important aspects from the successful Hawker aircraft that preceded it, but included many of the innovations that were being introduced into fighter design and construction during that era.

OPPOSITE Hurricane Mk IIc, BE500, *Cawnpore I*, of No 87 Squadron based at Charmy Down, Somerset, pictured on 7 May 1942. The aircraft is being flown by Sqn Ldr Dennis Smallwood, the squadron CO.
(Imperial War Museum (IWM) COL186)

35
THE HURRICANE STORY

ABOVE The prototype Hurricane was exhibited at the SBAC Display, Hatfield, in 1937, where it created much interest. Particularly noteworthy is the aircraft's heavy Watts two-bladed wooden propeller and early style exhaust apertures. *(RAF Museum/Charles E. Brown Collection)*

When it was designed in the early years of the 1930s, the Hurricane was one of the most advanced warplanes of its day. It was a product of evolution, drawing on the many fine fighters and light bombers that Hawker had already successfully manufactured for British military service and overseas export. In particular, new features such as the retractable undercarriage, enclosed cockpit with opening cockpit cover, and metal construction and skinning, were allowing many strides forward to take place in warplane design. Most significantly, the increasing adoption of the monoplane layout as opposed to the externally braced biplane was embraced by Hawker for its new fighter. However, the Hurricane was lacking in some of the modern refinements that were introduced from the first into the contemporary and legendary Supermarine

Spitfire. The designers at Supermarine had no evolutionary process to draw on, in contrast to Hawker, and so were able to build in features that were not present in the Hurricane, such as the monocoque all-metal fuselage construction. Overall, it has often been noted correctly that the Spitfire had far more development potential in its airframe and engineering than the Hurricane. This is one of the reasons why the Spitfire successfully continued to operate in some numbers after the Second World War, while the Hurricane was very much at the limit of its operational life as a front-line type by the end of the war. Nevertheless, the Hurricane was the right aircraft at the right time during the opening years of the war, and it is indeed fortunate for Britain that so many were operational, with many more being built when the war began.

The handling qualities of the Hurricane during take-off and landing were excellent due to the type's wide-track main undercarriage with relatively wide low-pressure tyres. This made the Hurricane an easier aircraft to land,

LEFT One of the excellent design features of the Hurricane was its wide-track main undercarriage, in complete contrast to the difficult narrow-track main undercarriage of such contemporary types as the Spitfire and Messerschmitt Bf109. This is the lower part of an early Hurricane Mk I, L1684, showing in particular the very strong and sturdy main undercarriage units. *(RAF Museum, Cyril Peckham Collection)*

LEFT Manufacture of the Hurricane took place in several different locations in Britain, including the Hawker factory at Langley in Buckinghamshire. In this view several Hurricane Mk IIcs, including LF774 nearest to the camera, are on the production line at Langley. (RAF Museum)

even on austere surfaces, without the danger of nose-overs or ground-loops, in sharp contrast to the Spitfire. Particularly during the campaign in North Africa, when Hurricanes were so important to the overall Allied victory, and during operations in Burma and India, the type was able to operate from all sorts of basic and very rustic landing grounds with ease. The wide-track main undercarriage was also more suited to landings on aircraft carrier decks, as the Royal Navy discovered with its operations of specially converted Sea Hurricanes. The type's large, comparatively thick wing allowed the Hurricane to be a stable gun platform, much more so than the Spitfire.

The first Hurricanes began to reach front-line RAF squadrons from December 1937 onwards. This was a little sooner than the Spitfire, but was several months after the initial deliveries were made to front-line Luftwaffe units of the chief adversary of the Hurricane, the Messerschmitt Bf109. The Hurricane was considerably more advanced than many of its contemporaries in other air forces, which were mainly biplanes or early monoplanes of inferior performance. The Hurricane, for example, was a better aircraft in terms of power, performance and firepower compared to the French Morane Saulnier MS.406, which it fought alongside in the so-called Phoney War in late 1939/early 1940, and then during the Battle of France from 10 May 1940 onwards.

Manufacture of the Hurricane was undertaken by the parent company and a number of sub-contractors, in addition to widespread construction in Canada. A large number of smaller companies were involved in supplying components to the overall manufacturing effort, some of these in dispersed facilities to avoid the worst effects of German bombing. There exists the thorny problem of just how many Hurricanes were actually built. An often-quoted figure is 14,231, which appears to be the one that Hawker itself published. However, this must be qualified by a number of factors. For example, a small but significant number of Hurricanes were built from spare parts, utilising components from written-off aircraft, while some earlier machines were converted into later models and appear to have taken on new serial numbers as a result. Additionally, a major repair organisation existed in Britain during the Second World War, which brought back to life many wrecked aircraft

BELOW The Hurricane had a robust and substantial centre section that held fuel tanks and the undercarriage with its retraction mechanism. The outer wing panels were attached to it when the complete aircraft was assembled later in the manufacturing process. (RAF Museum)

ABOVE Two female workers at Hawker's Langley factory manhandle a Hurricane firewall from the rear of the engine compartment, and illustrate the fact that Hawkers, like most other aircraft companies in Britain, used a considerable number of women in the production process during the Second World War. *(RAF Museum)*

BELOW A considerable amount of recycling and rebuilding of damaged Hurricanes took place during the war. A civilian repair organisation was specifically created for this purpose and used a number of companies in Britain to carry out repair and reconstruction work. Hurricanes like the damaged example shown here (Mk I, P3154) were selected or actually worked on for possible return to front-line duties. *(RAF Museum)*

that had been officially Struck Off Charge, some of which took on new identities even though they were in effect the same aircraft. The 'Civilian Repair Organisation' was created in 1940, and within it a number of companies were seconded to repair and overhaul battle-damaged Hurricanes. The organisation also overhauled war-weary aircraft, which were later sent to training units or other air forces. One of the factories involved was the Austin Motor Company at Longbridge, Birmingham, which also built 300 new Hurricanes; another was David Rosenfield Limited, based at Barton aerodrome, near Manchester. Further, before the Second World War some of the export Hurricanes sold abroad began life with RAF serial numbers; these numbers were then replicated on new aircraft on the production lines that replaced the exported examples. Therefore the often-quoted figure of 14,231 must be viewed with scepticism, but it does exist as probably the only real guide as to what was roughly the final total of 'new-build' Hurricanes.

In another footnote to the Hurricane story, the designers who were responsible for the aircraft, and Sydney Camm in particular, went on to continue their distinguished careers by creating such famous British types as the Typhoon, Fury and Sea Fury, and arguably one of the finest jets of all time, the Hawker Hunter.

Hurricane: Variations on a theme

Compared to the Spitfire, which progressed through many versions, as its basic design was developed and its power and capability were increased, there were few production versions of the Hurricane. Nevertheless, the type similarly went through progressive upgrading and was given increasing capability, particularly in the field of armament. The Hurricane was built by several different manufacturers apart from the parent company, either under licence or due to the increased output necessitated by wartime requirements for mass production, and this had an effect on the various marks that were produced. Like the Spitfire, the Hurricane was 'navalised', leading to several important marks of Sea Hurricane. In the early war years, the factories producing Hurricanes were subject to German bombing, but the effects were not as serious as the difficulties faced by the German aircraft industry as the war progressed, when Allied bombing increasingly disrupted production, necessitating fragmentation and dispersal of manufacture, and sub-contracting. Disruption on this scale never took place in Britain, despite the attentions of the Luftwaffe. There was a considerable amount of dispersal of aircraft manufacturing and component fabrication in Britain, but not sufficient to interfere with production in the way that it eventually did in Germany.

The following is a brief description of the principal production versions of the Hurricane, excluding the limited production in such countries as Belgium and Yugoslavia. More thorough details of the weapons and power plants fitted in these different models are given in the accompanying sections.

Hurricane Mk I (early and late production)

The Mk I was the first Hurricane series production version, but there were significant differences between the early and the later production examples in this initial type of Hurricane. The very first production Hurricane Mk I examples that reached No 111 Squadron in late 1937, and the aircraft that followed them to that unit and other early RAF users, were austere machines. Powered by the Merlin II, they featured a two-bladed, wooden, Watts fixed-pitch propeller, fabric-covered outer wings, and a ring-and-bead gunsight. Initially, the tailwheel was intended to be retractable, but it was soon discovered during early testing and service use that a larger rudder area was required to improve control characteristics, particularly during spinning. Introduced into production, and retrofitted to some of the early

BELOW In 1938 the initial RAF Hurricanes of No 111 Squadron were shown off to a delegation of MPs and other dignitaries at RAF Northolt, their home base. In this scene, an antiquated-looking Handley Page Harrow, K7009, '214-Z', of No 214 Squadron, flies over one of 111's Hurricane Mk I aircraft. *(RAF Museum/Charles E. Brown Collection)*

two-bladed, fixed-pitch propeller, but this was only an interim measure. The big change came with the installation of the Rotol constant-speed, three-bladed, metal propeller unit, which gave a dramatic improvement in performance. 'Ejector' exhaust stacks were fitted, which were believed to give a little additional thrust. The fabric-covered outer wings were replaced by slightly redesigned metal-covered wings, which had a different gun bay access panel shape, but retained the eight-gun layout. It is often claimed that the first Hurricane to be fitted with the metal-covered wings on the production lines was L1887, a Hawker-built machine, but there is conflicting evidence of this in company records, especially as many older Hurricanes were fitted with the new wings to replace their fabric-covered outer wings at any convenient point in the future. An armour-glass panel was incorporated in the front of the windscreen, and from the summer of 1940 some 70lb of armour-plate protection was added (including pilot's head and back armour). The wing fuel tanks in the wing centre section were also given a measure of protection, as was the reserve gravity-feed fuel tank in the forward fuselage, just ahead of the cockpit.

Other changes included better radio equipment, the installation of IFF equipment, and the replacement of the original upright rod-type aerial mast behind the cockpit with a distinctive, streamlined tapered mast. Early Hurricanes were fitted with TR9 HF radio

ABOVE This early production Hurricane Mk I, L1683, shows features of the first production batch of Hurricanes including the simple radio mast behind the cockpit and Watts two-bladed wooden propeller. This particular aircraft survived long enough to become a ground-based instructional airframe in 1943. *(RAF Museum, Cyril Peckham Collection)*

machines, was an extension at the base of the rudder, and a distinctive keel was added to the lower rear fuselage. This effectively made the rudder taller, and thereafter the tailwheel was fixed and non-retractable due to the new keel. The early Hurricanes also lacked any significant armour or self-sealing fuel tanks. They were armed with eight 0.303in Browning machine-guns, four in each wing outside the arc of the propeller disc and therefore not requiring to be synchronised.

Successive improvements were made to the Mk I as production continued. During 1939, the power plant was changed to the more powerful Merlin III. The de Havilland (Hamilton Standard patent) three-bladed, two-speed, metal propeller unit replaced the Watts wooden,

RIGHT The ubiquitous and ever-present RAF starter trolley was a necessary part of the ground equipment that would surround a Hurricane Mk I on the ground, as shown by this Gloster-built mid-production Mk I with the later production-standard radio mast aft of the cockpit and Rotol propeller unit with Jablo blades. *(RAF Museum, Cyril Peckham Collection)*

equipment, but this began to be replaced in the late summer of 1940 with new T/R Type 1133 VHF radios. The IFF equipment, which also started to be incorporated in the late summer of 1940, was an important addition to the electronic warfare side of operations, making the Hurricane easier to spot as friendly by other defending fighters. An unfortunate incident had taken place shortly after the declaration of war in September 1939 in which two North Weald-based Hurricanes of No 56 Squadron were shot down by defending Spitfires; the use of IFF equipment theoretically guarded against this type of occurrence. It did, however, result in wire aerials needing to be run between the Hurricane's horizontal tailplane tips and the rear fuselage, which caused some undesirable drag and were a nuisance to ground crews. The use of the new VHF radio equipment, on the other hand, deleted the need for a wire to be run between the aerial behind the cockpit and the vertical tail.

These later-standard Mk I Hurricanes bore the brunt of the aerial fighting during the Battle of Britain, the earlier Mk I Hurricanes having seen action during the 'Phoney War' and the Battle of France. Overall, the Hurricane was well-liked by its pilots, and its manoeuvrability and ability to pull quite tight turns gave it a marked advantage over the Bf109E and Bf110 fighters that were its potentially deadliest adversaries during this period. In terms of top speed it was bettered by the Bf109E by up to some 30mph, depending on the altitude of the fight, especially above some 15,000ft.

Nevertheless, it was a comparatively easy aircraft to fly, which turned out to be a good thing when many pilots arriving in the front-line during the Battle of Britain had comparatively limited flying experience.

In mid-1940, the first Hurricane Mk I version specifically for operations in hot, dusty areas of conflict started to be included in Hurricane production. These so-called 'Tropical' or 'Trop' Hurricanes were fitted with a Vokes air filter to the carburettor air intake in a prominent 'chin' fairing under the nose and forward fuselage. Initially, until the French capitulation, some of these aircraft were ferried to North Africa and Malta via France, using a non-jettisonable, cylindrical 40gal fuel tank beneath each wing for long-range ferry flights.

Hurricane Mk II

From the start, Sydney Camm and his design colleagues at Hawker looked for ways to improve the Hurricane, without indulging in unnecessary redesign work that would have made the aircraft more time-consuming and difficult to manufacture. The more powerful and improved Merlin XX (sometimes written as Mk 20) engine became available in 1940, and this gave the possibility of improving the Hurricane's performance without complicating the design and slowing production. Among the engine's enhanced features was a new two-speed supercharger that could have its impeller speed altered by the pilot depending on the altitude and other flight characteristics. At approximately 18,000ft it could be switched to a higher or Full Supercharger (FS) speed rating for added compression. For flying at below that altitude, the lower or Moderate or Medium Supercharger (MS) speed rating was the optimum setting. The result was more power at both lower and higher altitudes, the latter being particularly welcome and significantly increasing the overall performance of the engine: this was a maximum of 1,260hp. Somewhat ironically, by the time this new combination was available, some Hurricanes were being increasingly switched to low-level fighter-bomber operations where the enhanced performance at higher levels was rarely needed.

The Merlin XX and its related equipment took up a little more room compared to the earlier Merlins and so the engine/equipment compartment in front of the cockpit was lengthened by several inches (for full official Specifications for the Mk IIc, see page 65). The carburettor air intake under the forward centre section was redesigned and moved back by some 3in. Coolant for this more powerful engine was provided by a 70% to 30% water/glycol mix, rather than pure glycol used for earlier Merlin versions. This and the increased cooling requirements required a larger radiator and a redesigned, circular oil cooler. There were tropical versions of most of the Mk II series for operations in North Africa and the Far East, including a survival kit for the pilot and, most prominently, an increased size carburettor air intake beneath the nose, giving a 'chin' – some of the Hurricanes supplied to the Soviet Union had these features, too, because a number of them had been earmarked for transportation to the Middle East prior to being diverted to the Soviet Union.

This limited but important redesign work led to the Hurricane Mk II series, which became the most numerous variant of the Hurricane and was built in several specific models. The prototype was P3269, a converted Mk I, which first flew on 11 June 1940. In addition to the different mark of Merlin engine, several other changes were made during the long Mk II production run, visibly including a slight modification to the tailwheel leg arrangement and attachment area, and the addition of an altered spinner, which also slightly affected the length of the aircraft. Initial deliveries were made to the RAF of the first Mk II Hurricanes before the end of the Battle of Britain. Subsequently, significant orders were received by Hawker in the autumn of 1940 for large numbers of Mk IIs, although it is interesting to note that some of these contracts did not differentiate between the specific marks of Mk II, which are listed below.

Hurricane Mk IIa

The initial Mk II Hurricanes were similar to the Mk I, with the eight-gun wing armament, but with the Merlin XX engine installed. They are sometimes referred to as Mk IIa Series I. In addition, some of the early Mk II Hurricanes introduced what was called a universal wing. This was a slightly redesigned wing compared to the later production Mk I Hurricanes, which had the capability for carrying beneath the wings a pylon on each side that could accommodate fuel tanks for extended range flying, or unguided rocket projectiles (RPs), or gun pods. This represented a considerable up-gunning of the Hurricane, which was continually extended throughout the Mk II production run, and was fortunate considering that the Hurricane in north-west Europe was increasingly switched to fighter-bomber and intruder missions during 1941. The universal-wing Mk IIa Hurricanes are sometimes referred to in official documents as Mk IIa Series II aircraft. It must also be stressed that some Mk II Hurricanes were converted from a number of surviving Mk I airframes, making the possibility of arriving at a definite total for overall Hurricane production a difficult proposition.

Hurricane Mk IIb

The developments that Hawker made with the Hurricane's wing were most important in giving the type extra capabilities and the possibility for additional armament to be carried. The Mk IIb had the initial eight-gun Hurricane armament layout increased with two additional 0.303in machine-guns outboard of the landing-light installation, making six guns in each wing for a grand total of 12.

Hurricane Mk IIc

The Mk IIc was probably the most important mark of Hurricane aside from the Battle of Britain-winning Mk I, and is the type that many associate most closely with the operational mid-war Hurricanes. Hawker's designers had been interested for some time in the idea of beefing up the type's firepower from the rifle-calibre 0.303in machine-guns of the initial production Hurricanes by incorporating a

Increasing the capability of the Hurricane took place throughout production, with one of the most important changes to the type's internal armament being the adoption of four 20mm cannons (two in each wing) during Mk II production. This development aircraft, Z3888, was used by Hawkers to pioneer various weapons concepts including the carriage of under-wing stores. *(RAF Museum)*

cannon armament. With the introduction of the all-metal outer wings into Hurricane production this became a more realistic possibility. The established wing machine-gun armament was removed altogether, and was replaced by four Hispano 20mm cannons, two in each wing, with up to 364 rounds of 20mm ammunition. This gave the Hurricane a greater striking power, particularly for ground-attack and intruder missions (including those at night). The altered wings also included an underwing attachment for a 250lb bomb (later, 500lb bombs could be carried by the Mk II-series), and the provision for underwing fuel tanks. The Hurribomber had been well and truly developed by this point, underlining the growing importance of the Hurricane for ground-attack work by 1941/2. The initial production Mk IIc Hurricanes were issued to the RAF in April 1941.

Hurricane Mk IId

The Hurricane Mk II-series was capable of being up-gunned, and with the type's success in the ground-attack role a wide range of armament possibilities was looked at by Hawker. An operational necessity that increasingly became apparent – particularly in the North African desert – was the ability to attack German tanks, in addition to the wide variety of 'soft-skinned' ground targets that intruder and ground-attack Hurricanes normally found as targets. German tanks in the open battlegrounds of North Africa generally had armour capable of warding off attack from the then current range of Allied tanks that were almost all inferior in firepower and armour. A solution was to fit a large-calibre cannon to ground-attack aircraft, and so the Hurricane Mk IId was born. This mark was modified to carry a Vickers Type 'S' 40mm cannon in a pod beneath each wing. An initial conversion was flown in September 1941, and the type entered service in April/May 1942. Only one wing machine-gun was retained in addition to the cannons for sighting purposes with tracer ammunition.

Hurricane Mk IIe

Further wing modification was introduced in the planned Mk IIe, but the changes soon became extensive enough that the Mk II designation was finally dropped and this new mark was rebranded as the Mk IV.

Hurricane Mk III

The Mk III was to have been an emergency layout of the Mk II powered by a US Packard-built Merlin engine, in case home-produced Merlins started to be in short supply. By the time production was to have commenced, Merlin production had increased to the point where the concept was rendered unnecessary. Packard Merlins were installed in some of the Canadian-built Hurricanes.

LEFT The Hurricane grew into being a very important ground-attack aircraft after its days as a pure fighter were over. The Mk IV was the greatest expression of this transformation, with the 'universal' wing able to carry and mount a variety of different weapons options. Some Mk IVs were fitted with 'dust' filters for operations in austere environments. This Mk IV, KX877, was used for development work and was temporarily known as a Mk V. (RAF Museum)

Hurricane Mk IV

The Mk IV was the last major production mark of the Hurricane – although the final Hurricanes to be completed on the production lines were of the Mk IIc variety. The Mk IV represented how far the Hurricane had developed during the war into a dedicated ground-attack type. The universal-wing arrangement of this mark allowed for a wide variety of ordnance to be carried, including underwing bombs, unguided rockets and other stores such as long-range fuel tanks and the 40mm cannons also used by the Mk IId. This new mark was powered by the improved and more powerful Merlin 27 engine of 1,620hp, and was equipped with dust filters for desert operations. Some 350lb of additional armour plating was added to the airframe for low-level operations (although the early production examples were fitted out with similar armour to the Mk IId), for the cockpit, radiator, fuel tanks and engine compartment. According to the official *Pilot's Notes* for the Hurricane (AP 1564B&D), under no circumstances should the Mk IV (or indeed the Mk IId) Hurricane be entered into a spin when fitted with the underwing cannons. The first Hurricane Mk IV examples flew in March 1943 and the type was eventually replaced by the big, powerful, dedicated ground-attack Hawker Typhoon.

LEFT The Hurricane Mk IV introduced the so-called 'universal' wing which allowed for a wide variety of ordnance to be carried, including under-wing bombs, unguided rockets (as seen here) and other 'stores' including long-range fuel tanks. BP173 began life as a Hurricane Mk IId, but performed development work for the Mk IV and was assigned to the A&AEE at Boscombe Down from April 1942 as a part of this work. (RAF Museum)

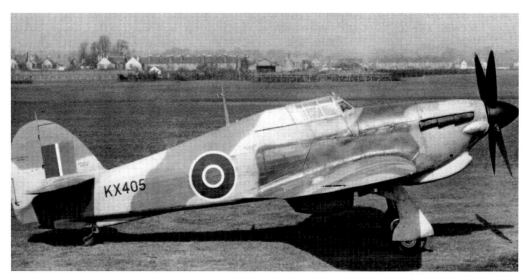

Hurricane Mk V

Only three Hurricane Mk Vs were built, two of these as conversions of Mk IVs, and featured a Merlin 32 engine and four-bladed propeller. The Mk V was intended to be a yet more capable ground-attack Hurricane, particularly for operations in the Far East, but more than enough Hurricanes were available there by late 1943 and in the event production did not commence.

Canadian-built Hurricanes

Hurricanes were built in Canada by the Canadian Car & Foundry Company Ltd. More than 1,400 were produced, and further details are included elsewhere in this chapter. Initially known as Mk I, the first aircraft were renumbered as Mk X and production continued through several marks to the Mk XIIa. Some were converted into Sea Hurricanes. Power was provided by US-built Packard Merlin 28 and 29 engines.

Sea Hurricane

There was a separate, but related line of development of the Hurricane for naval use, known as the Sea Hurricane. Britain's Royal Navy was in need of modern fighters capable of operating from aircraft carriers from the earliest days of the Second World War, and the Hurricane, with its wide-track main undercarriage and comparatively easy handling,

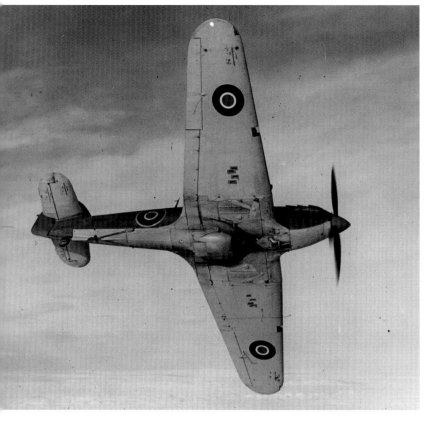

LEFT Hurricanes played a central role in the Catapult Aircraft (or Armed) Merchantman concept, which intended to provide aerial protection to convoys until aircraft carriers were sufficiently widespread and available to do the job more effectively. Here, what is believed to be a Sea Hurricane Mk Ia, is hoisted from a lighter onto a CAM ship, while a second example awaits its turn on the lighter. *(RAF Museum)*

was a natural choice for conversion for naval use. All Sea Hurricanes were conversions from standard land-based Hurricanes of various types, although some of these conversions were made on the production line in both British and Canadian factories. Contracts for some 800 conversions were eventually made, but the exact number of Sea Hurricanes that existed has never been satisfactorily determined. The first naval Hurricanes, however, were to go to sea not on aircraft carriers, but as expendable catapult aircraft aboard armed merchant ships.

Sea Hurricane Mk Ia

The earliest Sea Hurricanes were simply Mk I examples that were handed over to the Royal Navy from RAF stocks mainly for training. It is interesting to note that there was rarely a shortage of Hurricanes – Hawker's production organisation always kept up well with demand, allowing for surplus aircraft to be available for situations such as this.

The Sea Hurricane Mk Ia was a Mk I modified either by Hawker, Gloster, or mainly by

BELOW Although of poor quality, this interesting photograph shows a Hurricane or Sea Hurricane installed and ready to be launched on the catapult of a CAM ship, looking down the line of launch. In this case the merchant ship is the SS *Empire Franklin*. *(RAF Museum)*

RIGHT A Hurricane or Sea Hurricane ready to be launched from the catapult of the SS *Empire Franklin*. For anyone watching these launches the spectacle was most interesting. In this case the ship is still in port but the concept is nonetheless very clear. The installation of the catapult and rail is particularly noteworthy, as it tended to vary from one ship to another depending on the design of the ship itself. *(RAF Museum)*

General Aircraft Ltd for operation aboard specially converted Catapult Aircraft Merchantmen (CAM ships), whose crews were civilian and whose Hurricanes were piloted and serviced by RAF personnel. There was also a small number of Fighter Catapult Ships, which were crewed by Royal Navy personnel, whose aircraft were operated by the Fleet Air Arm. All of these were cargo ships equipped with a catapult for launching a Hurricane, but without any facilities to recover the aircraft once it had been launched. If the aircraft was not in range of a land base, pilots were forced to bail out or ditch after completing their mission. Ditching a Hurricane was not easy, because the radiator housing beneath the centre section acted as an unfortunate water brake, pitching the nose of the fighter downwards when it hit the water. The escaping pilot then had to be picked up by a ship, so it was advisable to land near to one. Over 80 modifications, some small, were needed to convert a landplane Hurricane into a Sea Hurricane, including new radios to conform with those used by the Fleet Air Arm and new instrumentation to read in knots rather than miles per hour. These aircraft were popularly known as 'Hurricats'.

Sea Hurricane Mk Ib

The Sea Hurricane Mk Ib was the first real naval Hurricane, as it had both catapult spools and an arrester hook, enabling it to be operated from aircraft carriers. The prototype was converted from a Canadian-built Hurricane Mk I,

LEFT An extremely rare colour photograph of a Hurricane on the catapult of a CAM ship. As can be seen, the whole contraption appeared to be very precarious. Although some of the catapulted Hurricanes had to land in the sea (they could not land back on the CAM ship), in a number of cases the fortunate pilot managed to use the Hurricane's good range qualities to find land and make a much safer conventional landing. *(RAF Museum/Michael Lyne Collection)*

P5187, and, it is believed, first flew in this configuration in March 1941. Operational Mk Ib Sea Hurricanes were converted mainly from Mk I-series Hurricanes from May 1941, but also included were some Mk IIa and IIb aircraft, as well as a number of Canadian-built, machine-gun-armed Hurricanes. By the end of 1941, four Fleet Air Arm squadrons were operational on the type on aircraft carriers, allowing the existing Fairey Fulmars to be largely phased out of service, the Sea Hurricane being a major step forward in performance and capability over these two-seat fighters.

Sea Hurricane Mk Ic

A number of Hurricane Mk I airframes were converted with the addition of outer wings mounting the four-cannon armament of the standard Hurricane Mk IIc to become the Mk Ic Sea Hurricane. They were also fitted with catapult spools, an arrester hook and other naval equipment and were operational on aircraft carriers from early 1942. Some of these aircraft-carrier capable Sea Hurricanes were delegated in 1943 to bolster the dwindling numbers of CAM ship Hurricats, which by then were starting to wear out.

Sea Hurricane Mk IIc

The Sea Hurricane Mk IIc version was equipped
with naval radio equipment, catapult spools, an
arrester hook and other naval equipment. This
was a 1942 modification and was probably the
best of the Sea Hurricanes as it had the Merlin
XX engine and four-cannon combination that
worked so well with the standard land-based
Hurricane Mk IIc.

Sea Hurricane Mk XIIa

This designation is sometimes used to describe
Canadian-built Hurricane Mk XIIa converted into
Sea Hurricanes.

Two-seat Hurricanes

Bearing in mind the rear fuselage structure
of the Hurricane consisted of metal
tubes and a wooden framework covered in
wooden stringers and then fabric, it seems

impossible that there could possibly be a two-
seat Hurricane. Nevertheless, several two-seat
Hurricanes did exist, with their second cockpits
in the rear fuselage aft of the normal pilot's
cockpit. There was also at least one *three*-seat
Hurricane.

The 'official' two-seat Hurricane was an
adaptation by Hawker for the Persian military.
The company had already looked in detail in
the early 1940s at the prospect of a two-seat
Hurricane advanced and conversion trainer
for British service, possibly as a Miles Master
Mk I replacement. Hawker's designers had
gone so far as to investigate a layout with a
second cockpit placed behind the normal
pilot's location, separated by a bulkhead and
crash pylon and with full dual controls. Persia
had been an early export customer for the
Hurricane, but the onset of the Second World
War prevented the original order from Persia
being completed. After the war, a new Persian

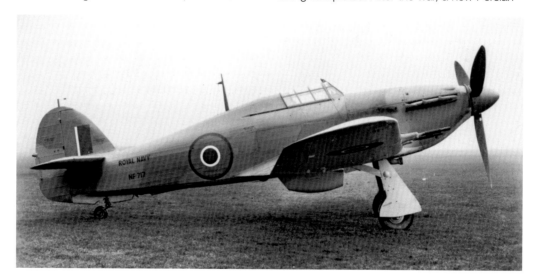

order was placed, which included two two-seat Hurricanes as a result of the investigations already carried out by Hawker's designers. Originally, both cockpits were to be open, but turbulence for the rear occupant (the instructor) was found to be such that a fix was arranged in which the rear cockpit was covered with an adapted Hawker Tempest teardrop – like a rearwards sliding canopy, the front cockpit remaining open. Hawker had looked at the possibility of a Hurricane single-seat fighter arrangement during the war with the rear fuselage cut down and a teardrop canopy installed (in similar fashion to the later Spitfires and later P-51 Mustangs), and some of this

experience also found its way into the Persian two-seat configuration. This seemed to work and both aircraft, which were equivalent to Mk IIc Hurricanes, were delivered to Persia in this configuration, although one of them was originally completed with both cockpits open. The first flight was made on 27 September 1946.

In the Soviet Union, necessity came first on many occasions during what the Russians called the Great Patriotic War, and several of the many Hurricanes supplied to Russia during the Second World War were converted into two-seaters. The Russians identified the need for a two-seat conversion trainer Hurricane

The 'official' two-seat Hurricane conversion by the parent company was this Hawker layout, with a second crew position cut into the fuselage behind the normal cockpit location. Two examples were converted after the Second World War for Persia. Although the open cockpit format shown here was at first intended, eventually a specially-adapted 'teardrop' canopy was fitted to the rear crew position. *(RAF Museum/Cyril Peckham Collection)*

RIGHT The Russians made good use of the Hurricanes that were supplied to them by Britain during the war, including converting some of them into two-seaters, with the second cockpit located behind the first as in the later 'official' Hawker two-seat conversions. This Russian two-seater was intended for general reconnaissance and artillery spotting, and was based on a Canadian-built Mk XIb, BW945. It was armed with a flexible-mounted 12.7mm ShKAS machine gun in the rear cockpit, with the rear gunner/spotter seated facing aft. (Nikolay Baranov Collection)

due to the large number of Hurricanes that were entering Soviet service, and to that end an initial batch of ten were converted – the work being Russian with no apparent input from Hawker. Dual controls were fitted, some of the armament was removed (it is believed that some of the Hurricanes were Mk IIb, which had at least eight of the wing machine-guns removed) and the conversion was not unlike the two Hawker aircraft that were later configured for Persia, albeit retaining fully open cockpits. The Russians also converted further two-seaters (the exact number may never be known for sure), some being used for liaison, while at least one was employed as an air ambulance and another was fitted with a rearwards flexible-mounted machine-gun and used for reconnaissance. Several others were configured as glider tugs at Saratov, to tow gliders such as the Antonov G-11 and A-7 light transport.

The three-seat Hurricane was a non-flying aircraft, converted with a seat mounted on each side of the cockpit on the outside. The conversion was made in India, it is believed near to the end of the war, to allow prospective Indian pilots the chance to literally sit-in on ground taxiing and see exactly what the pilot was doing.

Other Hurricane versions and projects

The operational Hurricane's shape changed little over the long production run of the type, which was always an encouraging sign with any aircraft as it showed that the basic

design was good from the start. Most of the changes made during manufacture regarded the fitting of more powerful versions of the Merlin engine, and the provision of different types of armament. As mentioned before, Hawker looked at the possibility of cutting down the high fuselage line behind the cockpit for the fitting of a better-vision teardrop canopy, but this concept was not carried through, although some prototype work was started, and it was finally abandoned in 1942 as large-scale production continued of the basic Hurricane design. A number of other ideas were looked at either for testing new concepts, or ideas that came about through military necessity for the provision, for example, of extended range or endurance.

Perhaps the most bizarre experiments involved the aircraft being towed in the air to extend ferry range. At one stage during the Second World War the concept of ferrying aircraft direct from Britain to Malta and North Africa appeared to be well intentioned, resulting in some strange ideas to try to achieve this non-stop, long-flight concept. A number of towing aircraft alternatives were proposed, including the Consolidated B-24 Liberator bomber. The entry of the US into the war, and the subsequent provisioning of aircraft carriers for British use, from which Hurricanes could be transported long distances and then flown off to distant war zones, nullified the continued consideration of this bizarre and potentially highly dangerous plan. Similarly unusual, and also reflecting the lengths that some dreamers go to in warfare to try to meet a perceived demand, was the biplane Hurricane. Also referred to as the slip-wing Hurricane, this peculiar plan involved a Hurricane being fitted with a detachable upper auxiliary wing, ostensibly to improve short-field performance at high weights (such as carrying fuel for long ferry flights) and to increase range. The modification of a Hurricane Mk I, L1884, was made by F. Hills and Sons Ltd of Manchester (a woodworking company which also had aviation connections, particularly through the licence production in the 1930s of a Czechoslovak light aircraft known as the Hillson Praga). Named the Hillson F.H.40, this Heath Robinson-like contraption was test-flown, but wiser heads prevailed and the concept did not proceed.

A number of re-engining projects were also pursued, partly due to the perceived but groundless fear that Merlin engines might come into short supply, with those available being diverted specifically for use in the Spitfire. To that end several alternative engine types were envisaged for the Hurricane, including the Napier Dagger inline engine and the Bristol Hercules radial engine. There was also a plan for an uprated, ground-attack Hurricane derivative powered by the Rolls-Royce Griffon inline engine, but this was discontinued when development of the Hawker Typhoon dedicated low-level, ground-attack aircraft gained momentum and eventually led to the successful production and operation of the Typhoon later in the war. Interestingly, one of the Yugoslav-operated Hurricanes was converted to Daimler Benz DB 601A power. This German inline engine was the same power plant as that of the Messerschmitt Bf109E (the Yugoslavs also operated Bf109Es) and the conversion was tried out in the period prior to the German invasion of Yugoslavia, at which point further development ended.

Aerodynamic research was carried out using a converted Hurricane Mk IIb, Z3687, which was fitted after the Second World War with a laminar-flow wing, and quite extensively tested at the Royal Aircraft Establishment, Farnborough, Hampshire, during the later 1940s. Various odd types of armament were also envisaged for the Hurricane but not carried in service, including an upwards-firing rocket installation aft of the cockpit for anti-bomber operations, similar in concept to the German *Schräge Musik* weaponry carried operationally in some German night-fighters during the war.

A floatplane conversion of the Hurricane was considered in the early part of the war as a result of the problems encountered when operating landplanes during the ultimately unsuccessful Norwegian campaign in 1940. To allow a trial conversion to be made, Hawker was supplied with a pair of floats applicable to the Blackburn Roc fleet fighter. Some work was made on this conversion, but the idea was abandoned later in 1940, which is perhaps fortunate as the resulting modified Hurricane was envisaged to have had a maximum speed

BELOW The biplane Hurricane. This bizarre contraption, otherwise named the Hillson F.H.40 or 'slip-wing' Hurricane, was conceived during the Second World War to give the Hurricane greater ferry range for delivery flights using a detachable upper auxiliary wing. Thankfully it was not tried out except in experimental form. *(Malcolm V. Lowe Collection)*

RIGHT A modified
Hurricane layout
that did work well
was the fitting of
some Canadian-built
Hurricanes with a
substantial fixed ski
main undercarriage
and fixed 'snow
shoe'-type tail ski for
operations during
snow conditions
in Canada. The
example shown
here also exhibits
a particular feature
of many Canadian-
built Hurricanes, a
Hamilton Standard
propeller unit without
a spinner *(David Harvey
Collection)*

of only 210mph. Among Canadian Hurricane production, more successful was the concept of putting the Hurricane on skis for operations on snow. A number of Hurricane Mk XIs were converted in this way, with a substantial fixed ski main undercarriage and fixed 'snow-shoe' type tail ski. The resulting aircraft were used only in Canada, but were successful in service.

Foreign employment and manufacture

The Hurricane was widely exported, and was also built under licence in three countries apart from Britain: Belgium, Yugoslavia and Canada. The latter was responsible for the construction of more than 1,400 Hurricanes, which represented a significant contribution to the overall number produced. The Hurricane was a comparatively straightforward aircraft to manufacture, with its mixture of old and new technology, and was well suited to operation by air forces that were less conversant with the most up-to-date technology. Hurricane export sales began before the Second World War, and during the war a number of Hurricanes were handed over to friendly countries from RAF stocks – the RAF rarely seemed to have a shortage of Hurricanes. Following the Second World War, Hawker was again successful in selling Hurricanes on the export market. They were also flown by a significant number of foreign nationals who had joined the RAF to continue the fight against the Germans after their own countries had been defeated, or who were members of the British Commonwealth –

their contribution to the eventual Allied victory in Second World War should never be overlooked.

Aviators from the British Commonwealth participated either through joining RAF squadrons made up of Commonwealth personnel, or by being a member of the squadron service actually under the banner of their particular country. Among the former were units such as Nos 450 and 451 Squadrons, RAF, which were made up primarily of Australian personnel and served in the Middle East. Only one Hurricane was ever actually flown in Australia in Australian colours (V7476), this sole example being a refugee from the fighting in Java, although No 3 Squadron, RAAF, did fly Hurricanes for a brief period in the Middle East. Among the latter category, several Commonwealth countries had significant numbers of Hurricanes under their own auspices. The first to do so was South Africa, which was undergoing its own military expansion in the later 1930s. Initially seven Hurricanes were shipped to Cape Town from Britain in November 1938 – one of many hasty reactions to the so-called Munich Agreement several weeks beforehand. During the war, South Africa was supplied with substantially more Hurricanes, some being shipped through Takoradi in West Africa, allowing five SAAF squadrons to regularly fly Hurricanes in combat in various parts of Africa, including the major fighting in North Africa. Another Commonwealth country, New Zealand, was associated with the Hurricane in much the same way as the Australians, with two New Zealand-manned RAF squadrons, Nos 486 and 488, briefly operating the type in 1942.

India was also a major Commonwealth recipient of Hurricanes, resulting in eight Indian air force squadrons flying the type, primarily in the armed reconnaissance and fighter-bomber roles. The first Indian squadrons to fly Hurricanes, Nos 1 and 2 Squadrons, became operational in the latter months of 1942, and the growing stocks of Hurricanes in India for British and Commonwealth use allowed more than 100 Mk II-series aircraft to be passed to the Indians by the end of 1943. Much of the reconnaissance for the XIV Army fighting the Japanese in Burma was provided by Indian Hurricane pilots, some of these aircraft being fitted with an oblique camera installation in the lower port fuselage. It was an Indian Hurricane pilot, Flying Officer J. C. Verma of No 6 Squadron, Indian air force, who achieved his service's only air-to-air victory of the war, when he shot down a Nakajima Ki-43 'Oscar' in February 1944. Some of the Indian Hurricanes served into 1946, when eventually replaced by more modern types, No 4 Squadron being the last to cease flying its Hurricanes.

One of the lesser-known operators of the Hurricane was Egypt, of whose fledgling air force No 2 Squadron flew Hurricanes supplied by Britain, albeit after the fighting in North Africa had largely died down. Turkey was one of the

ABOVE As a part of the British Commonwealth, India was a major user of the Hurricane, with the Indian Air Force eventually operating eight squadrons against the Japanese. These Indian-operated Hurricane Mk II (apparently Mk IIb) aircraft were photographed in Assam during 1944. Although the Hurricane by that time was generally being replaced in North West Europe, in the continuing fight against the Japanese the Hurricane still had much to offer. Note the internal structure of the main gun bay hatch, which is lying on the outer wing surface. *(RAF Museum)*

BELOW Two 'tropicalised' Hurricanes of the Indian Air Force, apparently eight-gun Mk II airframes, prepare for take-off in 1943. The Indians used their Hurricanes primarily in the armed reconnaissance and fighter-bomber roles, in conjunction with other Allied air assets in the often bitter struggle against the Japanese in the China–Burma–India theatre. *(RAF Museum)*

BELOW Yugoslavia was the first foreign country to place an order for Hurricanes when it signed up in early 1938 for twelve of the early Mk Is with fabric-covered wings. This Yugoslav Hurricane from that first batch is cavorting on a test-flight prior to delivery. Yugoslavia also licence-built Hurricanes before production ceased with the German invasion of the country in 1941.
(Hawker Aircraft Ltd)

early purchasers of the Hurricane, being in the process of attempting to modernise and expand its armed forces during the 1930s. An order was placed for 15 Hurricanes in the first half of 1939, and all of these were delivered between August and October 1939 even though the war commenced in September 1939 – Hawker's records suggest that approximately ten more aircraft than the original order were also delivered, or at least earmarked for delivery to Turkey. These aircraft were all allocated RAF serial numbers. Considerable efforts were made during the course of the war to encourage the Turks to remain neutral, and to this end a large amount of bribes in the form of more military equipment were supplied to the Turkish armed forces. Among the supplies, more Hurricanes were sent in 1943 from RAF stocks in the Middle East, including several Mk IIc Hurricanes with tropical modifications.

Many Polish aviators escaped the destruction of their country in September 1939 to fight again with other Allied air forces, and several RAF Hurricane squadrons were manned by Polish nationals. Some of these fought bravely in the Battle of Britain, and eventually nine RAF Hurricane squadrons were Polish-manned. Poland had requested a Hurricane for evaluation purposes in 1939, some months before the German invasion on 1 September. The aircraft was shipped in July 1939 and apparently arrived at Stettin in early August, but nothing further is known about it. There have been persistent rumours that nine further Hurricanes were shipped to Poland at roughly the time of the outbreak of war, but the episode remains shrouded in mystery.

In addition to the Poles, pilots from several other countries that had suffered at the hands of the Germans also joined the RAF and manned Hurricane squadrons, including Czechoslovaks, Greeks, Norwegians and Yugoslavs. In the case of Yugoslavia there was also a very considerable export story that related to the Hurricane. Yugoslavia was no stranger to Hawker aircraft, having ordered the Hawker Fury biplane in the early 1930s (with Hispano-Suiza rather than Rolls-Royce power), and was the first country to place an order for Hurricanes when it signed up for 12 early Mk Is with fabric-covered wings in early 1938. The first two of these were delivered on 15 December 1938. They were flown out from Brooklands and reached Belgrade in stages; both aircraft were from the first batch of 600 Hawker-built Hurricanes and had previously been earmarked for RAF service, with the RAF serial numbers L1751 and L1752 allocated to them. The Yugoslavs were very impressed with the Hurricane, and subsequently ordered a second batch of slightly later standard Mk Is with metal outer wings and Merlin III engines – and also applied for, and were granted, a licence to build the Hurricane in Yugoslavia. This was a major success for Hawker. Indeed, it is worth noting that if the war had not intervened, the Hurricane would have proved to have been excellent value as an export sales success for Hawker. As it was, two factories in Yugoslavia were intended as the airframe manufacturers, the Rogozarski facility in Belgrade and a second plant in Zemun. Unfortunately for the

Yugoslavs, production started comparatively slowly, and there was also a problem with the supply of Merlin engines, leading to one of the Hurricanes being re-engined by the Yugoslavs with a Daimler-Benz DB 601 engine as a test to see if this power plant would be suitable for the Hurricane and easy to install.

The Yugoslav air force was hardly prepared when the German hammer blow fell on the Balkans in April 1941. Realising that the Yugoslav air force could pose a real threat, the Germans attempted to bomb Yugoslav military facilities and the manufacturing plants as soon as possible. At the time of the German attack, the Yugoslavs had approximately 38 Hurricanes available, with around 15 of these being from local production – the Yugoslav records from that period are very sketchy, and this information has been pieced together subsequently by local historians. In the event, the Yugoslav air assets were largely destroyed on the ground by the Germans, or lost in fruitless combats against overwhelming numbers of German fighters. Later in the war, Yugoslav personnel manned the RAF's Nos 351 and 352 Squadrons, of the Allied-manned Balkan Air Force, fighting with Hurricanes and Spitfires over the Balkans in support of Yugoslav partisans, and eventually these aircraft were handed over to the Yugoslavs for their own

service as the Germans were ousted. Several Hurricanes remained in service for a time post-war, with one of the Yugoslav air force units having Hurricanes on charge (on paper at least) as late as 1951. One of these aircraft is now preserved in the aviation museum at Belgrade's international airport.

A second country that intended to build the Hurricane under licence before the Second World War was Belgium. Like many nations in the late 1930s, Belgium woke up to the danger of Nazi Germany too late, and started to rearm with whatever modern equipment was available. She had an established aircraft industry that was capable of building Hurricanes, and in the event was able to operate both Hawker-built and home-produced examples of the Hurricane. Belgium ordered 20 Mk Is from British manufacture in March 1939. The first aircraft were delivered in the following month, seemingly there never being a shortage of Hurricanes from British factories. These were early Mk Is with Watts wooden propellers and Merlin II engines. A manufacturing licence was also purchased by the Belgians, for the manufacture of Hurricanes by Avions Fairey at Gosselies, with Merlin engines supplied from England. The Belgian government subsequently placed an order for 80 Hurricanes with Avions Fairey, which if they had been built would have

ABOVE Yugoslavia had a comparatively long association with the Hurricane. In this view, the exiled King Peter II of Yugoslavia is taxiing out in a Miles Magister Mk I (T9673), with a Hawker Hurricane Mk IIb of the RAF's No 71 Operational Training Unit and a Westland Lysander in the background, at Ismailia, Egypt, in October 1943. In various forms, Yugoslav personnel flew Hurricanes before, during and after the Second World War. *(RAF Museum)*

was a major export
customer for the
Hurricane before the
Second World War
and also undertook
licence-production
before the German
invasion in May 1940.
Most Belgian-operated
Hurricanes were
swiftly destroyed on
the ground by German
pre-emptive air strikes,
but this example with
a two-bladed propeller
was captured by
the Germans in the
early days of their
advance into the Low
Countries.

represented a significant fighter force. Deliveries
of Merlin III engines to Belgium commenced
from early 1940 and, indeed, supplies of Rotol
constant-speed propellers also appear to have
been made. A plan was devised to up-gun the
Belgian-produced Hurricanes with 12.7mm
FN-Browning machine-guns instead of the
0.303in armament, but it had no time to come
to fruition before the Germans attacked on 10
May 1940. At that time the Belgians could field
about 23 or 24 Hurricanes (although these
figures are vague due to the loss of documents
from the period), but only around a dozen of
these are believed to have been serviceable. The
first German attack included air raids on military
installations and factories to blunt any possible
military action, and within three days most of the
Belgian Hurricane force had been destroyed.

This was by no means the end of Hurricane
operations by Belgian pilots. Rarely if ever
mentioned in published works on the Hurricane
is the fact that the Belgians used a number of
Hurricanes *after* the Second World War. They
comprised six aircraft, all Mk II Hurricanes,
three of which had been used for fast
communications duties between RAF Hendon
and Brussels near to the end of the war,
operated under the auspices of the Metropolitan
Communications Squadron. These three aircraft
were later transferred to the newly reconstituted
Force Aérienne Belge, and subsequently served
principally in a liaison capacity. Later they were
added to by three further aircraft, which appear
to have been used as ground instructional
airframes. One of the six is now displayed, in a
non-airworthy condition, in Brussels.

From 1936 onwards the kingdom of
Romania embarked on a major programme of
rearmament and sent delegations to a number
of European countries, including France, to
purchase armaments of various kinds. Following
a royal visit to Britain in November 1938, the
Romanians ordered 50 Hurricanes, with the first
12 required as soon as possible. It appears that
only the 12 urgently requested Hurricanes were
ever supplied to Romania, the last of these in
September 1939 when Britain needed every
Hurricane that was available. These Hawker-
built aircraft had already been assigned British
military serial numbers as they were intended for
the RAF, and so the British numbers allocated
to them were subsequently reassigned to other
new Hurricanes.

Research of Romanian records by co-author
Malcolm Lowe suggests that at one stage in
1941 the Romanians listed *13* Hurricanes as
being active. Most published sources on the
Hurricane claim that these aircraft were little
used by the Romanians, but this is untrue.
The Hurricane was a major front-line type for
the Romanian armed forces, and equipped
the air force's Escadrila 53 at the time of the
German invasion of the Soviet Union, Operation
'Barbarossa', on 22 June 1941. As an ally of
Nazi Germany, Romania was fully committed
to 'Barbarossa', with her forces fighting
alongside her German allies in the southern
front of the 'Barbarossa' operations. The
Romanian Hurricanes were divided between
front-line operations and the coastal defence
of the strategically vital port and naval base
of Constanta on the Black Sea. On the first
day of 'Barbarossa' operations the Romanian
Hurricanes were in the thick of the fighting, with
pilots Petre Cordescu and Constantin Pomut
achieving four confirmed victories over Soviet
aircraft. The Romanians were well-pleased
with their small force of Hurricanes, which
were more than a match for the Soviet aircraft
they encountered in combat, including the
diminutive Polikarpov I-16. On the second day
of 'Barbarossa' operations, 23 June, Romanian
Hurricane pilot Horia Agarici instantly became
a national hero when he single-handedly shot
down all three Soviet Tupolev SB bombers
that were attempting to raid Constanta. The
Hurricanes were subsequently in the thick of the

aerial fighting over Bessarabia and the ultimately successful German-Romanian operations later in 1941 to take the port of Odessa, operating alongside Romanian-operated Messerschmitt Bf109Es and indigenous IAR 80 fighters, as well as Luftwaffe air assets. A lack of spares, and the appearance of better Soviet fighters during the course of 1942, resulted in the small Romanian Hurricane force being withdrawn from front-line operations.

Somewhat ironically, the country that the Romanian Hurricanes had seen much action against, the Soviet Union, became the largest user of Hurricanes outside British and Commonwealth service. Following the Axis invasion of the Soviet Union in June 1941, Britain began to supply the Soviets with what would become a considerable amount of materiel, including aircraft. Two principal routes were used to deliver the warplanes to Soviet forces: the safest was overland through Persia (modern-day Iran); the more direct but perilous route was by sea to northern Russian ports such as Archangel and Murmansk. A significant number of convoys of merchant

ships were dispatched on what became known as the North Cape route, into the Arctic Circle, protected by Royal Navy vessels. In the early days these convoys were protected by Hurricats aboard converted merchant vessels, but later in the war aircraft carriers took over the main part of the protection task. Not surprisingly, the Germans attempted to stop this line, and many British merchant seamen and service personnel lost their lives trying to supply the Russians – a point that received little recognition from the Soviet Union after the war.

To protect the northern Soviet ports from air attack, two squadrons of RAF Hurricanes, Nos 81 and 134, were sent aboard two convoys to the airfields of Vayenga and Keg-Ostrov in August 1941 with 40 Hurricanes. Comprising No 151 Wing, they provided local air defence for Murmansk, going into action on 12 September against Finnish-operated Bf109s. The stay of No 151 Wing was brief, and while in action British ground personnel provided instruction on the maintenance of the Hurricanes while the RAF pilots tried to pass on their wisdom to the local Russian pilots.

BELOW RAF Hurricanes and personnel were shipped from Britain to northern Russia in August and September 1941 to provide local air defence for the vital Soviet northern ports through which British supplies were being sent. This Hurricane Mk IIb, which appears to be Z5208, belonged to No 134 Squadron ('G' code) of the RAF's No 151 Wing, and was being filled up at Vaenga (Vayenga) in September or early October 1941 from a Soviet BZ-35 fuel truck. *(RAF Museum)*

LEFT, TOP A Soviet-operated Tupolev SB bomber takes to the air as a backdrop to two RAF-operated No 151 Wing Hurricanes, from No 134 Squadron, Vaenga, in September or early October 1941. The nearest Hurricane is a twelve-gun Mk IIb, Z3763, with a 'tropical' filter beneath the nose. *(RAF Museum)*

LEFT, CENTRE A No 151 Wing RAF Hurricane flies over a fellow Hurricane bearing the fuselage 'G' code of No 134 Squadron, in suitably cold conditions at Vaenga in September or early October 1941. When RAF personnel were withdrawn from northern Russia in October 1941 the remaining No 151 Wing Hurricanes were handed over to the Soviet authorities. *(RAF Museum)*

LEFT, BOTTOM The Soviet Air Force flew large numbers of Hurricanes. Here a Hurricane Mk II of a unit of the Soviet Northern Fleet is refuelled under cold and primitive operating conditions. The fuel truck is a Soviet BZ-38 using a modified GAZ-AAA chassis. *(Nikolay Baranov Collection)*

BELOW The official Soviet caption to this image states that Major General A.A. Kuznetsov, the commander of the Soviet Northern Fleet's air elements (VVS SF) was about to make the first official flight in a Hurricane by a Soviet pilot. The date was 25 September 1941 and the Hurricane was a Mk Ib, Z5252, '01'. It is known, however, that Soviet pilots had already flown some of No 151 Wing's RAF Hurricanes before this time. *(Nikolay Baranov Collection)*

The final British sorties were flown on 8 October, after which the surviving 36 Hurricanes were handed over to the Soviet authorities on 14 October and served with the newly formed 78 IAP of the Soviet VVS SF (which later became 2 GSAP and was a major user of Hurricanes for some time). No 151 Wing RAF personnel returned to Britain on a convoy. In due course, the Soviet Union received large numbers of Hurricanes, enough to equip at least 29 fighter regiments on several war fronts. It is often said that the Russians did not want Mk I Hurricanes, but instead, after evaluating a Hurricane Mk II-series aircraft (Z2899), decided that all deliveries should be of the Mk II variety. This appears to have occasioned Hawker to convert some of the Mk I Hurricanes earmarked for sending to Russia into roughly Mk II-standard. The Soviets subsequently went about up-gunning their Hurricanes, with around 1,200 of the eventual total of Soviet Hurricanes being rearmed with a variety of armament options. Some of this took place at unit level, but maintenance depots at Monino and Gorky carried out the 'official' conversions. The most favoured option was the fitting of four 20mm ShVAK cannons (two per wing) and two 7.62mm ShKAS machine-guns, plus underwing racks for three RS-82 ground-attack unguided rockets beneath each wing. Some of the later deliveries to Russia comprised 40mm cannon-armed anti-tank aircraft of the Hurricane Mk IV variety, but the Soviets preferred their indigenous Ilyushin Il-2 'Shturmovik' for close-in air-to-ground work against tanks and the type was not widely favoured. Some Soviet Hurricanes were used as rudimentary night-fighters, often for the nocturnal protection of Russian cities, and as reconnaissance aircraft. A number of Soviet Hurricanes were converted into two-seaters.

There is controversy as to how many Hurricanes were supplied to the Soviet Union. Many Western historians claim a total of 2,952 Hurricanes from both British and Canadian production. However, research into former Soviet archives by co-author Malcolm Lowe confirms a figure of 3,082, which is a total also favoured by most Russian historians.

Another country that used its Hurricanes in combat was Finland. Finnish procurement of the

Hurricane was limited to 12 aircraft, which were required as a result of Soviet aggression against the country from November 1939 in what is known as the Winter War. Shipped in early 1940, they were little used before the armistice in March 1940 between the two countries. When fighting again broke out in June of the following year, the Finnish Hurricanes operated with some effect against Soviet aircraft, and it is possible that there may have been combats between Finnish and Soviet-operated Hurricanes.

During the Second World War a small number of RAF Hurricanes force-landed in the neutral Irish Republic. The trend began in 1940 during the Battle of Britain with a Mk I and soon the Irish had three Hurricanes. A large amount of horse-trading resulted in two of these later being exchanged for three older examples and a fourth added, and then in 1943/4 Britain supplied seven Mk Is and six Mk IIcs. Eventually the Irish No 1 Squadron at Baldonnel operated the type, some surviving until 1947.

Another small-scale operator of Hurricanes was France. Initially, a number of Hurricanes were supplied from RAF stocks in the Middle East to Free French units during the fighting in North Africa, including GC 1 'Alsace'. At the end of the war the French naval aviation (*Aéronavale*) was the recipient of a mixed bag of around 15 Hurricanes, including some Mk IIc examples.

A country whose Hurricane procurement spanned the war years was Persia. Initially, Persia ordered 18 early Hurricane Mk Is following a military mission to Britain in March

ABOVE A Hurricane with several owners. Originally intended for the RAF, Hurricane Mk IIa, Z2585, was instead one of the 3,000-plus Hurricanes supplied by Britain to the Russians. It was shot down by Finnish anti-aircraft gunners in February 1942 over Finnish-held territory while attached to the Soviet 760 IAP (Fighter Regiment). Repaired, it served with the Finnish Air Force in 1944. (*via Nikolay Baranov*)

1939. These were required with tropical filters, but problems in developing adequate equipment meant that only one example was delivered before the war broke out in September 1939. A second Hurricane appears to have been delivered in 1940, and during the war ten were transferred to the Persians from RAF stocks (again underlining the fact that there never seemed to be a shortage of Hurricanes). When the war ended, the Persians renewed their intention to obtain Hurricanes and 16 Mk IIcs were purchased, in addition to two unique, company-converted two-seaters, which were based on the Mk IIc layout.

An often-overlooked operator of the Hurricane was the US Army Air Force. Only a small number of Hurricanes were ever used by the Americans, usually as fast liaison aircraft or 'hacks', but it is an aspect of the Hurricane's story that receives little attention. In England, three Hurricanes are known to have been flown by the Eighth Army Air Force during 1943, two of them being withdrawn before the end of the year and the third (V6844) returned

The post-war order from Persia for Hurricanes included two unique company-converted two-seat trainers which were based on the Mk IIc layout. Hawkers had hopes of selling two-seat Hurricanes more widely than was eventually the case, the two Persian two-seaters being the only ones that were ordered from the company. Initially, the two Persian aircraft were finished with open cockpits as shown here, but later a canopy was fitted over the rear cockpit. *(RAF Museum/Cyril Peckham Collection)*

to the RAF in early 1944. One of the three appears to have been used by the Eighth Air Force's headquarters staff at Bovingdon, in Hertfordshire. Several Hurricanes are also believed to have been used, on a more ad hoc basis but for the same purpose, by the Twelfth Army Air Force in the Mediterranean theatre – that particular area of operations having been especially well populated by Hurricanes.

A post-war user of Hurricanes was Portugal. During the Second World War ostensibly neutral Portugal allowed Allied forces to use installations on the Portuguese islands of the Azores. This enabled British and US long-range anti-submarine patrol aircraft to operate from the Azores, thus helping to close the 'Atlantic Gap' that had been exploited by German U-boats previously to attack Allied shipping without fear of return fire. In return, Portugal was promised military assistance after the war, and as a part of this a batch of Hurricanes was supplied. Fifty comparatively new Hurricane Mk IIc aircraft were released from maintenance units and returned to Hawker at Langley for overhaul. The best 40, plus a large supply of spares, were shipped to the Portuguese. Interestingly, when the last of these Hurricanes was retired in the early 1950s, several returned to Britain and subsequently starred in the movie *Reach for the*

Sky, the film biography of the famous Battle of Britain pilot Douglas Bader.

Three countries flew Hurricanes 'unofficially'. These were Germany, Japan and Italy, all of which operated captured examples mainly for evaluation or sometimes simply as trophies. At least one example captured by the Japanese was test-flown by an operational unit, the highly successful 64th Sentai, for familiarisation purposes.

Possibly of greatest significance to the Hurricane story in terms of procurement and manufacture was Canada, where major

ABOVE A number of Hurricanes were captured by the Germans in different theatres of operations. Hurricane Mk I, V7670, was captured in the Western Desert and was painted in German markings. It is seen here having been 'recaptured' by British forces in a rather dilapidated state – the official caption claiming the location as Gambut in January 1942. *(RAF Museum)*

LEFT At least one Hurricane Mk I is known to have been captured by, or on behalf of, the Italians during the invasion of Yugoslavia and subsequently painted in Italian camouflage and markings. It is seen here in full Italian regalia, under evaluation in Italy late in 1941. *(RAF Museum)*

ABOVE Canada was
a major operator
and producer of
Hurricanes. Canadian-
built Hurricanes
served with Canadian
forces in Canada, but
were also supplied
to the RAF in Britain
for service there
and elsewhere. This
twelve-gun Canadian-
built Hurricane Mk XII,
5658, has a glare
shield ahead of the
cockpit and a feature
common to many
Canadian Hurricanes
– a Hamilton Standard
propeller unit without
a spinner. (Malcolm V.
Lowe Collection)

production took place in addition to widespread service. In keeping with other Commonwealth countries, many Canadian airmen flew under the umbrella of the RAF during the Second World War, manning a number of RAF squadrons, including at least five of the Canadian-manned RAF squadrons operating Hurricanes at one time or another. In addition, No 1 Squadron, RCAF, flew Hurricanes from early 1939, and was based in Britain from mid-1940 onwards in time to participate in the Battle of Britain. However, Canada had developed an excellent and efficient aviation industry of its own in the inter-war period, and was well placed to build the latest generation of modern warplanes.

Canada first asked for Hurricanes in 1937, but at this stage the Hurricane production programme was in its infancy and no aircraft could be spared – in sharp contrast to following years, when there were many Hurricanes available. The Munich Crisis of 1938 brought into sharp focus, at least for those who were willing to listen, the reality that war was inevitable. The Canadian requests were looked at again, and with mounting pressure from Canada 20 Hawker-built Hurricane Mk Is were shipped across the Atlantic, with the first departing in October 1938. Arrangements were also made for the Hurricane to be manufactured under licence in Canada, and no time was wasted in setting up this potentially difficult

task. The company chosen to perform the licence manufacture was the Canadian Car & Foundry Company Ltd (CCF), based in Montreal, with additional works at Fort William, Ontario. Sometimes known by the abbreviation Can-Car, the company went about setting up the necessary production facilities, and a pattern aircraft was supplied by Britain in March 1939 to help the procedure. Also useful was the rapid copying onto microfilm of all the relevant drawings for the Hurricane at Hawker's Kingston offices and their rapid dispatch to Canada.

The first Canadian Hurricane to come off the production line at Fort William was serial number P5170, which first flew on 9 January 1940. It was later shipped to Britain for evaluation, where it was found to have been very well put together. At first, Canadian-built Hurricanes were generally similar to the British-made Mk I, and were referred to as such. However, a new numbering system was soon devised to differentiate between the British and Canadian-manufactured Hurricanes, with the initial Canadian machines being named Mk X. There were, in fact, many detail differences between the British and Canadian Hurricanes, but none that was a major cause for concern. One obvious difference was in the power plant. In the US, the Packard Motor Car Company of Detroit was becoming a major producer of the Merlin in its Mk XX form, having signed agreements with Rolls-Royce for the manufacture of the Merlin in the US during 1940. This soon became the supplier of choice for the Canadian-built Hurricanes, with the Merlin 29 being most widely used in the Canadian production.

An often-quoted figure for Canadian production of the Hurricane is 1,451, split into several different marks:

Hurricane Mk X fighter and fighter-bomber, powered by a 1,300hp Packard Merlin 28, armed with eight 0.303in machine-guns.
Hurricane Mk XI, similar to the MkX, but with a number of armament options.
Hurricane Mk XII fighter and fighter-bomber, powered by a 1,300hp Packard Merlin 29. At first armed with 12 0.303in machine-guns (and thus similar to the British-manufactured Mk IIb), this armament was later changed to four 20mm cannons (as in the British-manufactured Mk IIc).
Hurricane Mk XIIa (sometimes written as Mk XIIA) fighter and fighter-bomber, powered by a 1,300hp Packard Merlin 29, many armed with eight 0.303in machine-guns.

Some of the latter version were converted into Sea Hurricanes. The 1,300hp rating mentioned here for the Merlin 28 and Merlin 29 refers to take-off power with 12lb of boost applied.

Many of these Hurricanes were shipped to Britain for onwards assignment – a number finding their way to the Soviet Union – but a significant quantity remained in Canada, where they were used by home-based RCAF squadrons for local air defence throughout the vast country. A distinguishing feature of some of the Canadian-built Hurricanes was the installation of a Hamilton Standard propeller unit, which was often to be seen without a spinner fitted.

Hurricane facts and figures

The following are representative specifications from official British documentation for two different marks of Hurricane. Included is material obtained during official testing of the Hurricane at the A&AEE at Boscombe Down, in Wiltshire. Altogether, some 67 Hurricanes were at Boscombe Down

at one time or another during the war for the testing of a wide range of standard features, modifications, weapons combinations and many other related experiments relevant to the Hurricane – this was in addition to the several Hurricane Mk I examples that were originally tested at Martlesham Heath, the pre-war home of the A&AEE. It is interesting to note the increase in available engine power from the early Hurricane Mk I to the later marks of Hurricane, and also the rise in take-off weights, which

Specification: Hawker Hurricane Mk I

Wingspan	40ft
Length	31ft 5in (Watts propeller)
Horizontal tail span	11ft
Maximum speed	305mph at 17,000ft (Watts propeller, Merlin II)
	324mph at 17,800ft (Rotol propeller, Merlin III)
Normal take-off weight	6,447lb (Rotol propeller, Merlin III)
Range (internal fuel)	c.440 miles
Service Ceiling	31,000ft (Rotol propeller, Merlin III)
Armament	Eight 0.303in Browning machine-guns, four in each wing
Engine	One Rolls-Royce Merlin II or III inline piston engine, of 1,030hp at 16,250ft
Crew	One

Specification: Hawker Hurricane Mk IIc

Wingspan	40ft
Length	32ft 3in (Rotol propeller, long spinner)
Horizontal tail span	11ft
Maximum speed	329mph at 17,800ft
Normal take-off weight	7,544lb
Range (internal fuel)	460 miles
Service Ceiling	32,400ft
Armament	Four 20mm Oerlikon or Hispano cannons, two in each wing
Engine	One Rolls-Royce Merlin XX inline piston engine, of 1,260hp at 11,750ft (MS – in Medium Supercharger)
Crew	One

in the case of the Hurricane was adequately covered with increased power. It must be stressed that the Hurricane's performance for any given mark from the MkII onwards depended on what ordnance the aircraft carried, and the external operating conditions; a fully-laden Hurricane that could take-off without problems in the cool and damp air of an English morning in early 1942 would have struggled with the same load if taking-off in the heat of the day from a hardly well-prepared surface in India. The average stalling speeds quoted for Merlin XX-powered Hurricanes in the official *Pilot's Notes* (AP 1564B&D) were 80–90mph for an aircraft with undercarriage and flaps up, and 60–75mph for an aircraft with undercarriage and flaps down, both figures relating to Hurricanes at weights of 7,600lb or more.

There are also several questions concerning the fuselage length of some marks of Hurricane. This is partly because different marks had different propeller and spinner combinations (a fact that is overlooked by many historians), indeed this was true even within the same production batches. When production began at the Longbridge factory of the Austin Motor Company, a small number of Mk II Hurricanes may have had a slightly longer fuselage compared to their exact contemporaries from other factories due to a different design of

coolant header tank for the type's Merlin engine being installed. This point has long been a source of argument and conjecture regarding Hurricane Mk II manufacture. On page 65 are figures for the Mk I and Mk IIc, which were two of the most important specific production models of Hurricane.

Hurricane weaponry

There was considerable debate from the start as to what armament should be fitted in the Hurricane, and several of the official Specifications that were released to the aircraft industry in the early 1930s tried to grapple with this problem. The type of armament and armament arrangement installed in the biplanes that had been successful in the First World War had persisted in the inter-war period. Machine-guns that were accessible to the pilot so that they could be cocked and fired by the pilot, and where jams could be manually cleared, were the order of the day. The idea of mounting guns in the wings of the aircraft, well away from the pilot, remained novel to some air forces even in the 1930s. In Britain, a great deal of faith was still placed in the old Vickers machine-gun layout, the design of which dated back to the First World War era, to the extent that a modern alternative was not readily to hand. Somewhat in desperation, attempts were made by British designers, manufacturers and the Air Ministry alike in the 1930s to find a good modern alternative abroad, and one was eventually located in the US: an American machine-gun manufactured by the Colt Automatic Weapon Corporation in Hartford, Connecticut. Unfortunately it fired American 0.30in ammunition, but further investigation revealed that it was capable of firing standard British 0.303in ammunition, which had a fairly wide tolerance. Protracted attempts were then made to obtain manufacturing licences for the weapon to be produced in Britain and after much time had been lost it emerged ready for use under British manufacture by BSA as the Colt Browning 0.303-in machine-gun – usually referred to with the Colt origin conveniently forgotten. This weapon was to become a standard machine-gun for the RAF for many years to come, although it had its drawbacks.

BELOW The four 0.303in Browning machine guns in the starboard, fabric-covered wing of this No 601 Squadron Hurricane Mk I at RAF Tangmere are replenished in this posed but nonetheless interesting photograph from July 1940. The eight-gun (four in each wing) configuration was the classic early Hurricane armament layout. *(RAF Museum/ Charles E. Brown Collection)*

The most obvious of these was its small calibre. Indeed, a criticism voiced by pilots of both Hurricanes and Spitfires, into the wings of which these guns were installed, was that their rifle-calibre properties were of comparatively limited value against modern metal and armoured warplanes. The use of these rifle-calibre machine-guns in British warplanes of the time was in complete contrast to German thinking, in which a smaller number of larger-calibre and potentially more destructive weapons was preferred. It sometimes took an awful lot of 0.303in bullets to bring down a German aircraft during the Battles of France and Britain.

The comparatively strong and roomy thick wing of the Hurricane Mk I allowed four of these machine-guns to be installed in each wing, the four grouped closely together. The Spitfire also featured this seemingly heavy armament, but in the Spitfire's very different thinner wing the four guns on each side were spaced apart. Some pilots preferred the Hurricane's layout of closely

spaced guns, which seemed to a number of pilots to offer a better concentration of fire. Early in the Hurricane's design it was intended that only four wing guns in total would be fitted, two on each side, in line with some previous official requirements, but the Hurricane's wing design easily allowed for four guns on each side. These weapons were unsynchronised as they were installed outside the arc of the spinning propeller. Up to 2,660 rounds of ammunition could be carried for the eight guns. Gun sighting was initially by the long-standing ring-and-bead method, a throw-back to the inter-war biplanes, with the 'ring' mounted above the instrument panel and the 'bead' set on a small post above the engine cowling. The standard GM2 reflector gunsight was introduced in mid-1939, but many Hurricanes retained the bead even with the gunsight installed.

As the Hurricane was developed, the original fabric-covered outer wing sections were replaced by the all-metal wing (with the

ABOVE Rearming the four 0.303in Browning machine guns in the metal-covered wing of a late Hurricane Mk I or early Mk II that has Jablo propeller blades fitted. The metal-covered Hurricane wing with 0.303 in Browning machine guns featured a hexagonal access panel for the guns. *(RAF Museum)*

exception of the fabric aileron covering), this layout having a different, hexagonal access panel on the wing upper surfaces for reaching the guns. A so-called 'camera gun' was located in the starboard wing leading edge, inboard of the guns, which was activated when the guns were fired for recording the results of the firing.

With some strengthening and slight modification, Hawker's designers found that the Hurricane's now all-metal outer wings could be adapted for the carrying of many kinds of ordnance. This led to the 'universal' wing layouts, as pioneered from the early Mk II aircraft onwards, with the ability to carry beneath the wings the pylons that could accommodate external fuel tanks for extended-range flying, or unguided RPs, bombs, or gun pods. The latter fitted in well with the Hurricane's increasingly adopted role after the Battle of Britain as a ground-attack and intruder aircraft in north-west Europe. A variety of trials were carried out to determine the optimum type and number of rockets that the Hurricane could carry under its wings, with eight (four beneath

ABOVE A leading edge panel could be removed to allow forward access to the four-gun 0.303in Browning gun installation in each wing of those Hurricanes fitted with this armament. Note the blast tubes of the four guns which are in line with the leading edge, even though the guns themselves were installed in a staggered arrangement within the wing. The Hurricane in this case is a No 601 Squadron Mk I at RAF Tangmere in July 1940. *(RAF Museum/Charles E. Brown Collection)*

BELOW The hexagonal access area for the four 0.303in Browning machine guns of the metal-covered wing of the mid- and late-production Hurricane Mk I and some early Mk II aircraft. Note how the guns are staggered to allow room for the ammunition box for each gun. *(RAF Museum)*

RIGHT The Hurricane Mk IIb with twelve 0.303in Browning machine guns had the normal four-gun installation in each wing beneath the hexagonal panel inboard, with the two extra guns in each wing well outboard. In this view the two outer guns are being rearmed. Needless to say, all twelve-gun Hurricanes were made from the start with metal-covered wings. *(RAF Museum)*

each wing on special launch rails) being particularly favoured – although this type of weapon did not start to see widespread service on RAF aircraft (except for Coastal Command types, which did not include the Hurricane) until 1943. The wing also proved strong enough for the initial eight-gun armament to be extended, so that some Mk II Hurricanes had each wing fitted with two additional 0.303in machine-guns, making six in each wing for a grand total of 12. This layout was common to the Mk IIb, and appears to have been pioneered in some of the Mk IIa initial Mk II-series Hurricanes. It was one of the heaviest wing gun armaments ever carried in a front-line fighter, although the rifle-calibre guns installed still had the drawback of being lightweight for aerial combat, as previously stated. There were up to 3,990 rounds for these 12 guns.

A major change came with the Hurricane Mk IIc, one of the classic marks of Hurricane. In this version the wing machine-gun armament was removed altogether, and was replaced by four Hispano 20mm cannons, two in each wing, with

up to 364 rounds of 20mm ammunition. This beefed-up armament was useful for ground-attack and intruder missions, but did come with the penalty of slightly impaired performance and necessitated the outer wings being somewhat redesigned to fit the new weapons – noticeable by two bumps on the upper surface. The RAF had shown an interest in a four-cannon

ABOVE Rearming the hard-hitting 20mm cannon of a Hurricane Mk IIc. The installation of the two cannons is well illustrated in this view, as is the recoil spring of each weapon ahead of the wing leading edge. The large size of the 20mm rounds is noteworthy. *(RAF Museum)*

LEFT Hurricane Mk IIc BE500, LK-A, of No 87 Squadron, has its 20mm cannons rearmed amid a busy maintenance scene. This was one of a sequence of photographs taken by the famous photographer Charles E. Brown when he visited the squadron in 1942 to photograph its night-fighting Hurricanes. *(RAF Museum/Charles E. Brown Collection)*

armament as long ago as 1936, and at last received this layout in the Hurricane during 1941. The first four-cannon armed Hurricane (possibly Mk I P2640) flew on 27 May 1940, with a specially modified test Mk II V7360 undergoing a brief RAF trial later in the year. The new mark of Hurricane to mount this revised armament was named the Mk IIc, and initial aircraft were issued to the RAF in April 1941 (to Nos 3 and 257 Squadrons, the latter led by the celebrated Bob Stanford Tuck, at RAF Coltishall). They were an immediate success, with this mark being the most numerous type of Hurricane built, and the last of the aircraft to be manufactured, in 1944. Initial Mk IIc Hurricanes carried four 20mm Oerlikon cannons rather than Hispanos, but the latter became more numerous as production continued. The Mk IIc was also the first widespread Hurribomber, capable of carrying a 250lb bomb beneath each wing on specially designed racks, although this capability had been pioneered in some of the early Mk IIa Hurricanes and was subsequently extended throughout the Mk II-series.

Some Hurricane squadrons flew a mix of the machine-gun-carrying Mk IIb and the cannon-armed Mk IIc aircraft. Examples of the Mk IIc that were used for TacR operations often had one of the cannons removed from each wing.

The Hurricane Mk IId was a further development of the Mk II series, and was fitted with underwing gun pods for the largest of the Hurricane guns, the 40mm cannon. The need for a hard-hitting cannon of this sort arose from the requirement for the Hurricane to play the role of dedicated tank-buster, in addition to the already successful Hurribomber configurations, particularly in North Africa where British ground forces were hard-pressed to fight against the latest generation of German tanks, including the Panzer III and Panzer IV. The very potent and especially well-armoured German Tiger tank also started to make an appearance in North Africa towards the end of hostilities there, providing an even more pressing requirement for aerial assets capable of taking on these increasingly more powerful and well-armoured monsters.

Two types of 40mm cannon were under development at the time, the Rolls-Royce BF and the Vickers Type 'S'. The initial installation of the latter was in Hurricane Mk IIa Z2326, thus making it the prototype of the new Mk IId version. It first flew in this configuration on 18 September 1941, with one of the large guns beneath each wing, and provision for only 15rpg. A single 0.303in machine-gun was retained in each wing, simply for sighting the big cannons with a mixture of normal and tracer ammunition. This installation was satisfactory and the type went into limited production, the first examples reaching No 6 Squadron in Egypt in April/May 1942. Aiming the weapons was not particularly easy, and although some Mk IIds also served in the Far East and in north-west Europe, many were later shipped to Russia.

There was no production Hurricane Mk III, but the series-produced Mk IV was important in including a further developed universal wing, which could carry a wide variety of ordnance. Powered by the Merlin 27, the first Hurricane Mk IV examples flew in March 1943, and could carry the widest range of underwing stores yet, including bombs of up to 500lb (one under each wing), up to eight unguided RPs (up to four under each wing, including the RP-3 variety), and various underwing fuel tanks up to the largest available to the Hurricane (88gal capacity for ferrying) – in addition to engine and radiator armour, which made this the best of all Hurricanes for ground-attack work, albeit at the expense of increased weight. The underwing stores could also be carried asymmetrically. Initial deliveries were made to No 164 Squadron at RAF Colerne, in Wiltshire, during May 1943.

A small number of Hurricanes built in Belgium under licence (equivalent to the British Mk I) were fitted with four 12.7mm FN-Browning machine-guns instead of the 0.303in armament – it was intended that this arrangement would be more widely used, but the defeat of Belgium in May 1940 ended the plan. A significant number of Hurricanes operated by the Soviet Union were rearmed with completely different armament fits, with some used specifically as ground-attack aircraft against German tanks, but without the benefit of the knowledge of some of Hawker's development of Hurricane armament in Britain, although they did have some of the big-gun Mk IIds to examine.

Hurricane aces

During its comparatively long service life, the Hurricane was flown by many of the RAF's most successful and best-known pilots, a number of whom became aces, and some racked up impressive scores of aerial victories while in the Hurricane. The British method of calculating aerial victories in the Second World War was straightforward (unlike that of some other countries), with official 'ace' status being granted to any pilot who achieved five or more aerial kills. There has always been considerable debate among historians about how authentic some of these scores were, particularly when Allied claims for particular days or even specific actions and combats do not tally with known or recorded losses of Axis aircraft – the same is true when German claims for aerial victories over Allied aircraft are cross-referenced against actual Allied losses. Nevertheless, post-war analysis of all known recorded claims for victories in air-to-air combat by RAF fighter pilots (although what constitutes a 'fighter' is a little loose in this analysis) in the Second World War shows that 55 per cent of the claims were made by Hurricane pilots. If nothing else, this illustrates how widespread and prolific Hurricanes were in aerial combat during the conflict.

The RAF's first air ace of the Second World War was a Hurricane pilot. The period before the German army invaded the Low Countries and France in May 1940 is often referred to as the Phoney War, but a considerable amount of

aerial activity took place over the border areas of France and Germany in the months before May 1940, leading to many combats. On 26 March 1940 New Zealand Flying Officer Edgar James 'Cobber' Kain, of No 73 Squadron, while based at Rouvres in eastern France, brought down two Bf109Es for his fourth and fifth victories to become the RAF's first ace of the conflict, although he himself was shot down and injured later in the same combat.

As mentioned in the Introduction, the highest-scoring RAF airman in the Battle of Britain was the Hurricane pilot Josef František,

SERGT JOZEF FRANTISEK   POLISH SQUADRON

LEFT Flight Lieutenant I.R. 'Widge' Gleed of No 87 Squadron in the cockpit of one of the highest-scoring Hurricanes, P2798. Featuring Disney's *Figaro* on its right-hand pilot access door, this long-lived Hurricane Mk I, coded LK-A, was used by Gleed in the Battle of France and on into 1941. He gained at least nine victories flying P2798 during the Battles of France and Britain. *(RAF Museum)*

LEFT Czechoslovak pilot Sergeant Josef František, who flew with the Polish-manned No 303 Squadron, achieved 17 aerial victories in Hurricanes during September 1940 to become the highest-scoring RAF pilot in the Battle of Britain. Few photographs have come to light of František, but in September 1940 Cuthbert Orde drew this charcoal portrait of the Czech pilot at RAF Northolt where he was stationed. *(RAF Museum)*

ABOVE One of the most famous Hurricane pilots of them all was the incomparable Squadron Leader Douglas Bader. After losing his legs in a flying accident before the war and subsequently flying with artificial limbs, Bader became the most famous of the RAF's fighter pilots from the Battle of Britain era, and scored a string of victories in Hurricanes at that time. He is seen here with his No 242 Squadron Hurricane, V7467, LE-D, during the latter part of the Battle. *(RAF Museum)*

BELOW No 242 Squadron, which was one of the many successful Hurricane-operating squadrons during the Battle of Britain, was led by the famous Douglas Bader (centre). He is seen here in late September 1940 with two of the squadron's aces, Flying Officer G.E. Ball (left) and Pilot Officer W.L. McKnight (right). McKnight was the squadron's top-scoring Hurricane pilot by the end of the Battle of Britain with 17 victories, several of these achieved over France earlier in the year. *(RAF Museum)*

from Czechoslovakia, with 17 aerial victories during September 1940. Many other highly distinguished pilots flew the Hurricane for all or a part of their combat careers, including Douglas Bader and Bob Stanford Tuck. Squadron Leader Bader flew Hurricanes with No 242 Squadron during the Battle of Britain, and finished the war with a total of 20 aerial victories (some sources claim 23), including 11 with Hurricanes during the battle itself (the remainder were at other times while flying Spitfires). Squadron Leader Robert Roland Stanford Tuck became the commanding officer of Hurricane-equipped No 257 Squadron during the battle, with little prior experience on the type, and eventually achieved 12 victories in Hurricanes, the remainder of his 29 aerial victories being scored while flying Spitfires. These two pilots have tended to gain the limelight in subsequent years, while many who scored important numbers of victories in several of the theatres of war where the Hurricane operated have remained virtually unknown even to the present day. They include Sergeant Hamish Dodds, who was the top-scoring pilot in the theatre that the Hurricane can virtually call its own, namely North Africa. Flying Hurricanes with No 274 Squadron, Dodds achieved 13 victories and was involved in much of the desert fighting in the early part of 1942, having achieved his fifth victory on 24 January 1942.

A number of American pilots who had volunteered to fly with the British or Commonwealth forces also successfully flew Hurricanes. Among them was Pilot Officer William Robert 'Bill' Dunn, who became the first American air ace of the Second World War. Dunn joined the RAF in 1940 and was a member of the RAF's American-manned Hurricane-equipped No 71 (Eagle) Squadron at North Weald in May 1941. He scored three victories in Hurricanes in July and August 1941, and achieved two more in Spitfires later in August 1941 to become an ace while the squadron transitioned on to the latter type. He later scored again while flying P-47 Thunderbolts with the USAAF's 406th Fighter Group. An American ace who achieved all of his five victories while flying the Hurricane was Sergeant John Frederick 'Tex' Barrick, who flew with No 17 Squadron against the Japanese

during the difficult retreat in Burma in the early months of 1942.

Perhaps it is an indication of how far the Hurricane has been overshadowed in the years following the Second World War that two of the British and Commonwealth's top-scoring aces of the war, including arguably the highest scorer, have been largely forgotten. Neither of these pilots flew Spitfires and have therefore received little of the limelight afforded to more well-known Spitfire aces. Due to the nature of the combats that both took part in, there has been the problem of verification of claims, as both fought in areas of the conflict where good book-keeping of claims and confirmed victories were at times impossible. Flying with a succession of Hurricane squadrons, from the frantic combats over France and England in 1940 to later operations in Burma, Frank Reginald Carey was not only an accomplished Hurricane pilot but also a seasoned fighter leader who rose to the rank of Wing Commander at the head of No 267 Wing in Burma. Carey achieved 25 confirmed aerial victories plus three shared (some sources quote 28 in total, again reflecting the problems of verifying claims in such areas of conflict as Burma), all of these scored in Hurricanes.

It is quite possible that even Carey's impressive tally in Hurricanes was exceeded by another flyer. The airman who is now generally acknowledged as being the highest-scoring

ABOVE LEFT Generally regarded as the highest-scoring British and Commonwealth air ace of the Second World War, Flight Lieutenant (later Squadron Leader) Marmaduke Thomas St John Pattle from South Africa achieved well over 40 aerial victories, if contemporary accounts and surviving documentary evidence are to be believed. These were made while flying Gloster Gladiators and Hurricanes, the latter with Nos 80 and 33 Squadrons. He may well have been the highest-scoring ace for both the Gladiator and Hurricane. *(Malcolm V. Lowe Collection)*

ABOVE A number of leading Soviet pilots and recipients of the Hero of the Soviet Union award flew the Hurricane, which was extensively operated by the Soviet Union. Here, Lieutenant Colonel V.I. Belousov (right), commanding officer of 17 GSAP (Guard's Ground-Attack Regiment), is seen with two of his pilots and several of the unit's Hurricanes in the summer of 1942. Belousov was a Hero of the Soviet Union recipient and a considerable enthusiast of the Hurricane. *(Nikolay Baranov Collection)*

British and Commonwealth ace of the Second War (and indeed the highest-scoring Allied ace of them all in that conflict, if one dismisses countries such as the Soviet Union that fought on both sides), was a Hurricane pilot from South Africa. Flight Lieutenant (later Squadron Leader) Marmaduke Thomas St John Pattle firstly flew Gloster Gladiators and then Hurricanes with No 80 Squadron over North Africa and Greece, principally against Italian forces, and later commanded No 33 Squadron on Hurricanes during the desperate fighting against the Luftwaffe after Germany intervened in the Balkans in early 1941. 'Pat' Pattle was involved in many of the major air actions of the increasingly losing battle against far superior numbers over Greece despite being in poor health, and achieved an incredible number of aerial victories during that time. He found the Hurricane to be an excellent gun platform for his fine marksmanship and flying skills, and he was certainly one of the most gifted fighter pilots of his generation. Sadly he was shot down and killed by Messerschmitt Bf110s during the massive air battles that have collectively become known as the Battle of Athens on 20 April 1941, not long before the British pull-out from Greece. Many of the RAF records were lost in the retreat, making it impossible to say for certain how many aerial victories Pattle achieved in the final days of the air battles. Indeed, German and Italian archives are also far from complete for that period. A number of theories now exist as to Pattle's final score, with 50 in addition to 2 shared being the most popular interpretation. If this total is true, it would give Pattle some 34 victories while flying the Hurricane (although some sources insist on 26), together with 15 or 16 on Gladiators. If the total of 50 is true, it would certainly make Pattle not only the highest-scoring British and Commonwealth ace of the war, but also the top scorer in Gladiators as well as Hurricanes.

One of Pattle's comrades-in-arms over Greece was Pilot Officer Roald Dahl, who achieved five victories while flying Hurricanes, and went on to international fame after the Second World War as a novelist and short-story writer. Clearly the Hurricane was flown by some very distinguished people.

Power for the Hurricane

Hurricane engines

All production Hurricanes were powered by versions of the legendary Rolls-Royce Merlin V-12 inline piston engine. At the time of the Hurricane's service introduction this engine was not yet 'legendary', but the Hurricane pioneered its use in high-performance fighter aircraft. It was for its time an advanced engine that drew on Rolls-Royce's considerable experience of designing and manufacturing high-performance power plants for front-line combat aircraft, and also included many of the lessons learned and knowledge gained from the successful Rolls-Royce racing engines that had powered Britain's world-beating Supermarine-built racing seaplanes in the inter-war Schneider Trophy races. Hawker Aircraft Ltd, and in particular Sydney Camm, had become an important advocate of the inline, liquid-cooled piston engine, long before the Hurricane came into being. Compared to bulky radial engines, the inline power plant imparted several advantages, one of the most important being the comparatively small frontal area. This allowed for a streamlined fuselage design from front to rear, and Hawker had come up with perhaps the greatest expression of this clean aerodynamic formula with the most beautiful of all pre-war biplane fighters, the Hawker Fury. Powered by the Rolls-Royce Kestrel inline engine, the Fury was an important step towards the development of the Hurricane, which retained all the aerodynamic refinement in fuselage design and engine integration that had been a feature of Camm's biplane combat aircraft of the late 1920s and early 1930s.

The Achilles heel of the inline engine, compared to the radial, was the need for liquid cooling, and so somewhere in the airframe a bulky radiator was required with its attendant intake. Camm, like many designers, placed this intake beneath the fuselage (others tried the arguably more aerodynamically efficient location of underwing air intakes, as on the Spitfire and Daimler-Benz powered versions of the Messerschmitt Bf109).

BELOW The Merlin engine installation on the Hurricane was functional, well-designed and streamlined, with neatly-fitting cowling panels, as shown in this production line view taken at Langley in 1944. The Merlin was the only engine type used throughout the Hurricane's long production run from 1937 to 1944. *(RAF Museum/Cyril Peckham Collection)*

In basic layout the Merlin was a liquid-cooled (glycol) V-12 inline engine with its cylinders mounted upright as opposed to inverted, augmented with a single-speed supercharger on Mks II and III, but with a two-speed supercharger on later models. Fuel was introduced into the engine by an up-draught SU-type carburettor that was subject to g-forces, meaning that the engine could cut out due to fuel starvation if the aircraft was flown inverted for any length of time.

The very first Hurricane, the prototype K5083, was powered by the 1,025hp Merlin 'C' engine. However, introduced at the start of Hurricane production was the later, production-standard Merlin II of 1,030hp. The basic fuel capacity for this engine was a maximum of 94gal. This comprised 66gal in two self-sealing fuel tanks, effectively each of 33gal in the wing centre section, between the main spars. The fuel was pumped from these into a gravity-feed tank, which held an additional 28gal in the forward fuselage, just ahead of the cockpit. This was the main fuel feed to the engine. Unfortunately, this latter tank proved to be vulnerable to return fire if the aircraft the Hurricane was attacking had a rear gunner, and eventually it was protected with a material named Linatex. A 9gal oil tank was built into the forward, port wing centre section. The main coolant radiator for the engine was housed in a prominent fairing under the wing centre section; the oil cooler was also incorporated into the main radiator (the latter was circular on later Hurricanes, but most if not all Mk Is had a squarer oil cooler shape). Later in Hurricane Mk I production, the Merlin III of similar output but improved capability was introduced, this version also having a universal propeller shaft allowing more advanced propeller units to be installed.

At the start of the war the Merlin engine ran on the then standard 87 octane fuel. From around March 1940 greater quantities of 100 octane fuel, imported from the US, became increasingly available. This allowed an increase in supercharger boost from 6lb to 12lb for comparatively short periods without damaging the engine. With the full 12lb emergency boost, the Merlin III was able to output 1,310hp at 9,000ft in short bursts (although some pilots apparently ran their engines with this additional

boost for up to 30 minutes. If the pilot used the emergency boost, he had to report it on landing, so that it could be noted in the engine's log book). This extra power gave a considerable additional edge in combat and was a useful addition to the available power for the Hurricane.

A major change took place with the introduction of the Hurricane Mk II series, which was powered by the Merlin XX. This was a more powerful engine, with an output of 1,260hp, but significantly it included improved supercharging, replacing the single-speed supercharger of the Merlin III with a two-speed unit. An RAE anti-g carburettor was also available for this engine type, preventing the problem of the engine cutting due to fuel starvation if flown inverted for any time. With 14lb boost, the Merlin XX could output 1,485hp at 6,000ft for short periods, this engine type performing best at low and medium altitudes.

In the Hurricane Mk IV, a new version of the Merlin, the Merlin 27, was installed. This had an output of 1,620hp for take-off, but this increased to 1,635hp with 18lb boost at 2,250ft, and was obviously optimised for low-level operations. Again it had an RAE anti-g carburettor.

The type of propeller fitted to operational Hurricanes went through a number of changes through the life of the aircraft. The original, austere Merlin II-powered Mk I Hurricanes were fitted with a Watts wooden, two-bladed, fixed-pitch propeller unit. This was a throwback to the biplane days of the 1920s and early 1930s, but what might have been good for aircraft of that era was outmoded for a modern warplane

BELOW Early Hurricane Mk I fighters were fitted with a wooden two-bladed fixed-pitch Watts propeller unit, and powered by the Merlin Mk II as shown by this early production example. The Watts propeller was not suitable for a modern, high-performance fighter aircraft and was soon replaced. (RAF Museum)

and could not adequately cope with the output of the latest high-performance engines. The Watts Z38, with a diameter of 11ft 3in, was fitted in early production Mk I Hurricanes, the Watts Z33 of 11ft 6in diameter having been fitted to the Hurricane prototype K5083. Both of these were right-hand rotation. It was obvious to Hawker's designers at an early stage that a variable-pitch propeller was essential to gain advantage for the Hurricane's performance potential, but a suitable propeller unit did not exist at that time in Britain. In the US, Hamilton Standard had developed a relatively efficient two-pitch propeller unit that promised some advantages, and it was subsequently produced in Britain under licence by the de Havilland Airscrew Company. It had a diameter of 11ft, right-hand rotation, and was fitted to early and mid-production Hurricane Mk I aircraft.

The real breakthrough came with the development by Rotol of a successful constant-speed propeller unit, which could allow the pitch of the propeller blades to change in flight to optimum position depending on the flight regime and engine power output at any given time. This could be used with the Merlin III engine onwards, the Merlin III being the first mark of Merlin with a universal propeller shaft onto which the more complicated variable-

pitch propeller unit could be fitted with its attendant hydraulic pipework – the variable-pitch mechanism of the Rotol propeller unit was hydraulically operated. The pilot was provided with a pitch control lever on the port side of the cockpit that could be adjusted depending on the power output of the engine at any given time with the aircraft's speed and flight regime – the related hydraulic constant-speed unit fitted to the engine ensuring that the pitch of the propeller blades was adjusted to allow the optimum blade angle. This was somewhat difficult to master at first for pilots who were not used to variable-pitch propellers, but when employed well it gave the Hurricane a considerable improvement in performance by more efficiently and effectively using the power output of the engine.

A prototype installation of the Rotol propeller unit was tried out on Hurricane Mk I L1606, civil registered as G-AFKX (Hawker paid for the development work for the installation of the Rotol propeller in the Hurricane, hence the civil status of this aircraft while under flight test), which first flew with the new propeller configuration on 24 January 1939. Throughout the life of the Hurricane a number of different types of Rotol constant-speed propeller units were used by the aircraft, depending on such factors as the likely mission profiles of a given mark and the engine installed. Later Mk I Hurricanes were fitted with a Rotol RMS.7 unit of 10ft 9in diameter with right-hand rotation, while many of the Merlin XX-powered Mark II series had a Rotol RS5/2 unit, or the RS5/3 with Jablo propeller blades, of 11ft 3in diameter and right-hand rotation. There was also a different spinner shape for the later aircraft, which affected the aircraft's overall length, as it was longer and more streamlined when fitted.

The only real engine change that affected the Hurricane during its entire production life was the installation of US-built Merlin engines, manufactured by the Packard Motor Car Company of Detroit. Packard had been producing the Merlin in its Mk XX form for some time, having signed agreements with Rolls-Royce for the manufacture of the Merlin in the US during 1940. After some initial setting-up difficulties, Packard emerged as a major producer of Merlin engines, and these were

ABOVE Within the comparative luxury of a hangar, maintenance work is carried out on the Merlin engine of a Hurricane Mk I, T9531, in Southern Rhodesia in 1944 or 1945. Much of the routine maintenance work at operational airfields had to be carried out in the open air in all weathers, but away from the front-line in training areas such as Southern Rhodesia there was a much greater degree of comfort for maintenance crews. This particular aircraft has a 'tropical' filter installation below the nose. *(RAF Museum)*

increasingly used in Canadian-built Hurricanes – and would also go on to power Canadian-built Lancaster four-engined bombers later in the war, as well as the Merlin-engined versions of the North American Mustang fighter. Packard production ensured that there was never a shortage of Merlin engines (the fear of an engine shortage haunted British officials and manufacturers in the early stages of the war, but it never materialised). There was a noticeable change to the Canadian-built Hurricanes, however, as far as appearance was concerned – some were fitted with three-bladed Hamilton Standard propeller units, and sometimes did not have a full spinner fitted. Some early Canadian Hurricanes had the Packard Merlin 28 installed, but most had the Packard Merlin 29. This engine was rated at 1,300hp for take-off with 12lb boost, and being closely related to the Merlin 28 it was therefore a Packard version of the British-made Merlin XX.

Chapter Two

Restore to Flight

Keeping an historic aircraft in the air, or completely restoring any historic aircraft back to airworthy condition is a major undertaking that demands time, patience, access to relevant spare parts, and know-how – and very deep pockets. With all these ingredients in place, it is then necessary to be prepared to put in many years of sheer hard work. The rebuilding of a Hurricane – if you can find one to take on – is surely one of the more difficult projects in the challenging world of aircraft restoration.

OPPOSITE Fabric covered elevator complete with trim tab on the BBMF's Hurricane Mk II, LF363. *(Paul Blackah/ Crown Copyright)*

The owning of any historic aircraft, and the maintenance required to keep it in airworthy condition is an expensive and time-consuming labour of love. The people who take on such a task are dedicated enthusiasts and professionals who need to have deep pockets and seemingly limitless time and patience – in addition to the back-up of a team of engineers, and the goodwill of a wider base of individuals and companies who specialise in one or more of the dozens of skilled jobs that are needed to put the many parts of an historic aircraft into perfect running order. Added to this is the singularly important issue of finding a display pilot to fly your historic aircraft – if you are not a suitably rated pilot yourself – and the many (and often time-consuming and frustrating) issues of gaining the relevant and cherished airworthiness permits from your local civil aviation administrators. All of these factors refer specifically to private individuals, but there is a notable exception – the official historic flight. In Britain, the Battle of Britain Memorial Flight (BBMF), based at RAF Coningsby in Lincolnshire, maintains in airworthy condition two Hurricanes, in addition to an Avro Lancaster and several Spitfires. These are officially military aircraft, even though they are historic aircraft, and are subject to many different parameters regarding their official status compared to civilian-owner aircraft. Nevertheless, they have to be looked after to the highest standards required of civil aircraft. Fortunately both of the Hurricanes of the BBMF have remained in good condition throughout their long lives – with the exception of the accident that befell LF363 in the early 1990s, necessitating a major rebuild – and neither has needed to be restored from the ground up from a pile of neglected metal in an Indian back-lot or from the depths of a lake in Russia. Keeping the BBMF's two Hurricanes in airworthy condition is a full-time job that demands all the skills and patience of the dedicated and highly experienced team of technicians that make up the ground staff of the Flight. The BBMF is also fortunate in being able to call on a pool of exceptional talent of current military pilots when it comes to flying both Hurricanes, and the testimonials of two of these experienced service pilots can be found in Chapter 6.

Until the last few years, the total number of airworthy Hurricanes was less than half a dozen. Now, due to the work of companies such as Hawker Restorations, the Hurricane has increased in popularity and there are about a dozen flying examples with a few more being restored to flight.

Sourcing a Hurricane project is becoming harder because there simply aren't any around. Some of the aircraft flying today have been found in Russia and brought back to the UK for restoration and another example – Peter Vacher's rare Hurricane Mk I R4118 – was discovered in the grounds of a college in India. The state of these aircraft is such that a total rebuild is required, but there is always, in any restoration project, the possibility that some original features may be used.

How do refurbished Hurricanes differ from their original state?

It must be said that this question is as relevant for the Hurricane as it is for all other airworthy historic aircraft. At first glance one would be correct in assuming that many currently airworthy warbirds will most likely contain a lot of 'new' components, and that very few of their original parts will still be within the airframe – even the engine is likely to be a 'new' reconditioned item. One notable point to make about the restoration of a Hurricane is that it was at least on the winning side. This is important because the restoration – and the maintaining in flying condition – of British and American aircraft from the Second World War era is a somewhat different proposition compared to similar activity with aircraft from Germany and other Axis countries. The sourcing of some parts is more straightforward, because a number of the companies (or their successors) that made components for Allied aircraft during the war are still in existence. This contrasts with much of Germany's industry, which was bombed virtually out of existence by the Allies, making the remanufacture of components and the sourcing of original drawings of historic German aircraft a much more difficult proposition. Nevertheless, it is still a challenging, time-consuming and often frustrating process to fully restore an historic aircraft of whatever origin to flying condition. In a limited number of cases, the job is made easier by the aircraft concerned having remained in good condition throughout their lives, as is the case with the two Hurricanes of the BBMF – although, as mentioned, LF363 did need a major rebuild in the 1990s as a result of an accident. The other aircraft, the famous PZ865, which was the last-ever Hurricane to be completed, is probably one of the most original of the currently airworthy examples in existence. Even so it is a continuing struggle to keep these two aircraft in the air, and to meet current airworthiness requirements.

Restoring a Hurricane – Tony Ditheridge

Tony Ditheridge is the man behind the Suffolk-based Hawker Restorations Limited of Milden, to the west of Ipswich. He has been responsible for the restoration of many of the Hurricanes that are flying in the world today. Tony set up the company in 1993 with the specific intention of rebuilding Hurricanes and since then has become one of the most respected restorers in the country. His work can be seen on Hurricanes owned by The Fighter Collection, Flying Heritage and the BBMF.

Hawker Restorations has been successfully rebuilding Hurricanes for the last 15 years, and can give an insight into the idiosyncrasies of restoring the Hurricane as against the Spitfire. Rather than going into extreme technical details, a general overview of the philosophy, mechanical construction and comparison with the Spitfire is more appropriate.

The Hurricane was designed by Sir Sydney Camm, who worked at one time with Tommy Sopwith and was instrumental in many of the original Sopwith aircraft. If you look carefully at the Hurricane you can see the continuation of the early aircraft that were made of wood with cross bracing internally braced, which was traditional right the way through to around 1937/8. The Hurricane is configured in a similar way in so much that it is made of tube, but squared at each bay enabling a

ABOVE The wooden 'dog kennel' cockpit assembly complete with canopy rails and windscreen rear frame. (Classic Aero Ltd)

similar construction to the early aircraft. It is also internally braced with streamline wires. In order to have the rigidity and strength for the higher weights and speeds involved with the more sophisticated fighters it was crucial that the aircraft was manufactured to extremely tight tolerances – typically less than half a thou. Furthermore, the main structure requires hundreds of additional brackets to support the secondary structure in wood, which gives the Hurricane its distinctive shape.

A further difficulty regarding the Hurricane in today's world is the manufacture of the 12-sided spring steel spar booms within the centre section: one is within the other and within this there is a special heat-treated liner tube. The 12-sided spring steel is roll-formed using 120 rolls in order to achieve the end

BELOW The intricate wooden structure in place on the fuselage framework. (Classic Aero Ltd)

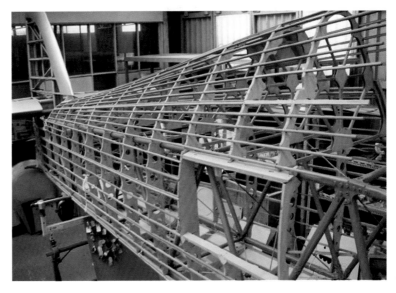

ABOVE The 'dog kennel' structure fitted to the fuselage framework and completed centre section. (Classic Aero Ltd)

ABOVE Framework construction progressing. (Classic Aero Ltd)

BELOW Fuselage framework and centre section. Coolant header tank is in place on engine firewall bulkhead. (Classic Aero Ltd)

ABOVE Centre section structure before restoration. (Classic Aero Ltd)

result. This represents a huge investment as the steel heat treatment and roll-forming has not been done since the 1930s. The same applies for the tailplane, fin and centre section. This work was achieved in conjunction with Guy Black of Aero Vintage, which experienced a similar problem in the restoration of their Hawker biplanes. The Hurricane is the direct descendant of the Hawker biplanes and this can clearly be seen when both aircraft stand side by side without their fabric covering.

The undercarriage assembly, which was the first retractable undercarriage used on a fighter, is an exceedingly complex arrangement, because, unlike the Spitfire, it consists of multiple joints, trunnions and sliding tubes in order to take it from the outermost position in the centre section and fold it within this area. The Spitfire simply has a pair of pintles and folds into the wing recess.

To compare the Hurricane and Spitfire in engineering parlance: the Spitfire is a monocoque construction in which a series of frames are placed in a jig and the frames are then skinned in situ, effectively manufacturing and assembling the aircraft at the same time. The Hurricane consists of over 1,000 parts that have to be manufactured to extreme engineering limits. Once these parts have been made there follows the lengthy process of assembling them, but due to the fine engineering limits in the manufacture of the parts the integrity of the aeroplane is maintained. Furthermore, there is a substantial amount of wooden structure required, fabric and systems. Therefore, a

restorer today will take at least twice the time to restore a Hurricane than a Spitfire, as we at HRL have done both.

Many documents state that the Hurricane is easier to build than the Spitfire and a number of articles quote a build-time which is slightly less than the Spitfire. This assumes that all the parts are ready to assemble and it is this aspect that adds at least the same time again (10,000–12,000 hours), making the actual restoration time for the Hurricane twice as long as the Spitfire. There are currently approximately 12 Hurricanes flying worldwide and more than 60 Spitfires.

Aspects of restoration

There are literally a hundred and one tasks to perform in historic aircraft restoration to achieve airworthy condition, and no corners can be cut either during restoration, or at the end of the process when the aircraft is successfully back in the air and gracing the skies once more. One of the many tasks is fabric covering. Early Hurricane Mk Is had fabric-covered wings, but even when these were replaced later in Mk I production with metal-covered wings, fabric

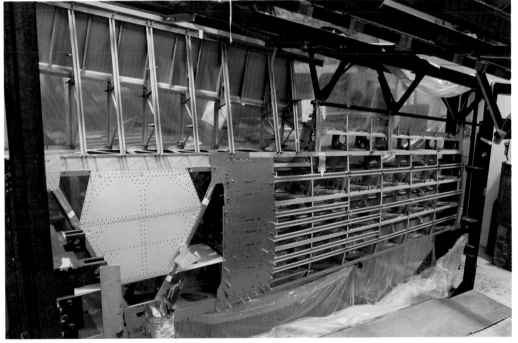

LEFT **Port outer wing being assembled in specially manufactured jig. Note the hexagonal gun bay access panel that covers the four .303in Browning machine guns.** *(Classic Aero Ltd)*

Fuselage structure with fin and tail plane assemblies in place and wooden framework fitted. *(Classic Aero Ltd)*

covering was still an important aspect of the Hurricane's construction, as the control surfaces of all hurricanes are fabric-covered. Now a disappearing skill, fabric covering is a vital task that is needed as a part of the restoration and maintenance reality for any Hurricane operator. Here, Clive Denny describes this fascinating skill.

Fabric covering – Clive Denny

Clive Denny is the owner of Vintage Fabrics, a company based at Audley End, in Essex, that specialises in the fabric covering of historic aircraft. He is also an experienced Hurricane and Spitfire pilot.

In 1988 a fabric-recover contract on a warbird was rumoured to be coming up for offer. The aircraft in question was a Canadian built Mk XII Hurricane G-HURI owned by the well-known warbird collector Stephen Grey. Vintage Fabrics was in its infancy and up to that time had concentrated its efforts on smaller classic types such as Tiger Moths, Chipmunks and Austers. Several companies tendered for the work and Vintage Fabrics was successful, with the project being carried out at Duxford. Little did I realise at the time how this one job would change our work careers and my flying career as well.

At the time Hurricanes were in fairly short supply; the BBMF had LF363 and PZ865, but civil-owned machines were rare. It was a great privilege to get the work, which was to be carried out in the original scheme using F1 Irish linen and red nitrate tautening dope.

The process of covering a Hurricane was to remain the same on every subsequent

Hurricane. You would start with the flying controls, ailerons, elevators, rudder, tailplane, fin, and then go on to the fuselage. Irish linen is expensive to use so you cut your fabric carefully. All trailing edges are hand sewn and, as you can imagine, it is fairly time consuming.

The fabric is left to settle and eventually shrunk with distilled water. After a period of 24 hours the first coats of red nitrate dope are brushed in. Shrinking time can vary due to various conditions such as temperature and humidity, but when the fabric is tight you can carry out the next process, which is rib-stitching.

Rib-stitching on a Hurricane only applies to the elevators and the rudder, the tailplane, fin and ailerons are secured with thin recessed strips of alloy pop-riveted through the structure – this turned out to be slightly quicker then stitching. The stitching between the ribs is to prevent the fabric ballooning in flight and to stop the spread of tear damage such as from a bird strike.

Once the fabric is taut and stitched it is time to apply the surface tapes, drain eyelets and inspection frames. The surface tapes cover and seal the fabric at the trailing edges and cover the ribs and anything else that protrudes above the level of the structure. They provide extra strength and also stop the risk of the base fabric chafing through. Drain eyelets are fitted at the trailing edge of the flying controls and various points on the fuselage to allow air to flow through the controls and lessen the risk of dampness causing mildew internally. The inspection rings are doped on as a means of inspection without damaging the fabric. Once all this has been carried out several coats of dope are applied and sanded down in between coats to bring the finish up to the desired result. Two coats of silver dope are applied to help protect against UV damage (one of the biggest killers of natural fabric) and the items are now ready to paint.

Attention is now turned to the fuselage. A Hurricane fuselage is made up of several pieces: the 'doghouse' (the area around the cockpit), the main fuselage itself, the right-hand emergency release door and the four lower fuselage trays. The doghouse is covered in madaplin, which is a lightweight cotton fabric. This is doped over the plywood structure using several coats and then taped.

The fabric on the fuselage is held in place by first doping or gluing the Irish linen into the recessed stringers and then securing the fabric with small wooden half dowels that run the full length of the fuselage, there are two dowels per side. Once fitted, distilled water is sprayed to shrink the fabric and the process starts all over again. Fuselage tapes start from the bottom, working your way up the side of the fuselage until you reach the spine, the spine tape being the last. The tapes are pinked and come in various sizes, unlike early aeroplanes where the tapes are frayed, but that's another method. The Hurricane is now close to completion; you carry on doping it until you are happy with the finish. Then UV silver is applied and it is now time to paint. The Hurricane is a fairly easy aircraft to paint in as much as the wings come off so there is less masking and less to get hooked up on when spraying. In today's world we use air-fed masks, which carry a lot of hose.

The process of fabricing a Hurricane is very time consuming. It is done by hand, there are no mechanical short cuts, but it is one of the most satisfying recovers you can carry out.

The process described above was performed in 1988. In 2004 we refabriced and painted the same Hurricane in preparation for its planned trip to Malta in 2005. We have now carried out 11 Hurricane recovers, which range from the BBMF to private owners and various museums worldwide, including Malta and the USAF Museum at Dayton.

If you build models of the Hurricane, or in fact any fabric aircraft, do not try to replicate the weave on your model; you do not see it on the real thing once it is doped, so you will not see it in any scale of model. Fabric should be smooth – if you can see a strong weave it needs more dope.

Like any painting project it has to be planned. Camouflage is not just applied; it conforms to a drawing, once all the information is obtained it is time to shoot the paint. All colours are standard BS381C, which are readily available today in various types of paint, so there is no need to research them.

My dream in 1988 was to fly the Hurricane. In 2005 I fulfilled that dream and was to go on to spend many hours flying the Hurricane, even to Malta and back, but that's another story.

Fabric covering

The fuselage wooden framework of Canadian-built Z5140, G-HURI, prior to the fabric being applied.
(Clive Denny)

Irish linen covering being applied to the fuselage wooden framework of G-HURI.
(Clive Denny)

Fuselage fabric covering in place on G-HURI.
(Clive Denny)

Fuselage fabric covering has coat of dope applied to tighten the fabric. Three or four coats will be applied before the final paint finish is carried out.
(Clive Denny)

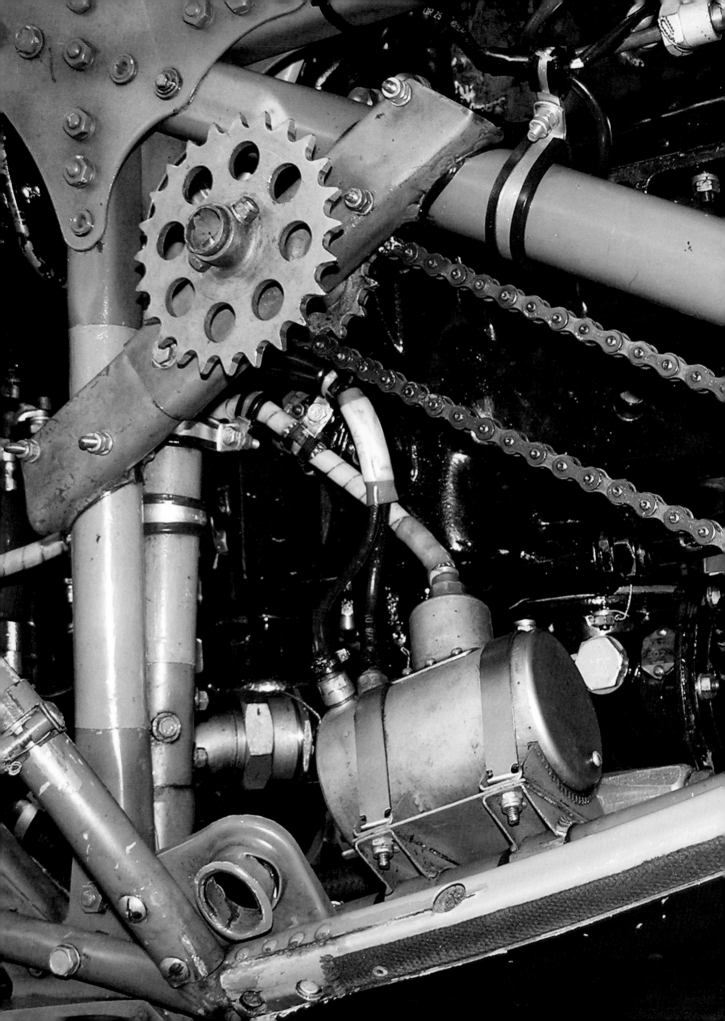

Chapter Three

Anatomy of the Hurricane

Many people look at the Spitfire and the Hurricane and see them as very similar aircraft – both are fighters and both played a pivotal role during the Second World War, especially during the Battle of Britain – but these aircraft are from different eras. The Hurricane is the last in the line of the tubular-framed, fabric-covered fighter aircraft. A closer look at the anatomy of the Hawker Hurricane will reveal the unique design features that made it such a successful fighter throughout the Second World War.

OPPOSITE Hand winding mechanism chain and sprockets. The top sprocket should have a chain that goes to the starter. This system has been disconnected and is not used. *(Paul Blackah/Crown Copyright)*

1 Starboard navigation light
2 Wing tip fairing
3 Fabric covered aileron
4 Aluminium alloy wing skin panelling
5 Aileron hinge control
6 Starboard outer wing panel
7 Inboard torsion box heavy-gauge skin panel
8 Starboard landing lamp
9 Rotol three-bladed propeller
10 Spinner
11 Propeller hub pitch change mechanism
12 Spinner back plate
13 Propeller reduction gearbox
14 Cowling fairing
15 Starboard machine-gun muzzles
16 Upper engine cowling
17 Coolant pipes
18 Rolls-Royce Merlin III V12-cylinder liquid-cooled engine
19 Exhaust stubs
20 Engine driven generator
21 Forward engine mounting
22 Ignition control unit
23/24 Engine bearer struts and joints
25 Starboard main wheel
26 Manual-type inertia starter
27 Hydraulic pumps
28 Carburettor air intake
29 Cooling air scoop
30 Rear engine mounting
31 Single stage supercharger
32 Port magneto
33 Coolant system header tank
34 External bead sight
35 Coolant filler cap
36 Starboard wing gun bay
37 Ammunition magazines
38 Starboard Browning 0.303in machine-guns (four)
39 Fuel filler cap
40 Engine bay canted bulkhead
41 Rear engine mounting struts
42 Pneumatic system air bottle (gun firing)
43 Wing spar centre-section carry-through
44 Lower longeron/wing spar joint
45 Rudder pedals
46 Pilot's footboards
47 Control column linkage
48 Fuselage (reserve fuel tank, capacity 28 Imp gal)
49 Fuel tank bulkhead
50 Control column handgrip
51 Instrument panel
52 Reflector gunsight
53 Starboard split trailing-edge flap
54 Bullet-proof windscreen panel
55 Canopy internal handle
56 Rear view mirror
57 Sliding cockpit canopy cover
58 Plexiglas canopy panels
59 Canopy framework
60 Canopy external handle
61 Starboard side 'break-out' emergency exit panel
62 Safety harness
63 Seat height adjustment lever
64 Oxygen supply cock
65 Engine throttle lever
66 Elevator trim tab control handwheel
67 Oil pipes to radiator
68 Radiator flap control lever
69 Cockpit section tubular
70 Coolant system piping
71 Pilot's oxygen cylinder
72 Boarding step
73 Seat back armour
74 Pilot's seat
75 Armoured headrest
76 Turn-over crash pylon struts
77 Canopy rear fairing construction
78 Sliding canopy rail
79 Battery
80 TR 9D radio transmitter/receiver
81 Radio shelf
82 Downward identification light
83 Flare launch tube
84 Handgrip
85 Plywood skin panel
86 Dorsal fairing stringers
87 Upper identification light
88 Aerial mast
89 Aerial lead-in
90 Wooden dorsal section formers
91 Fuselage upper longeron
92 Rear Fuselage fabric covering
93 Aluminium alloy tailplane leading edge
94 Starboard fabric covered tailplane
95 Fabric covered elevator
96 Aluminium alloy fin leading edge
97 Forward fin mounting post
98 Tailplane spar attachment joint
99 Elevator hinge control
100 Fin rib construction
101 Tailfin fabric covering
102 Diagonal bracing strut
103 Stern post
104 Rudder mass balance weight
105 Aerial cable
106 Rear aerial mast
107 Fabric covered rudder
108 Aluminium alloy rudder framework
109 Tail navigation light
110 Rudder tab

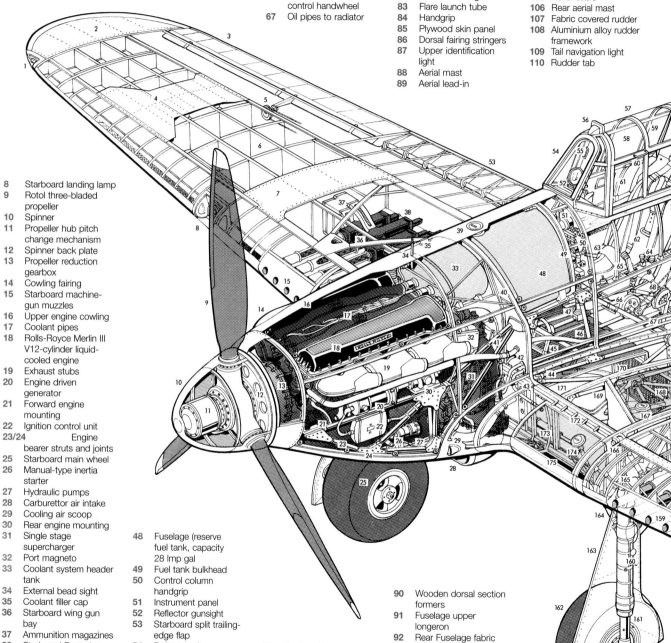

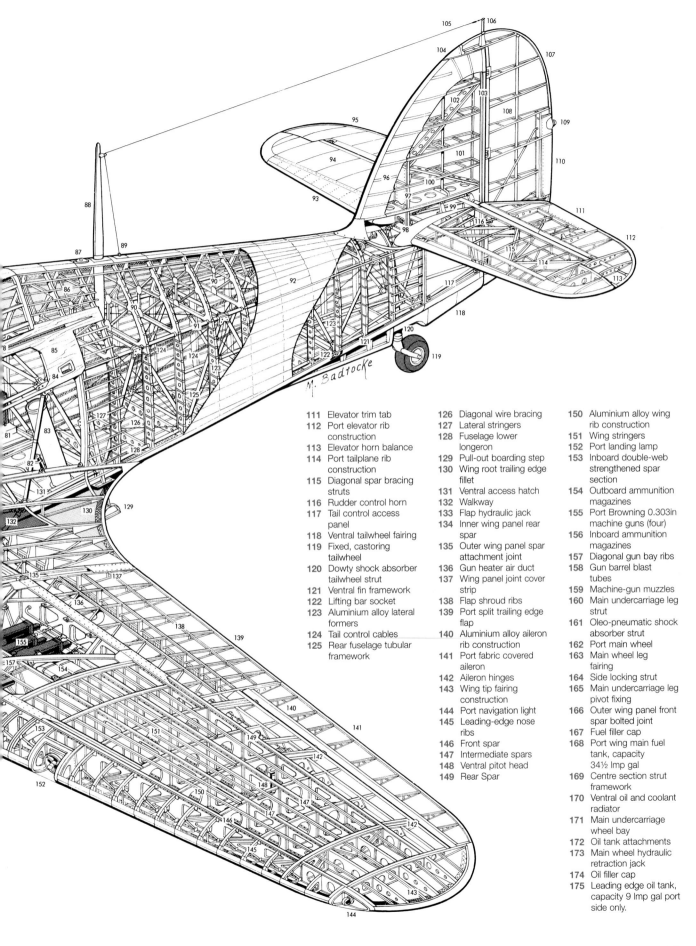

111 Elevator trim tab
112 Port elevator rib construction
113 Elevator horn balance
114 Port tailplane rib construction
115 Diagonal spar bracing struts
116 Rudder control horn
117 Tail control access panel
118 Ventral tailwheel fairing
119 Fixed, castoring tailwheel
120 Dowty shock absorber tailwheel strut
121 Ventral fin framework
122 Lifting bar socket
123 Aluminium alloy lateral formers
124 Tail control cables
125 Rear fuselage tubular framework

126 Diagonal wire bracing
127 Lateral stringers
128 Fuselage lower longeron
129 Pull-out boarding step
130 Wing root trailing edge fillet
131 Ventral access hatch
132 Walkway
133 Flap hydraulic jack
134 Inner wing panel rear spar
135 Outer wing panel spar attachment joint
136 Gun heater air duct
137 Wing panel joint cover strip
138 Flap shroud ribs
139 Port split trailing edge flap
140 Aluminium alloy aileron rib construction
141 Port fabric covered aileron
142 Aileron hinges
143 Wing tip fairing construction
144 Port navigation light
145 Leading-edge nose ribs
146 Front spar
147 Intermediate spars
148 Ventral pitot head
149 Rear Spar

150 Aluminium alloy wing rib construction
151 Wing stringers
152 Port landing lamp
153 Inboard double-web strengthened spar section
154 Outboard ammunition magazines
155 Port Browning 0.303in machine guns (four)
156 Inboard ammunition magazines
157 Diagonal gun bay ribs
158 Gun barrel blast tubes
159 Machine-gun muzzles
160 Main undercarriage leg strut
161 Oleo-pneumatic shock absorber strut
162 Port main wheel
163 Main wheel leg fairing
164 Side locking strut
165 Main undercarriage leg pivot fixing
166 Outer wing panel front spar bolted joint
167 Fuel filler cap
168 Port wing main fuel tank, capacity 34½ Imp gal
169 Centre section strut framework
170 Ventral oil and coolant radiator
171 Main undercarriage wheel bay
172 Oil tank attachments
173 Main wheel hydraulic retraction jack
174 Oil filler cap
175 Leading edge oil tank, capacity 9 Imp gal port side only.

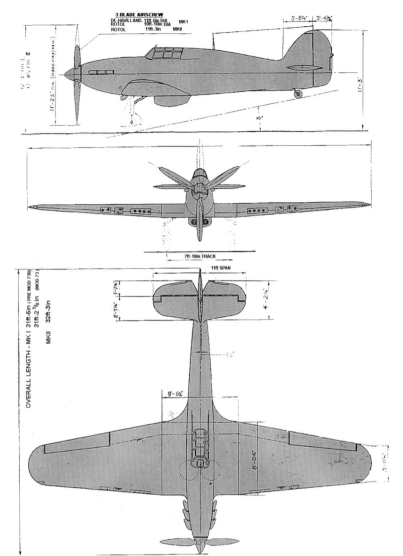

Airframe

The Hurricane is a low-wing, single-seater fighter, with a tubular-framed fuselage covered with wooden formers and stringers that are themselves covered with Irish linen fabric. The mainplane is built in three sections: a port and starboard outer and a centre section. For the purpose of this book we will examine each major section of the aircraft individually.

Fuselage

For ease of understanding, we will divide the fuselage into four sections: engine mounting, centre, rear and tail bay.

Engine mounting This is a detachable unit, of tubular structure, fitted to the centre fuselage at joints A and to the bottom boom of the centre section front spar at joint B1. The engine is supported between two side panels, connected at the bottom by two cross tubes. Four duralumin blocks support the engine feet, with the rear pair offset inboard from the main structure on two subsidiary struts to joint Z.

Centre fuselage The centre fuselage extends from joints A and B to joints G and H. The longerons are continuous between these two points, apart from joints F to joint H. At these joints the various tubular sections are bolted to the flanged U-shaped stampings, which house the upper booms of the centre section spars. Tubular bracing is employed, but wire bracing is also used in order to strengthen the centre section. The centre fuselage houses the reserve fuel tank, the cockpit area and the wireless.

ABOVE Aircraft plan view with dimensions. *(AP1564)*

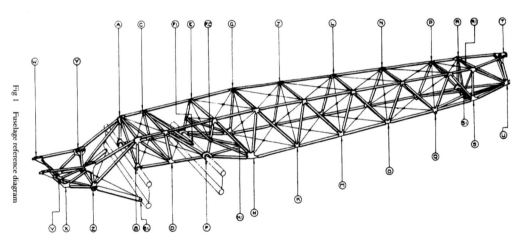

RIGHT Fuselage Framework Diagram. *(AP1564)*

NOTE
CENTRE SECTION
SHEWN CHAIN DOTTED

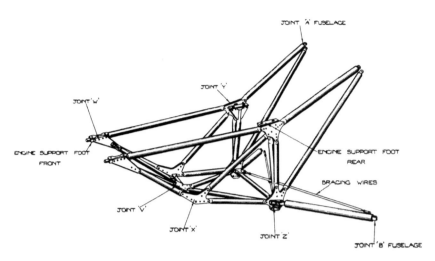

ABOVE **Engine bearer joint W.** *(Jim Douthwaite)*

LEFT **Engine bearer diagram.** *(AP1564)*

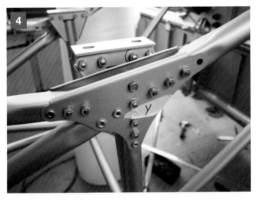

1 **Fuselage joint F.**
(Jim Douthwaite)

2 **Fuselage joint M.**
(Jim Douthwaite)

3 **Fuselage joint H.**
(Jim Douthwaite)

4 **Fuselage joint Y.**
(Jim Douthwaite)

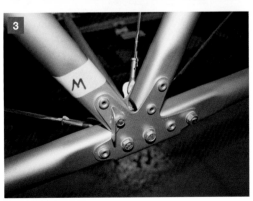

Dimensions and weights

These dimensions are typical for a Hurricane Mk IIc of the BBMF:

Length	32ft 3in
Wing Span	40ft
Propeller diameter	11ft 3in (Rotol)
Tailplane span	11ft
Basic weight	5,910lb (approx). This is taken with oil tanks full, coolant full and fuel tanks empty.

Flying controls – range of movements

Aileron movement	22° up and 21° down
Elevator	27° up and 26° down
Rudder	28° each way
Flaps	80° down (full travel)
Elevator trim tab	23° up and down
Rudder tab	15° (trimming movement, port only)
	20° (balance movement each way)

Tyre sizes and pressures

The main wheel tyre size is 10.25 x 8in, with a pressure of 45psi.
The tailwheel tyre size is 4.95 x 3.5in, with a pressure of 45psi.

RIGHT Front under-fairing diagram. *(AP1564)*

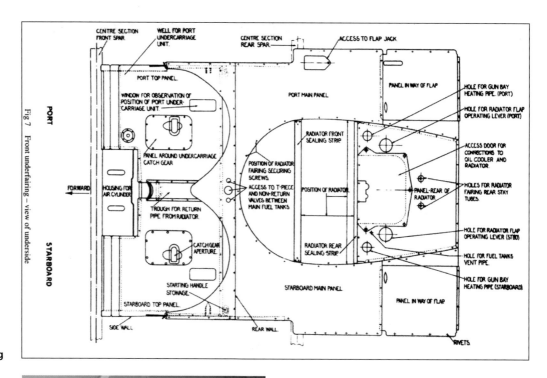

Fig 7   Front underfairing — view of underside

PORT

STARBOARD

FORWARD

- CENTRE SECTION FRONT SPAR.
- WELL FOR PORT UNDERCARRIAGE UNIT.
- CENTRE SECTION REAR SPAR.
- ACCESS TO FLAP JACK.
- PORT TOP PANEL.
- WINDOW FOR OBSERVATION OF POSITION OF PORT UNDER-CARRIAGE UNIT.
- PORT MAIN PANEL.
- PANEL IN WAY OF FLAP.
- HOLE FOR GUN BAY HEATING PIPE. (PORT)
- HOLE FOR RADIATOR FLAP OPERATING LEVER (PORT)
- PANEL AROUND UNDERCARRIAGE CATCH GEAR.
- RADIATOR FRONT SEALING STRIP.
- ACCESS DOOR FOR CONNECTIONS TO OIL COOLER AND RADIATOR.
- POSITION OF RADIATOR FAIRING SECURING SCREWS.
- ACCESS TO T-PIECE AND NON-RETURN VALVES BETWEEN MAIN FUEL TANKS.
- POSITION OF RADIATOR.
- PANEL-REAR OF RADIATOR.
- HOLES FOR RADIATOR FAIRING REAR STAY TUBES.
- HOUSING FOR AIR CYLINDER.
- TROUGH FOR RETURN PIPE FROM RADIATOR.
- CATCHGEAR APERTURE.
- RADIATOR REAR SEALING STRIP.
- HOLE FOR RADIATOR FLAP OPERATING LEVER (STBD)
- HOLE FOR FUEL TANKS VENT PIPE.
- STARTING HANDLE STOWAGE.
- STARBOARD MAIN PANEL.
- HOLE FOR GUN BAY HEATING PIPE (STARBOARD)
- STARBOARD TOP PANEL.
- SIDE WALL.
- REAR WALL.
- PANEL IN WAY OF FLAP.
- RIVETS.

RIGHT Radiator fairing complete with flap. *(Paul Blackah/Crown Copyright)*

BELOW, LEFT Fuselage joint U. *(Jim Douthwaite)*

BELOW, RIGHT Tail leg fitting on rear fuselage. *(Jim Douthwaite)*

COOLANT MIXTURE
GLYCOL   WATER
30%   70%

Rear fuselage This runs from joints G and H to R and S, and is a structure of triangulated side frames connected by cross struts, top and bottom, through plate joints. All the top and bottom panels are wire-braced except the rearmost panel, which is tubular-braced to withstand the loads from the tailwheel leg.

Tail bay Carried in the tail bay are the tail plane, the fin and the tail leg shock absorber unit. This structure runs from joints R and S to joints T and U.

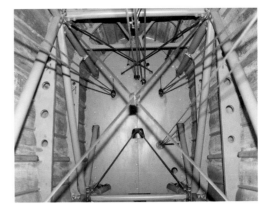

Tail unit

The tail unit is of metal construction and covered with fabric. A fixed tailplane is mounted over the rear end of the fuselage and has front and rear spars, which are parallel to one another, over its full length. It is secured to the fuselage by four bolts at fuselage joints R and T. The fin is positioned over the tailplane and is secured to the fuselage by its two fin posts. The rear fin post forms the fuselage sternpost. Attached to the tailplane and the fin are the elevators and rudder.

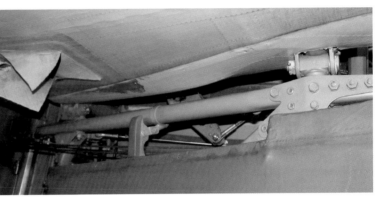

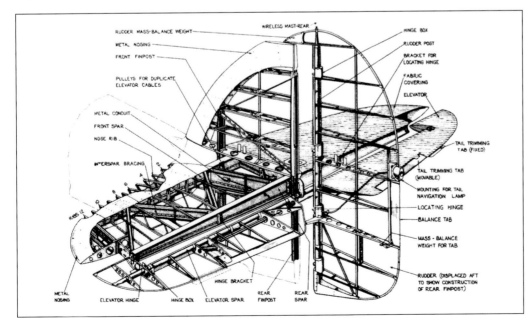

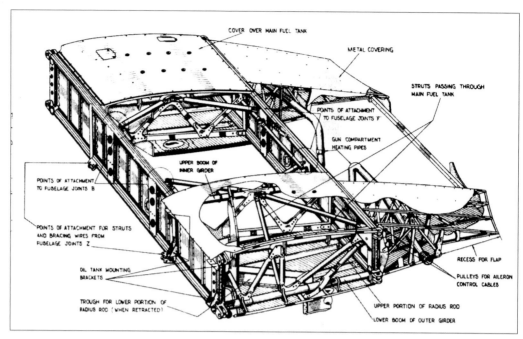

Mainplane

The mainplane is built in three sections: the centre section, port and starboard outer sections. The construction of the centre section comprises a pair of parallel high-tensile steel spars, braced by tubular girders and diagonal tubes. This unit is then attached to the fuselage at joints B, F, and by tubular bracing to joints Z and H. This section is metal covered.

The outer section comprises a pair of spars, braced at the inner end by two diagonal girders

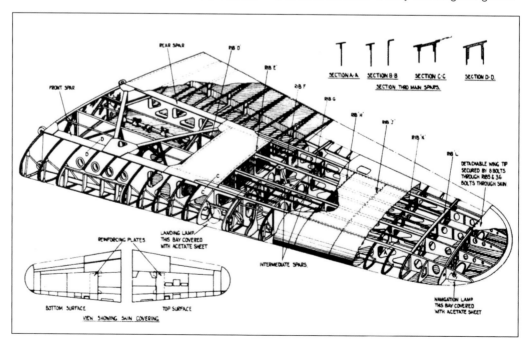

Fig 5. Cannon bay

MAGAZINE ACCESS DOORS

REAR SPAR

ARMOUR PLATING ON SUB SPAR

END RIB

INTERMEDIATE STIFF RIB

FIXED SKIN

FRONT SPAR

LEADING EDGE DOORS

SHOWING CANNON INSTALLED

SHOWING MOUNTING ONLY

BREECH BLOCK ACCESS DOORS

RIB D

RIB E

RIB F

REAR INTERMEDIATE SPAR

FRONT INTERMEDIATE SPAR

and at the outer by the sheet-metal skin, in conjunction with two intermediate spars. The distance between the spars decreases from root to tip to give the desired tapered shape. The spars and girders are manufactured from steel. The duralumin skin is riveted to the spars and ribs and is strengthened by a series of stringers, which are riveted to its inner surface. The outer sections are fitted to the centre section by four tapered bolts on each side.

Fuel system

The fuel system has three fuel tanks, with their own respective filler caps, including two main fuel tanks, effective capacity 33gal, in the mainplane centre section, and a further reserve tank, capacity 28gal, fitted in the fuselage immediately in front of the pilot's instrument panel. This tank also provides the supply for the engine-priming pump.

Although the aircraft has a capacity of 94gal, some operational Hurricanes, such as the BBMF aircraft, have an extra pair of tanks in the

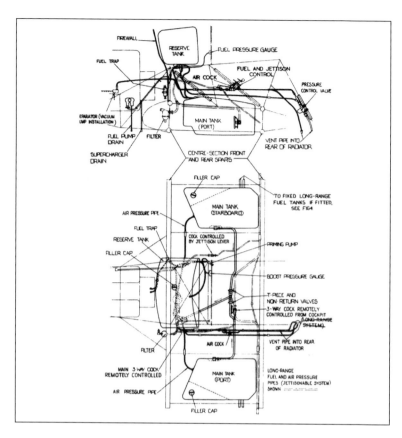

ABOVE Fuel system *(AP1564)*

1 Overload tank fitted in the inboard gun bay on the starboard outer wing.
2 Main and reserve fuel tank selector handle.
3 Overload fuel tank selector. The overload tanks are fitted in the gun bay on BBMF aircraft.
4 Port main fuel tank showing the green fabric covering.
5. Reserve fuel tank in front of instrument panel with the filler cap forward and contents indicator unit, rear, clearly visible.

(all photos Paul Blackah/Crown Copyright)

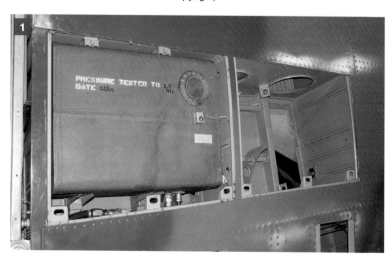

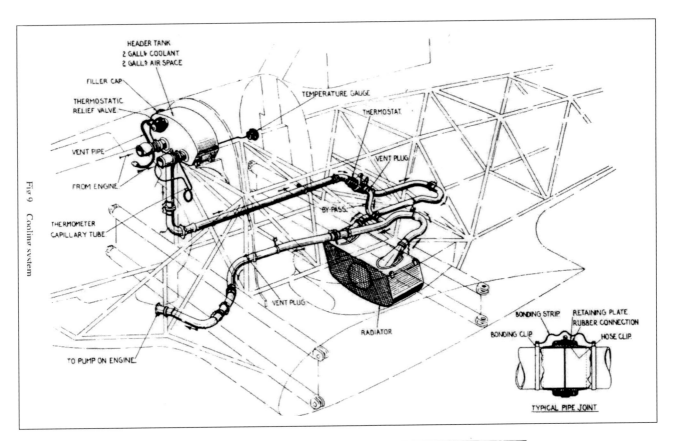

HEADER TANK
2 GALL. COOLANT
2 GALL. AIR SPACE

FILLER CAP

THERMOSTATIC
RELIEF VALVE

VENT PIPE

FROM ENGINE

THERMOMETER
CAPILLARY TUBE

TO PUMP ON ENGINE

TEMPERATURE GAUGE

THERMOSTAT

VENT PLUG

BY-PASS

VENT PLUG

RADIATOR

BONDING STRIP   RETAINING PLATE
RUBBER CONNECTION
BONDING CLIP   HOSE CLIP

TYPICAL PIPE JOINT

Fig 9   Cooling system

outer wing gun bays to provide a total capacity of 111gal. This gives the aircraft an extra 20 to 30 minutes' flying time.

A three-way valve, controlled from the cockpit, governs the supply from the main and reserve tanks. A two-way valve is fitted at each tank outlet; these valves are normally locked in the open position, except when a tank needs removing. The two main tanks are joined through a 'T' piece, with a non-return valve on each side. These prevent flow from one tank to the other. A fuel filter is fitted between the valve and the engine, which prevents any debris entering the engine.

Each of these tanks is constructed from sheet aluminium and covered with a protective, self-sealing covering and fabric.

The tanks have their own fuel contents gauge transmitter, enabling the pilot to check the contents of an individual tank at any time via the fuel gauge on the starboard side of the instrument panel.

Coolant system

The engine is cooled with a mixture of distilled water (70%) and ethylene glycol (30%). The coolant is circulated around the system by means

ABOVE Coolant system diagram. *(AP1564)*

LEFT Coolant pipe with thermostatic relief valve. *(Paul Blackah/ Crown Copyright)*

BELOW Coolant header tank. *(Paul Blackah/ Crown Copyright)*

of a pump, driven from the base of the engine
wheelcase. From the engine the coolant is passed
through the header tank, which is mounted on the
front face of the firewall. The capacity of the tank
is 4gal, although only half this quantity of coolant
is carried to allow for expansion. A thermostatic,
or spring-loaded relief valve is fitted to the tank
to control the pressure. If the pressure exceeds
30psi, then the valve will open.

From the tank the coolant passes to the

radiator, which is situated under the fuselage, and
then forward back to the engine pump. On some
aircraft a thermostat is incorporated into the
system to bypass the radiator when the coolant
temperature is low. Air to the radiator is controlled
from the cockpit by a flap fitted to the radiator
fairing. In the header tank, between the inlet
pipes, there is a connection for a thermometer
bowl. This bowl gives the temperature to a gauge
on the starboard side of the instrument panel.

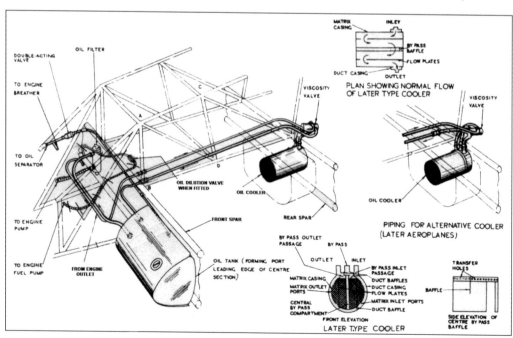

Oil system

The oil system has a main oil tank constructed out of light alloy sheeting to the profile of the centre section leading edge and has two baffles fitted internally. The tank is fitted to the port leading edge of the centre section. Towards the outer end of the tank is the filler cap.

A cylindrical oil cooler is housed within the centre of the coolant radiator. The cooler is constructed of a cylindrical casing of sheet brass, braced to it at the rear end is an eccentric rear duct, under which are situated the inlet and outlet ports to the cooler matrix.

An oil filter is fitted on the starboard front face of the firewall; it has a cylindrical body, which houses a gauze-covered filter element.

A pipe goes from the oil tank to the oil filter and then on to the engine suction pump, on to scavenge pump and to the viscosity valve, which is mounted on the fuselage at strut FH1.

LEFT Radiator and oil cooler on Hurricane Mk I, R4118. Note the oil cooler is rectangular, in the middle of the radiator.

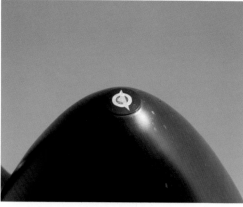

When the oil is cold, it flows through the bypass circuit of the cooler and when the oil has warmed up to temperature it is then diverted to the normal circuit of the oil cooler. The system has an actual capacity of 10.5gal although it is only filled with 9gal of oil. The 1.5gal airspace is to allow for expansion when the oil gets hot.

Oil pressure and temperature can both be read by gauges situated on the instrument panel.

Propeller

A Rotol, variable pitch, three-bladed propeller is fitted to the Hurricane. The hub forms the foundation of the whole propeller and consists of a hub shell and a driving centre. The driving centre is machined from a steel forging and runs axially through the hub shell and the two are bolted together to form one unit.

The driving centre is splined internally to fit the propeller shaft. At the rear end of the splined bore is an integral coned seating, which beds onto the rear cone on the engine propeller shaft. The hub-retaining nut screws onto the end of the engine propeller shaft and retains the front cone.

The mechanism for changing the pitch of the blades comprises a stationary piston and a moving cylinder mounted externally in front of the hub. The cylinder is connected to each blade-operating pin by an eyebolt coupled to a guided fork joint. The position of the fork joint in relation to the cylinder is adjustable to provide for the final correction of the blade pitch setting. The cylinder is attached to a tubular stalk, which projects rearwards from the rear cylinder wall and slides into the engine propeller shaft.

The piston is secured to the front forward ends of a pair of oil tubes, arranged one inside the other, which pass through the centre of the cylinder stalk. Oil, under pressure, from the governor unit (constant speed unit) passes along the bore of the inner tube to the front of the piston, to coarsen pitch, and along the annular space between the tubes to the rear of the piston to fine the pitch. The oil transfer plug, at the end of the engine propeller shaft, is fed by the governor unit (CSU) through oil ways in the engine reduction gear.

The propeller blades can be manufactured from three different types of wood:

Sitka spruce or Douglas fir The blade is shaped from spruce or fir boards of natural density, except for the root portion, which is made from boards of a high density known as Jicwood. The Jicwood boards are produced from packs of Canadian birch veneers, which, after being coated with synthetic resin, are heated and compressed to the required thickness and density.

Jablo wood The propeller blade is shaped from a block consisting of a number of compressed wood boards composed of Canadian birch, which have been interleaved with thin resin-impregnated paper and subjected to a combination of pressure and heat.

Hydulignum wood The blade is built up from a series of compressed Canadian birch veneer boards. The veneers are coated with a thermo-plastic resin and then assembled into a pack, which is heated and compressed to produce a board of constant density.

All wooden blades are spray-finished in matt black paint and the outer 4in of the blade are sprayed yellow, to ensure that the propeller is visible when rotating.

Electrics

The electrical system on the Hurricane is 12 volts, but most Hurricanes flying today have upgraded to 24 volts.

The power supply for the electrical components comes from a 24-volt, 750-watt engine-driven generator situated on the port side of the engine. A voltage regulator, fitted on the back of the armour plating at the rear of the pilot's seat, maintains a constant voltage whatever the engine speed and load fluctuations. A warning light, mounted near the undercarriage warning horn, gives the pilot indication of power failure.

The electrical system powers the following:
Landing lamps These are fitted in the centre of the leading edge of each wing and each lamp has a completely independent electrical circuit and is controlled by a two-way and OFF tumbler switch, which is mounted at the extreme port corner of the instrument panel.

ABOVE Prop blade with manufacturer's label, part number and setting angle. *(Paul Blackah/Crown Copyright)*

BELOW, LEFT Aircraft electrical power on/off switch. *(Paul Blackah/ Crown Copyright)*

BELOW, RIGHT External power socket with ground power unit plugged in. *(Paul Blackah/Crown Copyright)*

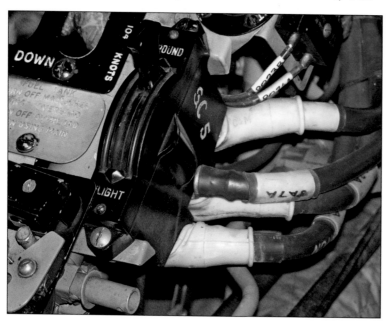

Electric starting An electric motor is mounted to the rear of the engine on the starboard side, while the booster coil is fitted on the starboard engine mounting strut XZ. Two push-button switches are mounted side-by-side on the port side of the instrument panel. One of these energises a relay coil, fitted on the starboard engine mounting strut AZ, and the other completes the circuit to the booster coil. When starting the engine these two buttons must be depressed together. The magnetos are controlled by a double switch, which is mounted close to the push switches on the instrument panel.

Cockpit lighting There are four lamps situated in the cockpit, each one controlled by a separate dimmer switch. One lamp is located on each side of the instrument panel, a third illuminates the compass and is located below the instrument flying panel and the fourth is at the port side near the cockpit seat.

Navigation lights There are three lights, one in each wing tip and one in the rudder. A switch at the port side of the instrument panel controls them.

Identification lights The upper and downward identification lamps are located midway along the fuselage in the upper and lower surfaces. The switch box is situated at the front end of the starboard side of the cockpit and provides steady illumination or more signalling from either or both lamps.

Fuel contents gauge A transmitter is fitted in each of the main fuel tanks and in the reserve tank. One indicator is provided and is situated on the starboard side of the instrument panel. A three-way selector switch is situated immediately above the indicator; by using this switch the pilot can check each tank for its respective contents.

Undercarriage indicator This is situated on the port side of the instrument panel. This indicator has two sets of red and green lights. One set is used as a back-up, should the other set fail. The red lights indicate the undercarriage is locked up and the green light indicates the undercarriage is locked down. The lights are operated by micro-switches on the undercarriage system. A warning horn, in the system, will sound when the undercarriage is not locked down and the throttle lever is in a

position of less than one-third open. The horn is mounted on the port side of the cockpit and is operated by a micro-switch, on a cam, at the end of the throttle lever.

Heated pressure head The heated pressure head is situated midway along the port outer wing. A switch on the port side of the instrument panel switches on the heater element.

Radio installation The radio is situated above the instrument panel, but may vary according to owner's preference. The BBMF aircraft are currently fitted with a Marconi AD120 radio. The power unit for the radio is situated in the bay immediately behind the pilot's seat.

Identification friend or foe equipment (IFF) An IFF system is fitted and is a modern transponder that is required for identification purposes when flying in controlled air space.

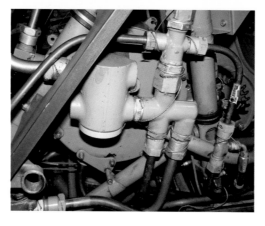

RIGHT Undercarriage and flap selector lever on the starboard side of the cockpit. The red guard stops selection of the undercarriage on the ground. *(Paul Blackah/Crown Copyright)*

FAR RIGHT Undercarriage and flap selector unit. *(Paul Blackah/Crown Copyright)*

RIGHT Hydraulic oil filter left and non-return valves in front of reservoir. *(Paul Blackah/Crown Copyright)*

FAR RIGHT Hydraulic reservoir, hand pump, pressure gauge and ACOV. *(Paul Blackah/Crown Copyright)*

Hydraulics

The hydraulics system is used to raise and lower the undercarriage and flaps, which are controlled by a dual selector unit, located on the starboard side of the cockpit. The system is powered by an engine-driven pump, which is situated below the crankcase on the centre line of the engine. A small hydraulic reservoir, complete with hand pump, pressure relief valve, filter and automatic cut-out valve is fitted on the starboard side of the fuselage just to the rear of the pilot's seat.

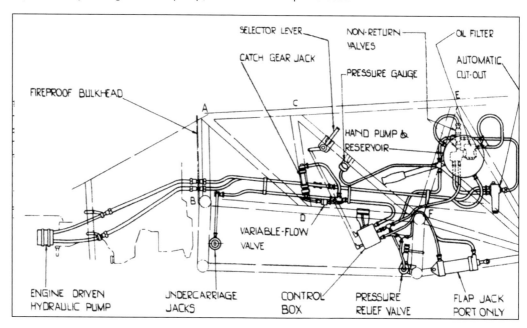

RIGHT Hydraulic system. *(AP1564)*

If the hydraulic pump fails, the hand pump can be used to raise or lower the undercarriage and flaps and, if a total hydraulic failure occurs, the undercarriage can be lowered by using the kick-down lever, which can be operated by the pilot's left foot.

Pneumatics

The pneumatic system operates the wheel brakes and on wartime Hurricanes it also operated the gun systems. This system is supplied with compressed air by an air cylinder located in the wheel bay. A Heywood compressor, mounted

FAR LEFT Hydraulic automatic cut out valve (ACOV) which controls the aircraft's hydraulic pressure. *(Paul Blackah/Crown Copyright)*

LEFT Hydraulic system pressure relief valve. *(Paul Blackah/ Crown Copyright)*

FAR LEFT Hydraulic pump fitted to the underside of the engine. *(Paul Blackah/ Crown Copyright)*

LEFT Undercarriage snap jack. *(Paul Blackah/Crown Copyright)*

FAR LEFT Air cylinder and coolant system pipe work. *(Paul Blackah/Crown Copyright)*

LEFT Oil and water trap left, fuel filter to the right. *(Paul Blackah/ Crown Copyright)*

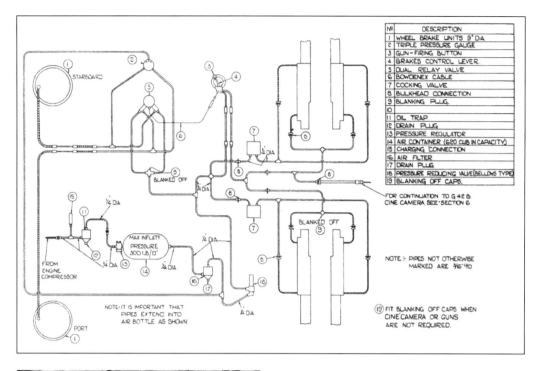

where any water or oil mist is collected. It then
passes through a filter on to a reducing valve,
which lowers the pressure to approximately
140psi. The main system pressure is indicated on
a triple pressure gauge, situated on the cockpit
floor between the rudder pedals.

Undercarriage

The undercarriage on the Hurricane consists
of two oleo pneumatic shock absorber struts,
which retract inwards and backwards into the
wheel bay beneath the fuselage, by means of
their individual retraction jacks, mounted on the
front face of the centre section. The oleo struts
are filled with oil and pressurised with nitrogen.

When the undercarriage raises, the hydraulic
jack moves inboard, the side stay folds and

on the rear of the engine starboard cylinder
block, charges the cylinder. The supply passes
through a regulator valve that limits the pressure
to 300psi, and then on to an oil-and-water trap,

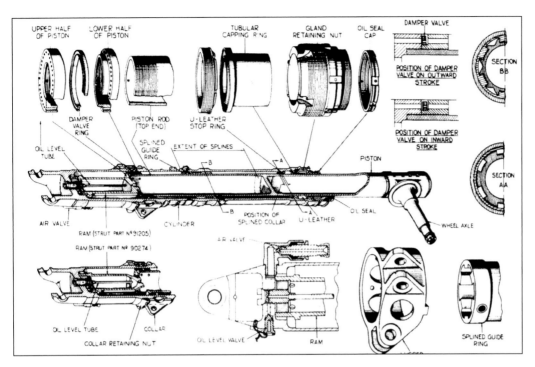

LEFT Main undercarriage oleo strut. *(AP1564)*

Labels in diagram: UPPER HALF OF PISTON, LOWER HALF OF PISTON, TUBULAR CAPPING RING, GLAND RETAINING NUT, OIL SEAL CAP, DAMPER VALVE, POSITION OF DAMPER VALVE ON OUTWARD STROKE, SECTION BB, DAMPER VALVE RING, PISTON ROD (TOP END), U-LEATHER STOP RING, POSITION OF DAMPER VALVE ON INWARD STROKE, OIL LEVEL TUBE, SPLINED GUIDE RING, EXTENT OF SPLINES, PISTON, SECTION AA, AIR VALVE, RAM (STRUT PART Nº 91205), RAM (STRUT PART Nº 90274), POSITION OF SPLINED COLLAR, U-LEATHER, OIL SEAL, CYLINDER, WHEEL AXLE, AIR VALVE, OIL LEVEL TUBE, COLLAR, OIL LEVEL VALVE, RAM, SPLINED GUIDE RING, COLLAR RETAINING NUT

forces the shock absorber strut to rotate about its bearing on the lower boom until the leg is horizontal. At the same time, the radius rod folds and its lower portion rotates about the lower boom. While this inward and upward movement is in progress the jointed radius rod is also providing the rearward component of movement. It is locked in place by two mechanical locks, which lock onto a stirrup assembly, fitted into the end of the axle.

On 'down' selection, hydraulic pressure to the snap jack disengages the locks and the release is affected by a system of cables and pulleys. The hydraulic jack extends outwards, pushing the leg down into the locked position. An assisting spring and triangular lever acting on the side stay lock the leg in place.

LEFT Tail leg fitted into rear fuselage. *(Paul Blackah/Crown Copyright)*

FAR LEFT 10.25 main wheel complete with brake drum. The white painted creep marks will show if the tyre moves on the wheel. *(Paul Blackah/Crown Copyright)*

LEFT 4.95 x 3.5 tail wheel and tyre. *(Paul Blackah/Crown Copyright)*

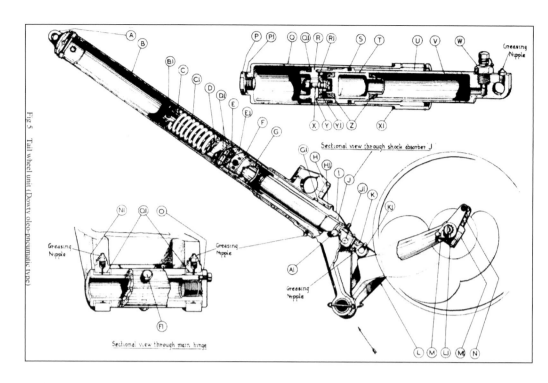

Fig 5 Tail wheel unit (Dowty oleo-pneumatic type)

Greasing Nipple

Sectional view through shock absorber 'J'

Greasing Nipple

Greasing Nipple

Greasing Nipple

Sectional view through main hinge

RIGHT Brake unit
complete with pads
covering the inflatable
bag. The up-lock
stirrup is shown fitted
in the end of the axle.
*(Paul Blackah/Crown
Copyright)*

FAR RIGHT Control
column spade grip
with gun firing button
and brake lever.
*(Paul Blackah/Crown
Copyright)*

The tailwheel unit is not retractable, but is fared into the underside of the fuselage tail bay. It comprises an oleo pneumatic shock absorber strut, which is fully castering and self-centring, and a tailwheel is carried on an axle, in a fork, at the lower end of the strut.

Brakes

The brake units are fitted to the undercarriage main axles and are operated by a bicycle type brake lever, which is fitted onto the control column spade grip. The lever is connected to the brake control valve with a Bowden cable. Operating the lever provides air to the drum brake air bags, which then inflate, pushing the brake shoes onto the brake drum, within the wheels, and thus stopping the aircraft. When the lever is fully applied, the brake pressure should be at least 100psi to each brake unit.

Movement of the rudder bar while the brakes are applied provides differential braking; this allows the aircraft to be steered on the ground while taxiing. A rod, leading from the rudder bar to the brake unit, enables this procedure to be carried out. The brake pressures are indicated on a triple gauge, positioned on the cockpit floor between the rudder pedals.

Flying controls

The flying controls consist of metal-framed, fabric-covered ailerons, elevators and rudder. A control column, mounted in the cockpit, operates the ailerons. The control column yolk operates the ailerons by chains and tie rods,

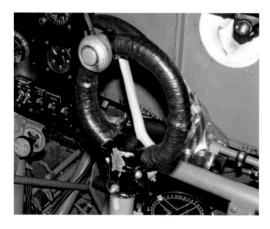

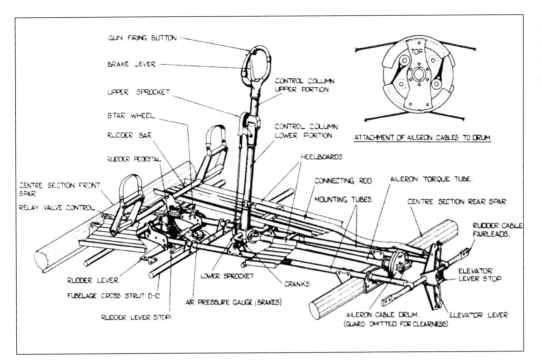

GUN FIRING BUTTON
BRAKE LEVER
UPPER SPROCKET
STAR WHEEL
RUDDER BAR
RUDDER PEDESTAL
CENTRE SECTION FRONT SPAR
RELAY VALVE CONTROL
RUDDER LEVER.
FUSELAGE CROSS STRUT D-D
RUDDER LEVER STOP.
AIR PRESSURE GAUGE (BRAKES)
LOWER SPROCKET
CRANKS
CONTROL COLUMN UPPER PORTION
CONTROL COLUMN LOWER PORTION
ATTACHMENT OF AILERON CABLES TO DRUM
HEELBOARDS
CONNECTING ROD
MOUNTING TUBES
AILERON TORQUE TUBE.
CENTRE SECTION REAR SPAR
RUDDER CABLE FAIRLEADS.
ELEVATOR LEVER STOP
AILERON CABLE DRUM. (GUARD OMITTED FOR CLEARNESS)
ELEVATOR LEVER
TOP

LEFT Flying control unit with rudder pedals and control column. *(AP1564)*

which are connected to a torque tube and then a cable drum, mounted rear of the control column. Cables and tie rods are then connected to a pulley in the outer wing, where they are then attached to an operating rod, which links to the aileron. Each aileron is mounted to the outer plane by three attachment brackets.

The ailerons have no trim tabs, so the aircraft is trimmed by gluing a length of cord up to 24in long, covered in a fabric strip, to the trailing edge of the aileron.

The elevators are operated by the control column via a connecting rod to a bell crank, aft of the centre section of the rear spar, and then by cables to a further bell crank in the rear fuselage and on to an operating rod to the elevator. The port and starboard halves

of the elevators are built on a single tubular steel spar, bolted together at the inner ends to form one unit. Five hinges are mounted on the elevator spar and then attached to the

LEFT Outboard aileron cable to aileron operating lever linkage. *(Paul Blackah/ Crown Copyright)*

FAR LEFT Fabric-covered aileron, note the covered cord strip. This is there to trim the aircraft. *(Paul Blackah/Crown Copyright)*

LEFT Fabric-covered elevator complete with trim tab. *(Paul Blackah/ Crown Copyright)*

RIGHT Elevator trim wheel sprocket and chain in the port side of the cockpit beside the seat, seen here from the outside looking into the cockpit with the fuselage outer covering removed. *(Paul Blackah/Crown Copyright)*

FAR RIGHT Elevator and rudder trim operating wheels in the port side of the cockpit beside the seat. *(Paul Blackah/Crown Copyright)*

RIGHT Rudder bar adjusting star wheel. *(Paul Blackah/Crown Copyright)*

FAR RIGHT Pilot's foot boards and the control column with chains and tie-rods for the aileron system. *(Paul Blackah/Crown Copyright)*

RIGHT Elevator trim gearbox. *(AP1564)*

FAR RIGHT Rudder with trim tab. *(Paul Blackah/Crown Copyright)*

tailplane. The elevator trim consists of two tabs, one on each elevator, which are operated by a wooden handwheel on the left-hand side of the cockpit, connected to chains and cables to a

gear box in each elevator. This gearbox has a wormwheel, which drives a threaded quadrant attached to the trim tab.

The rudder is operated by the rudder pedals,

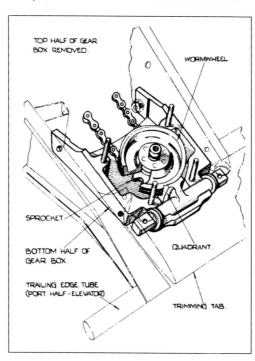

TOP HALF OF GEAR BOX REMOVED.

WORMWHEEL.

SPROCKET.

BOTTOM HALF OF GEAR BOX.

TRAILING EDGE TUBE (PORT HALF - ELEVATOR)

QUADRANT.

TRIMMING TAB.

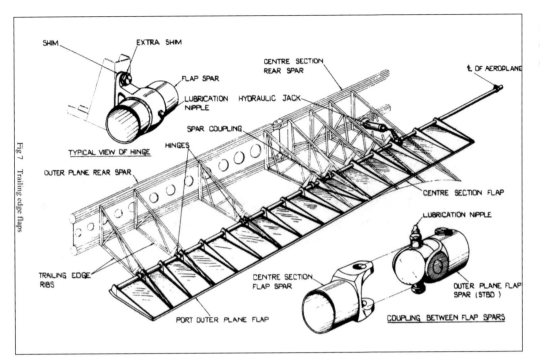

**LEFT Flap
construction diagram.**
(AP1564)

Fig 7 Trailing edge flaps

SHIM   EXTRA SHIM

FLAP SPAR

LUBRICATION HYDRAULIC JACK
NIPPLE

CENTRE SECTION
REAR SPAR

L OF AEROPLANE

SPAR COUPLING

TYPICAL VIEW OF HINGE   HINGES

OUTER PLANE REAR SPAR

CENTRE SECTION FLAP

LUBRICATION NIPPLE

TRAILING EDGE
RIBS

CENTRE SECTION
FLAP SPAR

OUTER PLANE FLAP
SPAR (STBD)

PORT OUTER PLANE FLAP

COUPLING BETWEEN FLAP SPARS

which move fore and aft about the rudder pedestal and lever assembly. Cables from the lever assembly go to an operating lever on the rudder assembly. The rudder is mounted to the fin posts by four hinge brackets.

The rudder trim tab is operated by a small handwheel, situated on the port side of the cockpit, via chains and cables.

The split trailing edge flaps are in three sections: one beneath the centre section and one beneath each outer main plane. These sections are connected by universal joints. The same selector box as the undercarriage hydraulically operates the flaps. A single hydraulic flap jack, located between the centre section rear spar and the operating arm on the flap spar, moves the flaps to the desired position.

**BELOW Trailing
edge split flaps in the
fully down position.**
*(Paul Blackah/Crown
Copyright)*

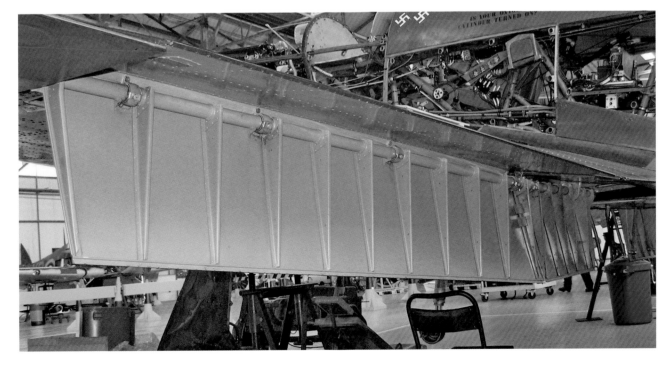

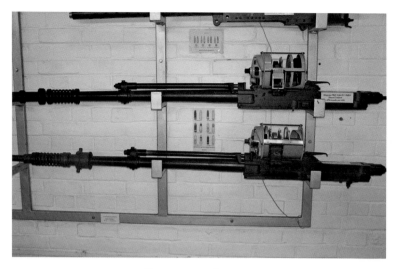

Armament

Although not fitted to the BBMF's Hurricanes,
the aircraft were originally equipped with four
20mm Hispano cannons. These were mounted
in sets of two in each outer wing and firing was
pneumatically controlled by a push button on
the control column.

Cockpit and instrumentation

The cockpit is housed in the centre fuselage

section. A two-part windscreen and canopy
assembly covers the cockpit. The windscreen
consists of a front armoured-glass panel and
the remainder is perspex. An inverted U-shaped
tube, fitted at its extremities to the fuselage
top longerons, supports the rear edge of
the screen. The front edge is screwed to the
decking. The sliding canopy is constructed of
perspex panels on a strip duralumin framework
and moves backwards and forwards on rollers,

ABOVE Windscreen assembly. *(Paul Blackah/ Crown Copyright)*

which run in channels fixed to each side of the decking. The canopy can be jettisoned by pulling on a handle located to the port side of the pilot's seat. When operated it disengages securing pins, which hold the canopy rail in place, allowing the canopy to be sucked into the air stream.

The pilot's seat is mounted on a pair of parallel links to allow adjustment of its height at any time. On the starboard side is a height

ABOVE Sliding canopy in open position. *(Paul Blackah/Crown Copyright)*

LEFT Emergency cockpit door, fitted on the starboard fuselage side beside the pilot. *(Paul Blackah/Crown Copyright)*

FAR LEFT Seat raising and lowering handle. *(Paul Blackah/Crown Copyright)*

LEFT Pilot's adjustable seat. *(Paul Blackah/ Crown Copyright)*

FAR LEFT Hand-hold. Door is open when the lower footstep is pulled down. *(Paul Blackah/Crown Copyright)*

LEFT The pull-out footstep in the down position. *(Paul Blackah/ Crown Copyright)*

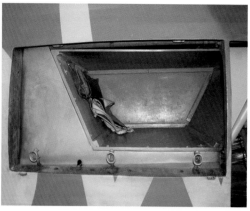

LF363 instrument panel. *(Paul Blackah/Crown Copyright)*

1 Airspeed indicator ASI	**9** Pressure head heater/ navigation lights switches	**17** Display stopwatch	**24** Low fuel pressure light illuminates under 5psi	**32** Slow-running cut-off
2 Artificial horizon	**10** Cockpit lights	**18** Port/starboard overload fuel tank warning light	**25** Oil pressure	**33** Undercarriage flap selector unit
3 Rate of climb indicator	**11** Ammeter	**19** RPM gauge	**26** Oil temperature	**34** P11 compass
4 Altimeter	**12** Accelerometer	**20** Start system light	**27** Coolant temperature	**35** Supercharger control knob
5 Directional indicator	**13** Air vents	**21** Press to test for overload lights	**28** Fuel contents gauge/ mains/reserve	**36** Landing light switch
6 Turn and slip	**14** Undercarriage lights and change over switch	**22** Fuel tank contents selector switch	**29** Ident light/Morse key	**37** Emergency boost
7 Starter/boost coil buttons	**15** Generator fail light	**23** Boost gauge	**30** Dimmer switch	**38** Throttle lever with press to transmit button
8 Magneto switches	**16** Radio AD120		**31** Priming pump	

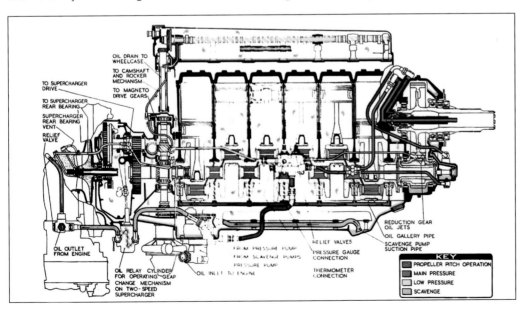

adjusting handle; by depressing a button at the end of the handle the seat can be locked into one of several positions by means of a ratchet gear assembly.

To enter the cockpit, two footsteps are provided; the lower one is retractable, while the upper one is fixed. When the retractable footstep is pulled downwards a bungee cord operates a trigger, which trips the catch holding the spring-loaded cover over the handhold. When the handhold cover is pushed back in it retracts the footstep.

Engine cowlings

Detachable duralumin panels cover most of the engine and are secured by quick-release fasteners.

Engine

The Rolls-Royce Merlin engine fitted to the Hurricane Mk IIc should be the Merlin XX-series, however the BBMF operates using Merlin 25, 225 and 500 engines. These are very similar in specification. The Merlin 25 is a 12-cylinder, V-12 liquid-cooled engine, weighing 1,430lb. Here we look closer at this specific mark of the Merlin.

Crankcase

The crankcase is cast from aluminium alloy and consists of two halves bolted together. The upper portion incorporates the rear half of the reduction gear housing at its front end and has a facing and spigot at the rear end, to which the wheel case is attached. The lower portion incorporates the scavenge pumps, filters and the mountings for the hydraulic pump.

Crankshaft

The crankshaft is manufactured from machine-forged chrome-molybdenum steel.

ABOVE LEFT P11 compass below instrument panel. *(Paul Blackah/Crown Copyright)*

ABOVE Right side of the engine magneto drive and exhaust ports are blanked. *(Paul Blackah/Crown Copyright)*

LEFT Engine oil circuit diagram. *(AP1564)*

Cylinders

The two cylinder assemblies, mainly the right and left-hand blocks, are known as the A and B blocks respectively. Each comprises six cylinders, the upper camshaft drive unit and the camshaft and rocker mechanism, which operates the valves incorporated in the cylinders. Each block consists of a separate alloy skirt, head and six detachable wet steel liners which, when bolted together, form the cylinder block proper. In addition to providing part of the coolant jacket, the head also forms the roofs of the six combustion chambers.

Cylinder liners

Each cylinder liner is shouldered and spigoted at the upper end to enter its respective recess in the bottom of the cylinder head. The cylinder liner is also provided with a sealing ring at its lower end to form a joint with the crankcase, to which the cylinder holding-down studs tighten it down to.

Cylinder block covers

The covers are secured to their respective cylinder blocks by studs and nuts, with a gasket between the two contacting faces. The main difference between the A and B covers is that the latter incorporates an engine speed indicator drive while the former is plain.

Camshaft

A single central camshaft for each cylinder block is mounted in pedestal brackets and operates both inlet and exhaust valves through rockers fitted with adjustable tappets. The camshafts, which are similar for both blocks, are driven from the wheel case by inclined shafts ending in bevel pinions, which mesh with bevel wheels at the end of each camshaft.

Camshaft auxiliary drive

The air compressor and hydraulic pumps for the turrets are mounted on the rear ends of the A and B cylinder heads. Both are driven from the spur gear wheels attached to the camshaft-driven bevel wheels.

Pistons

The pistons are attached to the connecting rods by fully floating gudgeon pins. The connecting rods are of the forked and plain type, the forked rod being fitted to the B-side of the engine.

The pistons are machined from light alloy forgings and are fitted with three compression rings above and one grooved scraper ring below the gudgeon pin. The gudgeon pins are made from hollow steel and are retained in the piston by spring wire circlips. A pair of oil holes are drilled obliquely and upwards towards the centre to meet in the metal above each gudgeon pin bore to assist in cooling the piston.

Valves

There are two inlet and exhaust valves per cylinder. Both valves are of the trumpet type

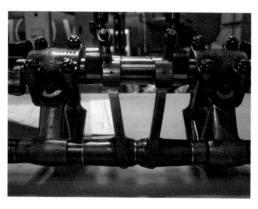

and have stellite-ended stems. The valve guides are cast iron for the inlet and phosphor-bronze for the exhaust. The valves are not interchangeable. Each valve guide is pressed into its respective bore in the cylinder block until a conical collar near its top end is seated on, and is flush with, the roof of the cylinder block.

Reduction gear

The reduction gear is of a single-spur layshaft type and is housed partly in a casing bolted to the front end of the crankcase and partly in the crankcase itself. The casing is located on the crankcase by means of a spigot concentric with the propeller shaft. The driving pinion is concentric with, and is driven by, a short coupling shaft from the crankshaft. All these shafts run in roller bearings, the propeller shaft having, in addition, a thrustable ball bearing, enabling the engine to be used with tractor (pulling) or pusher propeller. A dual-drive unit is fitted to the reduction gear cover for the purpose of driving the propeller CSU and vacuum pump unit, which are both bolted to it. The vacuum pump is used for the operation of certain navigational instruments.

Wheel case assembly

The wheel case is bolted to the rear end of the crankcase and carries the magnetos, coolant pump, generator drive, electric turning gear and fuel pump unit. It houses the spring-drive unit and certain shafts through which the magnetos, camshafts, electric generator, fuel, oil and coolant pumps are driven.

Fuel pump

The fuel pump unit, mounted on the facing on the port side of the wheel case, consists of two separate pumps operating in parallel. Each pump is capable of operating independently of the other and each is of sufficient capacity to supply more than the maximum amount of fuel required.

Electrical generator drive

The electrical generator drive is mounted upon a cast light alloy right-angled bracket that is located on the port side of the crankcase.

Coolant pump

The coolant pump is of the bottom-fed

LEFT Front of the Merlin engine with reduction gear, prop shaft (covered) CSU and vacuum pump. *(Paul Blackah/Crown Copyright)*

centrifugal type and serves each cylinder block from a separate outlet.

Carburetion

The SU twin-choke, up-draught type Merlin carburettor fitted to this engine is, with the exception of the separate boost control unit, entirely self-contained and is arranged to be fully automatic in its functioning, with the result that the responsibilities of the pilot are reduced to their simplest form and the danger of engine damage resulting from incorrect setting is reduced.

The SU type Merlin AVT40/93, or 214, carburettor embodies two complete carburettors in one unit. The flow of fuel through the left-hand carburettor main jet is directly controlled by the induction pressure-operated mixture control, while the right-hand jet is directly controlled by the atmospherically operated mixture control. Both these mixture controls are automatically controlled through linkwork by separate aneroid capsules incorporated on each side of the carburettor. The upper half of the carburettor casting is mounted on studs on the lower face of the

LEFT Port side of the engine with exhaust ports blanked. *(Paul Blackah/Crown Copyright)*

supercharger intake elbow. A large, specially shaped gasket is used at the joint faces to provide a gas-tight and fuel-tight joint.

Both the vertical intake passage and throttle barrels are coolant jacketed, these jackets being included in the coolant return from the B cylinder block to the inlet side of the coolant pump. A system of oil-heated throttle valves is also included to prevent freezing and to allow for a portion of the scavenge oil being directed through the hollow interior of the throttle valves before it is returned to the oil tank.

Supercharger

The two-speed, single-stage, liquid-cooled supercharger is of the high-speed centrifugal type, embodying a semi-shrouded impeller, which is driven from the rear end of the crankshaft through a two-speed gear.

Ignition system

The ignition system comprises two magnetos, which are attached to the wheel case, one on the left, and one on the right. Attached to these are the high-tension wiring harnesses for the spark plugs, which are metal-screened and serve a dual purpose by acting as a collector for the induced field around the high-tension wires and returning the resulting electrical current to earth, and also preventing radio interference. Each cylinder has two spark plugs – one magneto provides the spark for the inlet-side plugs and the other for the exhaust-side plugs. This ensures that if one magneto fails, the engine will still run using the other.

Engine controls

Throttle and mixture control

These engine controls are mounted on the port top longeron close to the pilot's left hand. The longer inboard lever is the throttle control and the shorter (where fitted) is the mixture control. The levers are moved forwards to open the throttle and to weaken the mixture. The knob on the mixture control lever projects in the way of the throttle lever to ensure that the mixture control is pulled back to 'rich' on closing the throttle. On some aircraft, such as the BBMF aircraft, there is no mixture control lever, as the system is fully automatic.

Boost control cut-out

Automatic boost control is provided to maintain a constant boost pressure without continual operation of the throttle lever by the pilot. In conditions of emergency, the automatic boost control may be cut out by pulling a knob on the port side of the instrument panel.

Propeller control

The constant speed propeller control is mounted on the port side just above the

FAR LEFT Landing light switch and supercharger changeover knobs. *(Paul Blackah/Crown Copyright)*

LEFT Slow-running cut-off control. *(Paul Blackah/Crown Copyright)*

LEFT Radiator cooler flap operating handle. *(Paul Blackah/Crown Copyright)*

throttle. The lever varies the governed rpm from 3000 down to 1800 by means of a Teleflex cable and the CSU, which is fitted on the starboard bottom side of the reduction gear casing.

Supercharger control

The supercharger two-speed gear is controlled from the cockpit through a Teleflex cable. The push–pull control is fitted below the left-hand side of the instrument panel and must be pushed in for low (M) gear and pulled out for high (S) gear.

Slow-running cut-out control

This control stops the engine when it is in idle, and consists of a Bowden cable connected to the cut-out control lever on the carburettor. Pulling out the knob immediately to the right of the undercarriage and flap selector lever operates the control.

Radiator flap control

A lever to the left-hand side of the pilot's seat controls the airflow through the coolant radiator and oil cooler. To operate the lever, a thumb button must first be depressed.

Priming pump

The priming pump is situated below the right-hand side of the instrument panel. It is a Ky-gas type pump, which takes its feed from the reserve fuel tank.

Engine starting

The starter and boost coil push buttons are to the left of the ignition switches on the instrument panel. An external power supply socket is accessible through a removable panel on the starboard engine cowling and two hand-starting handles are stowed in the undercarriage wheel bay under the centre section, although these are rarely used.

(The engine starting procedure for Hurricane pilots is described in detail in Chapter 6.)

FAR LEFT Engine priming pump. Handle shown stowed and screwed in; also shown is the oil and coolant temperature gauges. *(Paul Blackah/Crown Copyright)*

LEFT The hand starter in place on the right-hand side of the engine. *(Paul Blackah/Crown Copyright)*

Chapter Four

The BBMF's Hurricanes

The two beautifully maintained Hurricanes that form part of the Battle of Britain Memorial Flight are among the most well-known airworthy historic aircraft anywhere in the world. Based with the flight at RAF Coningsby in Lincolnshire, these two aircraft are regular participants at air shows and commemorative events all over Britain, and are among the best looked-after of all the warbirds worldwide. At the time of writing, they are 2 of approximately 12 surviving airworthy Hurricanes.

OPPOSITE The RAF Battle of Britain Memorial Flight's (BBMF's) Hurricane Mk IIc, LF363, minus its 20mm cannon. (Richard Paver)

You would have to go a long way to find two better looked-after historic aircraft. The care and dedication that goes into the maintenance and flying of the BBMF's two Hurricanes is second to none – indeed, for official reasons it has to be. Both the BBMF's Hurricanes are officially RAF aircraft, and as such are not present on the British civil register. On the contrary, as military aircraft they are maintained to the highest standards expected of RAF front-line combat aircraft.

The two aircraft have had very different careers prior to joining the BBMF, one of them being a genuine RAF combat veteran and the other having enjoyed an interesting career in civil life. While with the BBMF, each aircraft has worn a variety of colour schemes over the years. In recent times it has become an excellent trend in aircraft restoration that many airworthy warbirds wear fully researched and highly detailed authentic colour schemes and markings. This is in contrast to past times, when many historic aircraft were painted to suit the whim of their owners in fanciful colour schemes that had little to do with authenticity. The aircraft of the BBMF have been world-leaders in the representation of authentic colour schemes, and have commemorated a number of significant and historic RAF aircraft from the past. PZ865, for example, was recently painted in the colours of the Hurricane Mk IIc flown by

BELOW A pair of 1940s Form F700s when LF363 was with No 309 (Polish) Squadron. *(Paul Blackah/Crown Copyright)*

the famous and highly successful Czechoslovak pilot Karel Kuttelwascher.

The following is a brief history of each aircraft, with the most up-to-date information available of their current status in February 2010.

Hurricane Mk IIc, LF363

Hurricane Mk IIc, LF 363, was from the tenth and final production batch of Hurricanes built by Hawker Aircraft Limited. Hurricanes from this batch, which numbered some 1,357 examples of the Mk IIb, IIc and IV, were built in 1943 and 1944. It is widely held that LF363 was the last Hurricane actively to serve with the RAF, and may well have been among the last operational Hurricanes to enter regular RAF squadron service. The Hurricane first flew on 1 January 1944, and was delivered to No 5 MU on 28 January that year. It was in continuous RAF service from then, until a crash landing in 1991 interrupted its service while extensive repairs were made.

The Hurricane served with Nos 63, 309 (Polish) and 26 Squadrons before the cessation of hostilities in 1945. While with No 309 Squadron it was stationed at RAF Drem in Scotland on shipping protection duties. This Polish-manned squadron operated Hurricanes for several months during 1944 alongside its Allison-engined Mustangs until Merlin-engined Mustangs arrived in numbers late in 1944. No 26 Squadron was a unit that late in the war had a number of ageing but nonetheless still effective aircraft types on its inventory, including the Allison-engined Mustangs for artillery spotting in France and reconnaissance duties, again bolstered by Hurricanes. LF363 also served with some training units, including No 61 OTU at RAF Ouston, Northumberland.

Unlike many other Hurricanes, LF363 was not scrapped following the end of its front-line career. Instead, after overhaul by Hawker it subsequently served post-war on several station flights, including those at RAF Waterbeach, in Cambridgeshire, and Middle Wallop and Odiham, in Hampshire. The aircraft also appeared in the films *Angels One Five*, *Reach for the Sky* and

ABOVE LF363 in silver finish from the 1950s. This aircraft is now with the BBMF. *(Crown Copyright)*

RIGHT LF363 in flight alongside another famous Hawker design, the beautiful Hunter jet fighter. *(Crown Copyright)*

BELOW, LEFT LF363 being worked on by No 56 Squadron personnel in the 1950s. *(Crown Copyright)*

BELOW, RIGHT LF363 in flight with Spitfire TE476. *(Crown Copyright)*

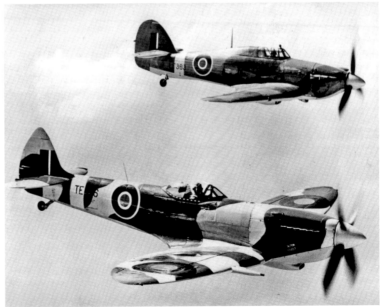

the *Battle of Britain*, as well as the television series *The War in the Air*.

LF363 became a founding member of the RAF Historic Aircraft Flight at RAF Biggin Hill, Kent, in July 1957. The Hurricane has been a member of the flight ever since, moving with the unit wherever it has been based, and seeing in the change of name to Battle of Britain Memorial Flight in 1973.

On 11 September 1991, while en route from the BBMF's base at RAF Coningsby to Jersey, LF363's engine suffered a mechanical failure and it started to run rough and to lose power, pouring smoke from the exhausts. The pilot diverted to RAF Wittering in Northamptonshire, but the engine failed completely at a late stage of the approach, resulting in a crash-landing on the airfield. The aircraft was seriously damaged by the crash and the ensuing fierce fire; fortunately the pilot escaped with only a broken ankle and minor burns. LF363 was completely

rebuilt by the private company and restoration specialists Historic Flying Ltd at Audley End, in Essex, between 1994 and 1998, when it flew again for the first time in seven years, subsequently rejoining the BBMF.

By February 2010, LF363 had logged 2,412.50 flying hours and 2,492 landings since 1944, and had recently worn a variety of accurately portrayed colour schemes in honour of several squadrons that flew the Hurricane in combat.

Hurricane Mk IIc, PZ865

This aircraft was the last of the 14,231 or more Hurricanes ever built. PZ865 rolled off the production line at Langley, Buckinghamshire, in the summer of 1944 with the inscription 'The Last of the Many' painted on its port and starboard fuselage sides next to the cockpit. Like LF363, it was from the large

BELOW

Photographed at Hawker's Langley factory in the summer of 1944, this is Hurricane Mk IIc, PZ865, *The Last of the Many,* as it moved along the assembly line as the last Hurricane to be built. Above the aircraft's fuselage a banner proudly proclaimed the places where the Hurricane had gained battle honours since the start of the war – there was certainly a good number of them. *(Hawker Aircraft Ltd)*

PZ865 was purchased back from the Air Ministry by Hawkers and used for some company flying before joining the British civil register as G-AMAU. Later it was used as a chase plane during the flight-testing of the Hawker P.1127 before joining the RAF BBMF. *(RAF Museum)*

final batch of Hurricanes built by Hawker Aircraft Limited.

PZ865 first flew in late July 1944 for 1hr 55mins. On completion, it was almost immediately purchased back from the Air Ministry by Hawker and used for some company flying before being mothballed. It was subsequently employed as a company communications and test aircraft, and joined the British civil register as G-AMAU in 1950 (its Certificate of Airworthiness was issued in May 1950). During that year, wearing its civilian registration G-AMAU and a smart blue and white colour scheme, it was entered in the King's Cup Air Race by HRH Princess Margaret. Flown by Group Captain Peter Townsend, it achieved second place. Townsend had flown Hurricanes during the war and it was thus appropriate that he flew PZ865 during this later stage in its career. The aircraft participated in other aeronautical events and air races, and was a part of Hawker Aircraft Limited's own flying museum, which included a number of historic Hawker types such as a Hart and Sea Fury.

During the early 1960s, following an extensive overhaul by Hawker at Dunsfold, Surrey, PZ865 was returned to its wartime camouflage scheme and continued to be used as a company hack and communications aircraft. The aircraft's useful days were not over by any means and it performed important work as a chase plane during the early flight testing of the Hawker P.1127 (which later became the Kestrel and matured into the Harrier), and also flew in similar fashion in support of the development work for the Sea Fury target-towing conversions for export to West Germany. It appeared in the movie *Battle of Britain*

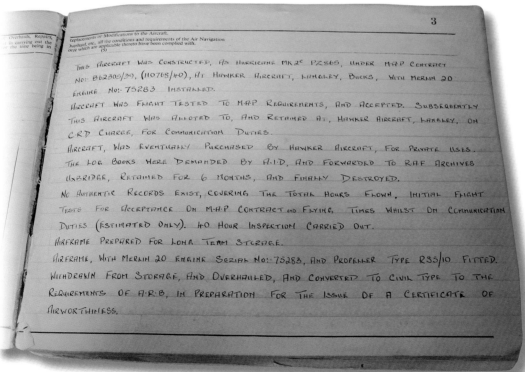

ABOVE PZ865's civil aviation aircraft log book, when she was registered as G-AMAU. *(Paul Blackah/Crown Copyright)*

BELOW Brief history of PZ865 from 1950, taken from the log book. *(Paul Blackah/ Crown Copyright)*

(alongside LF363) and also made numerous display appearances, often in the hands of the famous test pilot Bill Bedford.

After a complete overhaul, PZ865 was flown to RAF Coltishall, Norfolk, in March 1972 and given to the Memorial Flight by Hawker Siddeley – it was cancelled from the British civil register in December 1972. For many years the aircraft appeared as 'The Last of the Many', but eventually the inscription was removed from the Hurricane's fuselage and put on display in the BBMF headquarters. Like LF363, this aircraft has worn a number of colour schemes over the years, highlighting the diversity of RAF units that flew Hurricanes during the Second World War. As of early February 2010, PZ865 had achieved 2,466.25 flying hours and 2,227 landings.

BELOW The original fabric from PZ865, the last Hurricane built. This priceless exhibit is held by the BBMF. *(Paul Blackah/Crown Copyright)*

Power for the BBMF's Hurricanes

The heart of the Hurricane, as indeed any aircraft, is its engine. In the case of the two Hurricanes of the Battle of Britain Memorial Flight, the engine in question is the Rolls-Royce Merlin, in its XX-series form, which was one of the leading inline fighter engines of its day. Unlike the rival German Daimler Benz DB 601 inline engine, which powered the Messerschmitt Bf109E – the deadliest rival of the Hurricane in the early war years – the Merlin was not fuel-injected, but relied on a carburettor. In contrast, the DB 601 series engines, being fuel-injected, allowed the Bf109s fitted with these power plants to fly and fight upside down if need be, something that early marks of the Hurricane and Spitfire found impossible for more than a few seconds during the Battle of Britain – the arrangement of the carburettor fuel system in these aircraft prevented Spitfires and Hurricanes from flying inverted for any length of time due to fuel starvation in that attitude. This problem was later put right, but Hurricane pilots who flew within this limitation and instead used the Hurricane's excellent manoeuvrability and reasonably comparable performance at lower levels had a good chance of at least holding their own against the Bf109E – and in numerous cases of winning the argument. The following is a specific set of specifications for the Merlin XX series (actually referring to the Merlin 25, as used in the BBMF's two Hurricanes), based on official data.

Rolls-Royce Merlin XX series (specific to Merlin 25)

General

Type of engine	Supercharged, geared, pressure liquid-cooled V-engine, fitted with a two-speed supercharger
Number of cylinders	12
Arrangement of cylinders	Two banks of six cylinders each with an inclined angle of 60°
Bore	5.4in
Stroke	6.0in
Swept volume	1,648cu in.
Compression ratio	6.0 to 1

Supercharger

Type	Single stage, two-speed
Gear ratio	8.15 to 1 and 9.49 to 1

Propeller reduction gear

Type	Spur lay shaft, single reduction
Ratio	0.42 to 1

Direction of rotation

Propeller shaft	Right-hand
Crankshaft	Left-hand
Cylinder numbering	Propeller 1A, 2A, 3A, 4A, 5A, 6A, 1B, 2B, 3B, 4B, 5B, 6B
Weight of engine, nett dry	1,430lb + 2½% tolerance

Rated altitude

Merlin XX, 21, 22, 23	10,000ft low gear 18,000ft high gear
Merlin 24 and 25	9,250ft low gear 16,000ft high gear

Performance

International or climbing Power rating (Merlin XX, 21, 22 + 23)	Low gear 1,240bhp at 2,850rpm at 10,000ft and +9lb per sq in boost High gear 1,175bhp at 2,850rpm at 17,500ft and +9lb per sq in boost
(Merlin 24 and 25)	Low gear 1,210bhp at 2,850rpm at 9,250ft and +9lb per sq in boost High gear 1,135bhp at 2,850rpm at 16,00ft and +9lb per sq in boost

Oil

Type	OM270/W100
Consumption at max	6 to 20pt per hour cruising conditions

Pressures

Main	
Normal	60 to 80lb per sq in
Minimum	45lb per sq in

Ignition

Firing order	1A, 6B, 4A, 3B, 2A, 5B, 6A, 1B, 3A, 4B, 5A, 2B

Magnetos

Number	Two
Type	BTH C5SE 12-S or Rotax NSE 12-4
Direction of rotation	Port clockwise, Stbd anticlockwise
Speed of rotation	1.5 engine speed
Contact breaker gap	0.012in magneto fully advanced

Timing

Fully advanced (early type)	Stbd 35° before TDC, Port 45° before TDC
Fully advanced (later type)	Stbd 45° before TDC, Port 50° before TDC
Fully retarded	Stbd 25° before TDC, Port 30°before TDC
Sparking plug gap	0.012in

Carburetion

Carburettor	SU type Merlin AVT 40/193 duplex double entry
Fuel	100LL Avgas/F18
Max fuel demand	156gal per hour
Pump pressure to carb	6–10lb per sq in

Valves

Valve timing (0.020 in clearance all valves)

Inlet opens	31° before TDC
Inlet closes	51° after BDC
Exhaust opens	72° before BDC
Exhaust closes	12° after TDC

Tappet clearance

Running	0.010in inlet–0.020in exhaust

Accessories

The following accessories can be fitted to the engine:

Accessory	Speed ratio relative	Direction of rotation to crankshaft
Constant speed unit	0.828	Clockwise
Vacuum pump	0.828	Clockwise
Electric generator	1.953	Anticlockwise
Starter motor	101.7	Clockwise
Heywood compressor	0.5	Clockwise
Hydraulic pump (camshaft)	0.5	Clockwise
Hydraulic pump (crankcase)	0.5	Clockwise

Chapter Five

The Owners' Views

Anyone wishing to own a genuine airworthy Hurricane has to accept that there are not all that many possibilities any longer. Considerable good fortune is needed to find an airframe in a lake in Russia or other such location, and even in the unlikely event that one might suddenly become available, a very large amount of money would be essential to see the project to a successful conclusion.

OPPOSITE Peter Vacher's Hurricane Mk I, R4118, alongside Spitfire Mk I, AR213. *(Richard Paver)*

Acquiring a Hurricane

The most practical way of obtaining a Hurricane in airworthy condition is to buy one that is already fully operational, but with around only a dozen airworthy Hurricanes extant in the world, the possibilities are limited. The owners of these aircraft are very proud of their charges, and the price of a Hurricane in airworthy condition is likely to be in the high end of six figures – if indeed one of these precious aircraft ever were to become available on the open market in the first place. Sourcing an original Hurricane that needs restoration is not necessarily impossible, but nowadays unlikely. If you managed to find a project, and there always remains the remote possibility of a wreck being salvaged in Russia, or turning up in a barn in Canada, it would be possible to restore the aircraft – as long as you have money, and lots of it.

After you have sourced your project, verifying its provenance should be easy, providing that original makers' data plates are still fitted to major components. It is then a question of finding the skilled traders able to perform the many tasks needed during restoration, and to source suitable spare parts.

Obtaining spare parts and specialised services

There are many small companies that can support a restoration project. These range from firms manufacturing major components, such as mainplanes, to others which remanufacture smaller components, such as rubber seals.

If you are lucky enough to have original drawings, and the BBMF has over 6,000 original Hurricane drawings, then the process of manufacturing a part becomes much simpler.

Companies such as Dunlop still produce the original tyres. Rolls-Royce in Derby still gives advice on its engines, although it does not manufacture or overhaul any more. Retro Track and Air will carry out a thorough service and overhaul of the engine. Propeller blades are produced in Germany by Hoffmann and assembled in the UK by Skycraft Ltd.

There are a couple of companies that carry out fabric work, one of which is Vintage Fabrics. (Clive Denny, of Vintage Fabrics, explains the process of fabric covering a Hurricane in Chapter 2.)

Insurance costs

The cost of insuring a privately owned and operated Hurricane is approximately £50,000 per year.

Case History 1

Peter Vacher and Hurricane Mk I, R4118

Proud owner Peter Vacher found his Hurricane by chance during a visit to India in the 1980s. The aircraft was in a poor state of repair, obtaining permission to export it from India was problematical, and on its return to England a great deal of time and patience was needed to restore the aircraft to flying condition. It is a unique survivor, in being a genuine Battle of Britain veteran.

Running costs

Running costs depend on how much you fly your aircraft, but as a rough guide the following applies:

Oil	approximately £12–£15 per gallon (oil tank takes 7.5gal, after two hour's flying you could be putting in between 2–3pt to top up)
Fuel	approximately £1.30 per litre (tank holds 94gal, which gives approximately two hours' flying time)
Tyres	in 2009 the cost of a single main wheel tyre was £350, these will last 20–30 landings, more if you are using grass strips
Engine	an overhaul will cost roughly between £90,000–£130,000, depending on what needs replacing, although this is only necessary every 500 flying hours providing your engine remains serviceable
Propeller	is overhauled every 360 flying hours, or five years, and a set of blades will cost approximately £10,000–£15,000 per blade
Service	A major service, depending on what needs replacing, can cost upwards of £125,000

I stumbled upon the wreck of a Hurricane in India where it had been exposed to the elements for 54 years. There was no fabric, no wood, the wings were lying on the ground covered in leaves, the propeller was half buried and the tailplane had all but rotted away and yet here was a Mark I Hurricane standing proudly on its undercarriage, almost ready to take up arms again in defence of our country. I remembered how Hitler aimed to invade the shores of Britain in the middle of 1940. He only needed control of the skies. It was the Hurricane that thwarted his plans.

During the Battle of Britain, July to October 1940, the Hurricane accounted for 60 per cent of all enemy aircraft destroyed. Our Hurricane, Mk I R4118, undertook 49 sorties out of Croydon with 605 Squadron in the thick of the battle, destroying five enemy bombers, which were aiming for London. The few Spitfires in the skies at the time went for the bomber escorts of Me109s, but were very prone to damage from enemy fire. Due to its construction of metal tubes and wooden frame, the Hurricane could withstand much more battle damage and still fly. It was a stable gun platform with a greater 'concentration of lead' due to the compact grouping of its eight Browning machine-guns. It would also out-turn any other aircraft in the skies at the time.

The Hurricane was once described as 'a great big pussycat'. Certainly, with its thick wing and wide undercarriage, it was easier to land than either the popular Harvard trainer or the Spitfire. Being based on the design of the earlier Hawker biplanes, it was capable of only limited development later in the war. This did not prevent it serving in a wider world theatre than any other fighter. Hurricanes flew in India, Burma, South Africa, North Africa, Malta, Norway, Finland and France, and 2,500 were sent to Russia.

ABOVE R4118, Peter Vacher's Hurricane Mk I, as she was found in India prior to her restoration to fly again. *(Peter Vacher)*

BELOW R4118 nearing completion at Hawker Restorations Ltd. *(Peter Vacher)*

LEFT Cockpit of R4118 complete with gunsight.
(Jim Douthwaite)

ABOVE Siamese exhaust stubs on R4118.
(Jim Douthwaite)

BELOW Privately-owned and beautifully-restored
Mk I, R4118, taxiing with Squadron Leader Al
Pinner at the controls. *(Jim Douthwaite)*

Much of the pleasure from owning a Hurricane has come from meeting the veterans who flew these aeroplanes. When I initially found the aircraft I traced and interviewed five of the pilots who had flown R4118 in the battle. Sadly only one survives, Wing Commander Bob Foster who claimed three aircraft shot down from R4118. Bob is in great form and frequently joins UP-W, the aeroplane's squadron markings, at airshows.

It is a privilege to be the custodian of a true Battle of Britain fighter, which played its part in preserving our freedom.

Case History 2

Guy Black and Hurricane Mk XII, Z5140

Guy Black is an owner/operator of historic aircraft, which he runs as a joint operation with a friend, under the name of the Historic Aircraft Collection. His Hurricane is the Canadian-built Mk XII Z5140 (registered G-HURI), painted to represent a Hurricane Mk IIb of No 126 Squadron, and is normally based at Duxford, in Cambridgeshire.

ABOVE Looking down on Hurricane Mk I, R4118 with Spitfire Mk I, AR213. *(Richard Paver)*

BELOW Z5140 Mk XII, G-HURI, Guy Black's Historic Aircraft Collection Hurricane over Duxford. *(Richard Paver)*

ABOVE Hurricane
Z5140 lands at Malta in
2005. *(Clive Denny)*

Why did we buy a Hurricane? It is the unsung hero of the Battle of Britain, with more victories than the Spitfire and also it was the first successful monoplane fighter; it was the main linking design between the biplane fighters and the high-speed monocoque fighters such as the Spitfire – and so an extraordinarily successful aircraft of great historical importance, but undervalued historically by the Spitfire. Our rationale when adding an aircraft to the collection is that it should (a) be viable as an investment and (b) be of historical importance.

The Hurricane scores well on both counts.

However, our pilots all agree that it rattles, is hot and noisy to fly, and is ergonomically hopeless with the instruments and controls all over the place, but the overriding sense of history and the relatively benign handling and ease of landing make it an ideal display aircraft, though it is a lot heavier to handle and not as nimble and aerobatic as a Spitfire. It is like a carthorse next to the Spitfire, which is a racehorse – as a number of veterans have told us over the years – but we all have an affection for it.

RIGHT Four
Hurricanes at North
Weald in 2009.

Case History 3

Tony Dyer: Build – and own – your own Hurricane

As an 'RAF' child of the late 1960s and 70s, Tony Dyer grew up around aircraft. His father's postings (from Cyprus to White Waltham) gave a rich aviation foundation. In time-honoured fashion, Tony whiled away the hours making, using and abusing Airfix kits and gazing at warbirds as they flew overhead. He always dreamed of owning a Hurricane or Spitfire. A strong passion (obsession some might say!) for fighters and the Battle of Britain developed. In 1987, after university, Tony joined Boscombe Down as a flight test engineer and has continued to work as an FTE ever since on heavy aircraft, fast jets and rotorcraft. As well as the Hurricane, Tony's Air Defence Collection includes three Hunter cockpit sections (an F1, F2 and F6), a Spitfire fuselage and a motley collection of Merlin and Daimler Benz engines and Battle of Britain related artefacts. Here he describes his ongoing static Hurricane project, which began with his rebuild of a cockpit section.

The question I am often asked is why are you building a Hurricane? As a toddler, my parents took me to Booker, in Buckinghamshire, and I saw my first Spitfire (at Personal Plane Services). I have never forgotten that day. I was brought up, like many kids of the 1970s, reading *Commando* magazines, shooting cap guns, building Airfix kits, watching the Sunday afternoon war movies and listening to the stories of my grandfather who was a wartime Catalina pilot. I spent hours watching the *Battle of Britain* film and adored the Battle of France scenes, particularly when the arch-backed Hurri's lurch over the undulating grass, to the accompaniment of the Merlin's deep-throated popping.

In 1980, when I was 15, I bought a Hurricane tailwheel that had been used on the blanket trolleys at Witney; these wheels had originated from the old maintenance airfield nearby. My friends and I shared a passion for Second World War aircraft and would try to see inside aircraft at airshows, but no one would let us anywhere near the cockpit. One day, my friends said they were going to build a Spitfire,

LEFT Original manufacturer's data plates from P3554.

BELOW General view of the cockpit and instrument panel of P3554.

so naturally, I thought I would do a Hurricane cockpit. This would let me have my own aircraft to sit in. It seemed such an easy dream then. The more I read about Hurricanes, saw them fly, heard veterans speak, the more dedicated I became. My ongoing interest in these aircraft is now almost 30 years old and not a day goes by without me thinking something Hurricane related. The words that spring to mind are passion, obsession and compulsion!

Where to get parts?

In the 1980s, Second World War parts and instruments were freely available. Everyone wanted Spitfire parts – the Hurricane was the underdog so these parts were cheaper. I spent every penny available buying parts and also spare items for trade. Lucky breaks included getting several cheap canopies that had been used as strawberry cloches near North Weald, a large cache of wartime gunsights and several seats. The group I belonged to in Oxfordshire dug several wartime dumps, recovering large numbers of windscreens from Spitfires, Hurricanes, Whirlwinds and Second World War bombers. These all made handy swaps. Stainless steel 'fish plates' came from a Civilian Repair Unit (CRU) dump and from swaps with the many groups digging up Hurricanes shot down during the Battle of Britain. It is amazing how many parts from aircraft shot down can be incorporated into a static project. I also swapped potentially airworthy parts for static items from the team rebuilding 5589 (G-HURR), the IWM/Shuttleworth restoring Sea Hurricane Z7015, and the BBMF. The latter were particularly helpful with advice and, more importantly, static original woodwork and panels from PZ865. The doghouse from PZ865 still sports traces of Royal Blue paint from when 'The Last of the Many' was a racer in that fantastic blue/gold colour scheme. The parts with history give a rich historic depth to the project and must be the ultimate in recycling.

The identity came from a Mk I, P3554, that was shot down twice in the Battle of Britain. The first time was in July 1940, when it was damaged in a belly landing following combat and then repaired. On 5 October 1940, P3554 (flying with 607, County of Durham, Squadron) was shot down by a Messerschmitt Bf109E

over Swanage. The pilot, P/O D. Evans, baled out safely. The maker's plate, some structure and several cockpit controls came from P3554 and were incorporated into the project. The maker's plate (see photo) gives the aircraft serial number and is fitted to the port joint C (under the left-hand instrument panel).

The control column uses parts from eight aircraft: the spade grip from an early Mk I; the upper column from an ex-Portuguese Mk II scrapped after the *Angels One Five* movie; the lower column, elevator push rod and chain rods come from four different Battle of Britain Hurricanes; one gun tube comes from PZ865 and the elevator pick-off comes from LF363.

The problems

Restoring a static presents many of the same challenges as restoring one to fly: shortage of parts; complex polygon wing and tail spars; money and time. The one benefit is that scrap items that can no longer fly can also be used.

LEFT Port side of the cockpit.

BELOW All of Tony's Hurricane parts laid out in the garden in 1988.

However, as Hurricanes have increased in commercial desirability, owners are now less likely to release scrap/static parts, which is a pity. Drawings are a problem, but static restorers tend to help each other out. Most fuselage joints tend to survive crashes fairly well, although they can be badly bent and torn. Joint M on the lower rear fuselage frame joins two tubes together and is often damaged. My pair was built up from six aircrafts' worth of joint Ms! I would say that 50 per cent of my project time has been spent stripping down and straightening fishplates. I tend to reuse fasteners, ferrules, spacers and as much as I can, even down to nuts, bolts and washers. The whole idea is to make this as original as possible.

There are several parts that are incredibly hard to find; the most elusive is the hydraulic hand pump that fits to the starboard cockpit side. It took me 22 years to find one – actually it was the second as the first was far too good for a static and I suggested the owner talk to the BBMF. My pump came from a Hurricane that

ended up in a freshwater lake in Canada. The pilot's booster 'tit' (located on the left instrument panel) is also difficult to find; mine came from P3554. In fighter pilot memoirs they often talk of pulling the 'tit' to give added boost and chase the enemy.

Given its prominent position in the cockpit, it is essential to have a really nice spade grip. My grip is very early Dunlop-made grip (1939 vintage) and is absolutely immaculate. One in this condition is difficult to find.

Many things have got in the way over the years (university, marriage, house, kids, divorce – not the Hurri's fault! – etc), but the Hurricane has always been there. It is a member of the family, albeit an often annoying one.

The result

Armchair enthusiasts feel everything should fly and do not always realise that keeping an aircraft flying results in more and more of the original aircraft being replaced as the years go by. If some of these parts can be amalgamated in a museum aircraft, we can get the best of both worlds: static originals and flying (safe) Hurricanes.

P3554 is a complex composite; over 65 individual Hurricanes have 'donated' parts. This has resulted in the project being more than 85 per cent original Second World War material. All the parts are documented, so it is really a cross between a memorial and museum piece dedicated to the designers, builders, ground and aircrew. Since it is made up essentially of scrap, it is a bit of a metaphoric phoenix, allowing a humble flight test engineer to own a sizeable chunk of warbird.

In 2004, P3554 was named *Jessamy*, after my two daughters, and taken to the delightful CockpitFest Event at Newark Air Museum, Nottinghamshire, where she took first place. Has it been worth it . . . oh yes!

The Hurricane is finally coming out from the Spitfire's shadow and taking deserved credit for its true place in history. Britain needed the Spitfire, but it *had* to have the Hurricane.

The future

So what is the future? Well, I have amassed a huge kit of parts to continue the project to a full aircraft if and when I get time, space and the all-important money. I have a Merlin (that used to 'star' as a wind machine in many films), one-and-a-half wings, the rear fuselage tubing/joints and about eight tea chests of sundries. My wing centre section spars suffered a heavy force landing in Russia and will be a nightmare to restore. One day, I hope to have a fully serviceable (though non-flying) 85 per cent original Hawker Hurricane that can taxi under its own steam . . . a true phoenix rising from the scrap pile . . . we can all dream can't we!

The Hurricane spade grip

ABOVE AND RIGHT An early grip from a Hurricane that was written off before the war. The pilot was given the grip as a souvenir.

The most prominent part in the cockpit is the spade grip. This ring-shaped joystick allowed the pilot not only to fly the aircraft and fire the guns, but also to use the wheel brakes on the ground. Some people think that the stick design is archaic, especially compared to the pistol grip type stick fitted to the Bf109, but the spade grip was suited to the high lateral stick forces in dog-fighting and also allowed the pilot to change hands on the grip from the throttle to raise the undercarriage or flaps.

The Mk I and early Mk II aircraft had the AH2040 grip made by Dunlop in aluminium and this is highly prized by collectors and aircraft owners alike. Later Hurricanes had a similar grip, but cast in magnesium alloy and these tend to corrode.

The brass gun button had a knurled outer part that was turned between the SAFE and FIRE position. Depressing the button fired the guns pneumatically.

The brake lever was similar to a bicycle brake and could be used to brake the wheels individually or together (depending on rudder pedal position). A catch allowed the brakes to be left on for parking.

Chapter Six

The Pilots' Views

Flying an historic aircraft is a very demanding job that requires considerable experience, precision, concentration, and a true realisation of the limitations of the aircraft. Even a newly restored airworthy veteran, of whatever type, should be treated with respect and extreme care. The BBMF's two Hurricanes are flown by serving RAF pilots who have all the necessary qualifications, and who fly the Hurricanes at air displays and commemorative events to the very highest standards of airmanship that one would expect from serving RAF officers.

OPPOSITE Canadian-built Hawker Hurricane Mk XII, Z5140. *(Keith Wilson/SFB Photographic)*

Nowadays there are no Second World War era pilots who are able to fly existing airworthy Hurricanes – those who still survive are considered too old by the airworthiness authorities and do not hold the relevant up-to-date licence. It is therefore left to younger generations of pilots to take up the challenge of flying the Hurricane and getting to grips with its various characteristics. Fortunately, the Hurricane is a pleasant and stable aircraft to fly, and so long as it is flown within the limits that all service pilots knew during its time in front-line operations many years ago, it should hold few surprises for the experienced pilot. Its cockpit layout is unfamiliar to today's pilots, who are used to neat side consoles with all controls and equipment easily to hand, rather than the Hurricane's typical 1930's-style cockpit with controls and equipment tacked onto any available and suitable piece of framework.

The following eyewitness accounts give an illuminating insight into the flying of the Hurricane from a pilot's perspective, from a variety of piloting experiences.

Displaying the BBMF's Hurricanes

Squadron Leader Ian Smith, Officer Commanding, BBMF

Squadron Leader Ian Smith is the current (2010) Officer Commanding of the BBMF and has been

flying Hurricanes for the past four years. His RAF career has seen him fly a variety of aircraft types, including the BAe Hawk with the Red Arrows, and the SEPECAT Jaguar with No 41 Squadron.

Surely every boy's dream is one day to fly a Spitfire or a Hurricane? The Spitfire is a prettier aeroplane than a Hurricane and as such it has captured the world's imagination as an icon. The two were our saviours during the greatest air battle in the history of mankind, but it was the Hurricane that was responsible for destroying more enemy aircraft than all other air defence assets put together. My first sortie in a warbird was in a Hurricane and while the provenance of the type was not lost on me, it will remain as the most remarkable experience of my life. I have been extremely fortunate to have flown an aircraft that was fought in by 'The Few' and I am very proud to continue that heritage. As Winston Churchill said in 1944, 'A nation that forgets its past will have no future.'

We are very conservative with our Hurricanes and as such the display is tailored to show off the aircraft rather than the pilot's skill. In order to preserve both airframe and engine life we only use half the power that would have been available in wartime and less than half the positive g that would have been used. They were more likely to be shot down than run out of engine or airframe life. Our two Hurricanes have flown on the display circuit for over 50 years now and if we look after them they will fly for 50 more.

So, bearing all that in mind, if I take off from the display venue you will see me crowd front in a 'bogey gathering turn', gaining energy and positioning the aircraft on the 'B Axis', which is the one straight in front of you. The Hurricane coolant system is more efficient than a Spitfire's and as we don't need to 'cool down' I can get on with the display. Typically I will tip in onto the display axis at 2,500ft with 150kts and then accelerate down the hill. Levelling at not below 100ft I will have about 270kts depending on the temperature and pressure of the day. Before committing I will ensure that I have permission to display and I will set display power of 1,650rpm and +6in of boost. Temperatures and pressures are all good. I will then judge when to turn in order to line the Hurricane up accurately in front of you. Never a good idea to start in

ABOVE The BBMF's
PZ865 in the colours
of Karel Kuttelwascher
with Spitfire Vb,
AB910. (Richard Paver)

the wrong place! If I am arriving into the display from another airfield I will use my positioning time wisely to study the site for the crowd, the display line, display datum and see where the wind is coming from and at what strength. Any planning done at this stage will make my life easier when I get into the meat of the display.

The Hurricane is very noisy. Most of it is wind noise and while bearable at slower speeds when starting the display at high speeds it is deafening. Pitch trim is left alone at around 180kts, as is rudder trim, but the rudder forces vary considerably with speed and manoeuvre so one's feet are kept busy at all times. All display flying is strictly regulated and one must honour those rules. As a professional pilot it is a cardinal sin to transgress these rules and what's more there is a Flying Control Committee at every display site watching. They are responsible for safety in all respects, but they have the power to 'yellow card' or even 'red card' a pilot who is deemed unsafe or breaking the rules. It is always tempting to fly down to our absolute minimum of 100ft and, while that is very exciting and rewarding flying, nobody behind the front row can see a thing and it's important to remember that I am displaying for your enjoyment and not mine.

About 5 seconds before reaching the mandatory display line I will roll the Hurricane to 90 degrees of left bank and smoothly pull to +3gs. The stick forces in roll are heavy at higher speeds, but lessen as the speed reduces. I crane my head back and left to look for my roll-out feature 30 degrees off the display line. Such manoeuvring at very low levels requires ultimate concentration and you are not very far from your maker if you screw it up! Having rolled out I pause for up to 5 seconds, wind dependent, and pull the nose of the Hurricane up until it is well above the horizon, pause a few more seconds and then full left aileron control authority to roll the aircraft under through 270 degrees. The nose will drop about 40 degrees during the roll and I stop the roll in a timely enough manner to then begin the pull to get back onto the display line. Coming at you from your right now, I will power down the hill to complete the high-speed pass. You might see a Spitfire do this with his top wings showing, but it's not so easy in a Hurricane. Top rudder is required and any out-of-balance rudder forces at fast speeds cause the nose to tuck away from you, which is disconcerting at such low levels.

Having gone from right to left in front of you, I pause for a few more seconds and then start

RIGHT Underside of
BBMF's LF363 near
Blackpool Tower
showing how the
undercarriage fits
neatly into the wings.
(Jim Douthwaite)

another pull to complete another 270-degree
Derry Wingover. The wind has a marked effect
on a flying display and I will need to judge
it carefully to make sure that the display is
balanced in front of you. It is only balanced,
of course, if you are in the middle. This time,
though, I am turning right, having pulled up
in a straight line, and now need to get back
towards crowd centre and datum. The speed
is beginning to bleed off the Hurricane now so
I am grateful for having started with an energy
advantage. Having got myself back to datum
I will roll to 70 to 80 degrees of bank and then
gently pull to +3gs and then perform a level
360-degree turn in front of you. I will actually
cheat a little and climb by 200ft by the time
I get to the back of the turn, as if I didn't it
would look to you as if I were descending. This
manoeuvre is also very affected by wind so I
have to ackle it all the way around in order to
finish at crowd centre and not down wind.

All the way through the display I am
constantly moving my feet to keep the
Hurricane in balanced flight to cater for the
changes in speed and gyroscopic effects
of the massive propeller disc. You can, with
experience, feel that the aircraft is in balance
but I can check with a glance to the 'turn and
slip' instrument in the cockpit. A display pilot
must also have mechanical empathy. That
is to say he should understand his craft and

feel and listen and even smell how his aircraft
is behaving. The first signs of trouble might
be the faintest whiff of oil or a minor rumbling
noise. Notwithstanding this empathy, I am also
constantly scanning the engine temperature and
pressure instruments as these might also give
me a clue to impending trouble. All is well.

Onto the 30-degree off line and pull up,
but this time I do not have sufficient energy
left to do a Derry Wingover so I just roll right
and then pull down and to the right to achieve
the display line. A Spitfire would have enough
energy, but in order to keep it simple we will
always fly the same routine regardless of which
type we are in. Back to datum from right to left
this time and then I roll hard right and pull onto
the B axis but going away from you. I pause
for a few seconds and then pull until the nose
hits the horizon and then roll hard right and fly
a climbing 180-degree turn, which is the back
of the 'horseshoe'. Now pointing at the crowd,
but slightly off to the right, I wait a few seconds
and then judge my turn entry to show the
Hurricane's belly at datum as I continue onto
the 30-degree off line and pull up for the final
wingover. If I am with a Spitfire I will call to him
that I am 30 seconds from finishing my display
so that he can position himself for a head on
takeover. Nose high in the air again and hard
roll left this time and I pull the Hurricane around
onto the display line from left to right. I need to

judge when to pull, as I want the Hurricane to be inverted at crowd centre when I am doing the victory roll. Nose up for the last time, very light on G now as the speed is relatively slow having run out of energy. Imagine heels on the horizon and then start a very slow roll left which allows the nose to drop during the roll. There is nothing more iconic than a Hurricane or a Spitfire doing a victory roll and I can assure you that it is as pleasant to fly as it is to watch!

Flying and displaying the Hurricane

Squadron Leader Clive Rowley

Squadron Leader Clive Rowley MBE served as a pilot with the RAF for 36 years, during which time he flew aircraft ranging from the DH Chipmunk to high-performance jet fighters like the BAC Lightning and the Tornado. He was a display pilot with the RAF's Battle of Britain Memorial Flight from 1996 to 2006 and he regularly displayed the flight's Hurricane aircraft at air shows during those years. He was the Officer Commanding the BBMF during 2004/5.

As I walk out to the Hurricane I am struck again by the impressive shape and size of the aircraft, its hunched-back stance and height off the ground make it seem more imposing than other similar sized aircraft; it looks purposeful and potent. I wonder how the wartime pilots felt about it as they walked out for an operational mission in one. The pull-down step on the fuselage just behind the trailing edge of the port wing is very necessary to enable me to make the big step up onto the wing – clever the way it automatically opens up the hand hold in the fuselage side as you pull the step down. The cockpit switches are safe, so I jump down to the ground again to carry out my 'walk-round' external checks. This is more of a tradition than a necessity as the ground crew have already completed the most thorough of inspections before releasing the aircraft to me. As I walk round, conducting my checks, it is difficult to suppress the feeling of excitement and slight disbelief that I am about to go flying again in this truly classic and now very rare warbird.

External checks complete, I clamber back up onto the port wing and into the cockpit, pausing

ABOVE Clive Rowley with PZ865 in 1996.

to give the canopy an upwards tug to confirm its security. Settling into the seat, that wonderful smell of oil and petrol and I don't know what else, assails my nostrils; so different from the smell in a modern cockpit. I am assisted to strap in by the technician standing on the wing beside the cockpit, who then hands me my flying helmet (a modern departure from historical authenticity which provides much better head and acoustic protection than the original leather helmets). The ground crewman plugs in the lead and with a final pat on my shoulder in response to my thumbs up, he jumps down leaving me alone in the cockpit.

Despite the relative simplicity of the controls in the Hurricane compared with modern jet fighters, I am reminded as I scan the cockpit of how complicated it seemed when I first flew the aircraft. They obviously had not invented ergonomics when this cockpit was designed! Controls, instruments and warning lights seem to be scattered about in an almost haphazard manner. The cockpit is mainly original, although there have been some changes made over the years for very valid reasons. The left-to-right checks are simple and logical and are completed in a minute or two. I take a strange enjoyment in pumping the flaps down 20 degrees with the manual hydraulic pump handle (you can't do that in a jet). I leave the flap selector lever in the 'UP' part of the 'H' gate so that when the engine starts and the hydraulic pump comes on-line it will raise the flaps, proving the serviceability of the system.

As usual I have left myself some spare time before I need to start the engine to make my planned take-off time. I appreciate this time to myself in the cockpit, free from all outside distractions, able to focus on whatever it is I am going to do on the sortie. As I look around, I take the opportunity to refresh myself on the picture I will be seeing on landing, in terms of the height of my eye line from the ground and the nose-up angle of the aircraft.

It's time to start up. I load the KIGAS fuel priming pump by operating it in and out until there is resistance and then, as the engine hasn't been run today and taking into account the air temperature, I give it seven pumps of fuel. Signal for start clearance to the ground crew and a confirmatory signal from him means I'm clear to start. Confirm wheel brakes on, throttle just off the idle stop, control column held fully back to prevent nose-over, magneto switches on, press the boost coil button for 2 seconds with my index finger then, keeping it pressed, also press the start button with my middle finger. Meanwhile I'm holding the stick back with my legs and my right hand is ready either to use the priming pump or to move the throttle (a third arm and hand would be useful!). The prop turns very slowly and jerkily for three or four blades then the engine kicks and the Merlin V12 bursts sweetly into life, with puffs of smoke from the exhaust stacks and a cacophony of noise, or is that music? What a wonderful sound – I always get a buzz from that on start-up. The engine instruments, particularly the oil pressure, show that all is well so I set the 'holding' rpm of 1,000 with the throttle. The after-start checks are completed in seconds. The flaps have travelled up so the flap selector lever is set to neutral and then the magnetos are checked individually. A quick radio call gets me clearance to taxi so I throttle back to idle and signal for the chocks to be removed. The ground crewman removes the chocks carefully, avoiding the lethal propeller arc and then flings them any old where out of the way.

Taxiing the Hurricane is easy, the view over the nose is not bad at all, although it can be improved by weaving slightly from side to side. The brakes, controlled by a lever on the control column spade grip, are easy to use and give differential braking via the rudder pedals for steering. It is important to keep the stick fully back though, especially when braking or opening the throttle as nose-over could otherwise occur. The Hurricane is not prone to overheating on the ground because the large radiator is sensibly located on the centre line, under the fuselage behind the prop wash. Indeed, it is necessary to allow enough time for the engine to warm up for the engine run-up. Once the engine run-up checks are complete and we are cleared by air traffic control, I line up on the centre of the runway slightly canted off for a clear view down the strip. I won't put the aircraft straight until I'm about to roll, it wouldn't do to run into something unseen over the nose. I set the throttle friction very tight so that the engine will not throttle itself back after take-off when I take my hand off the throttle to raise the undercarriage. With the Hurricane, the final important check on the runway is to move the undercarriage safety catch to 'SELECT' – this catch prevents the inadvertent up selection of the landing gear while on the ground (nothing else does), but needs to be in the 'SELECT' position to permit the gear to be raised after take-off.

It's take-off time and I'm cleared to go. I release the brakes and gently open the throttle to give +6in of boost (less power than might originally have been used, but more than adequate for take-off and the maximum I will use in the interests of engine conservation). On take-off the aircraft tries to swing to the left as power is applied and again when I raise the tail at about 50kts, but the rudder control is powerful and it is easy to keep straight with right rudder. Acceleration is moderate and at 70kts I ease gently back on the stick to lift off, the aircraft feeling quite heavy on the controls.

When safely airborne I squeeze the brakes to stop the wheels rotating and then comes the tricky part. I take my left hand off the throttle and place it on the spade grip of the stick – it's now that you'll regret it if you forgot to tighten the throttle friction, because the throttle will gradually close and the aircraft will sink earthwards! Now, flying the aircraft with my left hand, I find the undercarriage lever with my right hand without looking in and, pressing the thumb catch, I slam it hard into the 'UP' gate, trying not to replicate the movement of my right hand with my left, but to continue to fly the aircraft smoothly. The air speed is increasing rapidly towards 100kts as the gear slowly begins to retract and I have to pull the aircraft up into quite a steep climb or the undercarriage limiting speed of 104kts will be exceeded and the gear will fail to lock up, because of the aerodynamic load on the doors. After what seems like an age, two thumps and the red 'UP' light on the undercarriage position indicator tell me that the gear is locked up. These undercarriage indications do not conform with the modern convention of green for down, red for travelling up or down, lights out for locked up. With the undercarriage locked up I can now lower the nose to a more normal climbing attitude, permitting the speed to increase to 140kts, while selecting neutral with the undercarriage lever and then setting +4in boost with the throttle and 2,400rpm with the prop pitch control lever. This reduction in engine rpm slightly reduces the absolute cacophony of engine noise, which has been present during the take-off run at maximum rpm, but the noise levels are still unbelievably high even inside a modern flying helmet. As the speed reaches 140kts, I start a climbing turn away from the airfield and then when I reach the cruising altitude I level off and set the power to maintain 150kts.

Even at cruising rpm the Hurricane cockpit environment is an extremely noisy place. The engine makes a tremendous racket and there is always a small gap between the windscreen and the canopy (which can be locked open but not shut) that creates considerable wind noise. I have the radio volume control turned up high in the air and I may still sometimes have difficulty hearing incoming radio calls, particularly if what is said is unexpected. I'll always try to avoid flying through rain because of the potential for damaging the airframe, paintwork or the propeller, but sometimes this is unavoidable and then, inevitably, I'll get wet inside the cockpit. There is absolutely no heating or cooling system in the Hurricane and the cockpit can become either very hot or very cold depending on the ambient conditions outside. As I become accustomed to the cockpit environment again, I can't help wondering, as I have done on many occasions, how the wartime pilots coped with these problems on operational sorties. My

discomfort at low altitudes and in temperate climes is a small price to pay for the pleasure of flying this wonderful machine; theirs would have been of a different order.

While cruising, I do not relax for a moment, I am constantly monitoring the engine instruments for any hint of an engine problem and I continually update my forced landing plans in the event that such a problem should occur. Where is the nearest runway and which field is the best within gliding distance for a wheels-up forced landing? Every few minutes I check the fuel tank contents by turning the fuel gauge button to the tank I wish to interrogate and pressing it in. I am also keeping a check on the navigation. However, there are still some moments when I can snatch a few seconds just to look out through the Hurricane's latticed canopy at the wingtips, twist round to see the tail, imagine I am transported back in time and wonder how it might have been.

Prior to flying a display in the Hurricane I complete my pre-display checks including setting 2,650rpm with the prop pitch lever and +6in of boost with the throttle, setting the throttle friction tight. I also press in the cage button on the directional indicator (DI). I will have no heading reference during my display other than what I can see out of the 'window' – the DI would topple as soon as I exceeded 60 degrees of bank if it was not caged. The artificial horizon will also topple and become useless during my routine and the altimeter will be of limited value in indicating height because of pressure errors. The only instruments I will be referring to during my display are the air speed indicator (ASI) and the engine performance gauges.

I trim the aircraft – elevator and rudder – at display power settings and at a speed of 180kts. From here on I'll maintain balanced flight with the necessary rudder inputs and I can retrim the elevator if I need to during the display. I run into the display in a shallow dive building up speed for the start. A final confirmation that I have display power set, 2,650rpm and +6in boost, and I tighten the throttle friction fully and put both hands on the control column spade grip. As I dive down to level off at 100ft on my run in, the speed builds to 250kts and the controls are becoming very heavy indeed. I will need both hands to roll and pull into the initial break turn. I wonder again how on earth the wartime fighter pilots manoeuvred these aircraft at speeds considerably in excess of the 270kts to which I am now limited. Approaching the display line, I roll the aircraft left with full stick and a large input of left rudder and pull into a level 3g break turn. In the interests of preserving airframe life the BBMF restrict the positive g on the Hurricane to a maximum of +3g. Even so this aircraft can really turn! I pull through 120 degrees and then max rate roll to wings level, wait 3 seconds and pitch up with a 3g pull to approximately 30 degrees nose up, judged by when my feet seem to be on the horizon. After 3 seconds in the climb, I roll to 120 degrees of right bank and pull down to 'wingover' back onto the line. As I'm rolling on the bank at the top of the wingover, I check the air speed. If the speed reduces below 110kts, the Hurricane can tend to 'tuck in' slightly, but if flown smoothly and gently with appropriate pitch-up angles the speed should not fall this low. On this wingover, started from high speed, I still have 140kts over the top. On the way down from the wingover I check the engine instruments – all is well – and then concentrate on rolling out on the display line and levelling off at 100ft. I'm enjoying myself! As I roar down the line on the so-called high-speed pass, the aircraft is bumping in turbulence and I have to feed on rudder to keep the nose straight as the speed builds up. Pull up into another wingover and on with the display sequence. The final move in the BBMF display routine is a victory roll. I position running down the line at 100ft and ensure that I have at least 180kts before pulling up. Just before display centre I pitch the aircraft nose up at 3g to 'feet on the horizon', wait until I'm passing 500ft and then roll left with full stick deflection and rudder to coordinate. As I pass inverted I look out of the top of the canopy at the ground to see if I've achieved the aim of passing inverted exactly at display centre. Not quite, missed by about 100 yards, my judgement didn't make enough allowance for the tailwind, but good enough for a crowd line of this length. I look back to the front as I complete the roll and regain level flight, display complete and I'm suddenly aware that I'm breathing quite hard. That was actually quite physical. The engine oil and radiator temperatures have risen slightly and I bring the rpm back to let the engine cool down.

Now I have to concentrate on the circuit and landing. For a 'tail-dragger' the Hurricane is relatively forgiving of pilots' errors of judgement on landing, because of its wide, strong undercarriage. Nevertheless, any tail-wheel aircraft demands respect when landing and today is complicated by a 10kts crosswind on this runway. These aircraft were really designed to land on grass airfields, more or less into wind, and are not ideally suited to hard runways. I level off downwind at 800ft, tight enough to the airfield to make the grass if the engine should quit, throttle back to just above idle to reduce speed and complete the pre-landing checks. When the speed is below 104kts, I lower the undercarriage. I select full flap down as I tip into the final turn and correct the big nose-down pitch trim change with a large movement of back stick and lots of nose-up trim. I fly the final turn at 85kts with about 30 degrees of bank, aiming to fly a continuous curved approach to roll wings level at about 200ft, enough time lined up straight-in on the approach to assess the effects of the crosswind. As the aircraft reaches the correct approach glide path, about 4 degrees, I apply a trickle of power to hold that runway aspect and then roll wings level for the final part of the approach. I gradually raise the nose, making sure that I am in trim, and let the speed reduce to 75kts by about 20–30ft. On this straight part of the approach I am 'crabbing' in sideways with the nose pointing into the crosswind, if I pointed at my touchdown spot I would drift sideways.

One final check of the speed at 70kts and I start the landing 'flare', gently raising the nose into the touchdown attitude and slowly closing the throttle. In the Hurricane, closing the throttle sharply causes the nose to drop and it takes back stick to prevent the aircraft touching the ground early, with an inevitable bounce, so it is important to throttle back gently here. Just before I believe that I am going to touchdown, I kick the aircraft nose straight with rudder, keeping the wings level with aileron as I do it. Now I am looking straight ahead to ensure that I keep the nose straight, but as the nose comes up in the flare it blocks my view and I have to use peripheral vision to monitor the runway edges either side of the nose. Hold it off, hold it off and with a squeak from the tyres and the gentlest of skips we are down. Stick right back now for maximum ground stability and concentrate on keeping straight with rudder, resisting the aircraft's tendency to swing into the crosswind. No time to relax yet. The ground roll after landing can be the most exciting part of the sortie in a strong crosswind. Now I'm down to taxiing speed and can relax slightly. Start weaving for a better view ahead and open the canopy to feel the welcome blast of fresh air. Park up and carry out a final engine run-down at 1,500rpm, checking the magneto switches for 'live and dead', before throttling back to idle and pulling the slow running cut-out control to stop the engine. Suddenly it seems very quiet and I'm ready for a cup of tea!

The RAF's point of view in 1938

Squadron Leader J. W. Gillan

In December 1937, No 111 Squadron based at Northolt in Middlesex became the first front-line squadron in the RAF to receive the Hurricane. Initially, four aircraft were taken on the squadron's strength and the full complement of Hurricanes for the unit was received in the opening weeks of 1938. This made No 111 Squadron one of the most modern and well-equipped fighter squadrons anywhere in the world. Both the RAF and the Hurricane's manufacturer, Hawker Aircraft Limited, were very keen to learn how the Hurricane settled in to life with this first squadron, and the following report was submitted by Squadron Leader J. W.Gillan of No 111 Squadron on 14 January 1938. It is reproduced here in its entirety, and makes for a very enlightening summary of the capabilities even of these early Hurricanes. Indeed, the small number of Hurricanes that were in service at that time were very early production aircraft, with fabric-covered wings, Watts two-blade wooden propellers and early production Merlin II engines. Underlining the necessary close communication between the service pilots and the manufacturer, Squadron Leader Gillan asks for a copy of his report to be forwarded to 'George' Bulman, the Hawker test pilot who made the first flight in the Hurricane prototype in November 1935, and who continued to be closely associated with the Hurricane programme.

BELOW Immaculate in their white pre-war flying overalls, the pilots of No 111 Squadron were the first in the RAF to fly a modern, high-performance monoplane fighter – the Hawker Hurricane. The impressions and experiences of these professional peace-time flyers were very important towards the widespread acceptance of the Hurricane into the RAF. A group of them is pictured here at RAF Northolt in 1938. *(RAF Museum/Charles E. Brown Collection)*

111 (Fighter) Squadron, RAF Northolt,
Station Headquarters, Northolt

(Copy to F/Lt BULMAN for information. Delivered by hand)

14th January 1938

1113/93/Air

Subject:
Tests to be made to determine the Operational Characteristics of
Hurricane Aircraft.

In reply to your letter N3/12/4/E dated 16th December 1937 on the
characteristics of the Hurricane Aircraft, this Unit has now been
equipped with Hurricanes for four weeks, and forwards herewith a
preliminary report on the flying characteristics of this aircraft.

2. FLYING CHARACTERISTICS.

(i)   The Hurricane is completely manoeuvrable throughout its whole
range, though at slow speeds between 65mph and 200mph controls
feel a bit slack.

Owing to its weight and speed some time is taken in coming out
of a dive and at high speed the turning circle is large.

On the ground the Hurricane is as manoeuvrable as is possible
and has the additional advantage of feeling secure across wind
or a strong wind owing to its high wing loading.

(ii)   Cross wind landings are particularly easy in the Hurricane.
Simplicity in cross wind landings is a characteristic of
aircraft with high wing loading.

(iii) VIEW

(a) Taxying with the seat full up and the hood back is
exceptionally good all round, better in front and above than
in fighter aircraft before in the service, and just as good
in all other directions.

(b) Taking off. The View is considerably better than the
Gauntlet and better than the Demon, both individually and
in formation. [These being the Gloster Gauntlet and Hawker
Demon biplanes.]

(c) Landing. The View is considerably better than the Gauntlet
and better than the Demon both individually and in
formation.

    (d) Flying in formation. The view is better than the Gauntlet or Demon with the hood open or closed, though at present no experience is available of flying in formation, in bad rain or damp cloud when it is thought the hood may fog or ice up.

    (e) The View is better than the Gauntlet or Demon.

(iv) Formation flying at height at speeds in excess of 200mph is very simple. It is thought the reason being that the air resistance at this speed is considerable and that the power used by the engine at this speed the pilot can slow his aeroplane up or accelerate it very quickly indeed.

At slow speeds in the neighbourhood of 100mph when only a small proportion of the engine power is in use and the resistance to the air of this clean aeroplane is comparatively small, some difficulty is found in decelerating the aircraft though no difficulty is found accelerating.

Landing in formation is similar to landing in formation in any other type of aircraft.

Taking off in formation is simple, but immediately after leaving the ground when pilots retract their undercarriages and flaps aircraft cannot keep good formation as undercarriage and flaps retract at different speeds in each aircraft. It is recommended therefore, that takeoff should be done individually in succession.

(v) The Hurricane is a simple aeroplane to fly at night. There is no glare in the cockpit, either open or closed, from the cockpit

lamps or luminous instruments. The steady steep glide at slow speed which is a characteristic of this type makes landing extremely simple. The takeoff run being longer than has been experienced in the past, it is recommended that the landing light should be at least 600 yards away from the beginning of the run instead of the normal 250 yards on ordinary flare paths. Opportunity has not arisen to test the landing lamp installed in this type, but experience is available to this unit of a smaller lamp installed experimentally in Hart aircraft when no difficulty was experienced in landing without any lights on the ground and it is anticipated that this will be the same with the Hurricane.

(vi)   The minimum size of aerodrome from which the Hurricane can be operated in still air in England must depend upon the obstructions surrounding the aerodrome. With good approaches and inexperienced pilots the Hurricane could be operated from an aerodrome 800 by 800 yards and with experience could probably be reduced to 600 yards.

(vii) The Hurricane without its engine running has a very steep glide and to the pilot inexperienced on this type judging the flattening out may be difficult. Therefore it is recommended for initial training that pilots should come in with their engines running. After they have become accustomed to an aeroplane of high wing loading and steep glide they should be able to land efficiently off the glide in the Hurricane as in any other aircraft. It follows that landing with an engine lengthens the period of holding off, making landing easier, and in the event of flattening out to high gives the pilot time to stop the aeroplane falling heavily on the ground as speed falls off.

(viii) The cockpit is large and comfortable and there is room for the largest man inside with the hood shut and by using the adaptable seat the smallest man can see everything comfortably.

It is thought that from an operational point of view that the system of having a selector box and a lever which each must be operated to move either the undercarriage or the flaps is unsatisfactory and furthermore it occupies for a period of perhaps half a minute the right hand of the pilot whilst he flies with his left and neglects his throttle. Should it be essential to take off in formation as in conditions of bad visibility the difficulties of the system are obvious, and it is recommended that two simple controls, one which moves the flaps to full up and full down position and the other which would move the undercarriage from full down to full up and vice versa could well be substituted.

All other controls are easily accessible and efficient and the instrument lay out is good and not complicated.

3. OPERATIONAL CHARACTERISTICS

With more experience on this type of aeroplane further figures will be submitted, but as far as can been seen at present the indicated airspeed at 2,000 feet is 270mph at 10,000ft indicated airspeed 260mph and at 15,000 feet indicated airspeed 240mph

The petrol consumption at 15,000 feet and economical cruising speed of 160mph indicated correcting to 200mph is 25.08 gallons per hour. Plus 2½ boost the maximum permissible cruising speed-petrol consumption approaches 60 gallons per hour.

At 2,000 feet an indicated air speed of 200mph petrol consumption is 30 gallons per hour at an indicated boost of plus one.

The remaining operational characteristics have yet to be investigated, but as yet the windscreen has shown no sign of oiling up and the cockpit is weather proof as far as can be seen at present.

        J.W. Gillan.
        Squadron Leader, Commanding, 111 (F) Squadron, RAF NORTHOLT

ABOVE Nine Hurricane Mk Is of No 111 Squadron (including L1555, L1558, L1560, L1564 and others), up from RAF Northolt in 1938, formate for the camera of Charles E. Brown. The squadron's pilots found the Hurricane a considerable improvement in most respects compared to the Gloster Gauntlet and Hawker Demon biplanes that many of them were used to. *(RAF Museum/Charles E. Brown Collection)*

Hurricane engine starting procedure

☐ **Initial checks**
☐ Check aircraft is in a suitable position for starting and taxiing and its wings are level
☐ No fuel, oil or coolant leaks
☐ Ground fire extinguisher available
☐ Chocks in position

☐ **Cockpit**

Hood	Operation and cleanliness
Hood jettison lever	Down, wire locked
Mirror	Secure and clean
Ignition switches	OFF
Ground/Flight switch	GROUND
Landing gear/ flap selector	Neutral, safety latch SAFE
CO detector	Normal
Parachute static line	Secured to seat harness fixed attachment ring
Dinghy, if fitted	In position
Pneumatic pressure	120psi minimum
Control locks	Removed

☐ **External checks**
Carry out a systematic check of the aircraft for obvious signs of damage, leaks, loose panels or fairings. At the same time make the following specific checks:

☐ **Port mainplane**

Flap	Up
Aileron	Full/free movement, leave neutral
Nav light	Secure, condition
Pitot ast	Secure, condition
Pressure head	Cover removed, condition

Landing gear

Wheel well	General condition
D door	Secure, undamaged
Oleo	Condition, extension
Brake pipe	Secure
	Check for leaks and chafing
	Ensure clear of wheel and ground
Tyre	Cuts, creep and wear
	Correct inflation, valve free
Oil tank filler cap	Secure
Radiator	Intake and matrix unobstructed
Engine cowling fasteners	Secure
Port exhaust stubs	Secure, no undrilled cracks
Propeller blades	Undamaged

Carburettor air intake	Unobstructed, no excess fuel or oil
Starboard exhaust stubs	Secure, no undrilled cracks

☐ **Starboard mainplane**

Stbd cockpit access panel	Secure
Stbd landing gear	As for port landing gear
Landing light	Condition
Aileron	Neutral, full/free movement
Flap	Up

☐ **Starboard fuselage**

Baggage locker panel	Secure
Radio mast	Secure, condition

Tail unit

Elevators	Full and free movement
	Condition of tabs
Rudder	Full and free movement
	Condition of tab
Tailwheel tyre	Cuts, creep and wear
	Correct inflation and valve free

☐ **Port fuselage**

Retractable step	Check operation

☐ **Starting**
Prime the engine as per SOPs, normally 5–7 strokes, then:

Groundcrew	Warn
Ignition switches	Off
Control column	Fully back
START and BOOST COIL Buttons	Press BOOST then both together

When the engine fires:

Ignition switches	Both ON

Release the START button keeping the BOOST COIL button pressed until the engine runs smoothly.
WARNING: Do not pump the throttle during engine start.

☐ **Failure to start**
1. Engine turns freely but does not fire. Check:

Ignition switches	Right ON until engine fires then both ON
Priming	Under or over-primed
Throttle	¼in open

If there is no obvious reason for failure to start, use one more stroke of the priming pump and try a further start.

2. Engine turns, flames appear from the exhaust banks but the engine does not run. **Continue to turn the engine on the starter until the flames are extinguished.** Then, if the engine does not start:

Ignition switches	OFF
Throttle	Fully open
START button	Press for nine propeller tips
Throttle	Set ¼in open
START and BOOST COIL buttons	Press BOOST then both together

When engine fires:

Ignition switches	Both ON

3. Engine does not turn. Check:

Start isolate switch	ON

(*note* the engine starter motor operating limits are):
a. Maximum 20 seconds continuous.
b. 30 seconds cooling time between each operation.
c. After three operations, each of 20 seconds, wait three minutes before a further operation.

☐ After starting, check

Oil pressure	Rising
rpm	Set 1,000rpm
Fuel pressure warning light	OUT
Generator warning light	OUT
Starter isolate switch	OFF, red light out
Priming pump	Screwed fully down
Flaps	UP, indicating
Flap selector lever	Neutral
Fuel cock	MAIN ON
Ignition switches	Check magnetos live and dead (rpm drops and recovers)
Radio	Taxi clearance
Altimeter	Set
DI	Synchronised, uncaged

☐ Taxiing checks

Flight instruments	Checked
Radiator temperature and brake pressures	Make frequent checks

☐ Testing the engine

Face the aircraft into wind, set the brakes on and parked and hold the control column fully back. Ensure:

Oil temperature	15° minimum
Radiator temperature	40° minimum
rpm	Set 1,500rpm

Ignition switches	Switch OFF each in turn (maximum drop 100rpm (NO)) 150rpm (NE)
Throttle	Closed, idle 550–650rpm
rpm	Reset 1,000rpm

☐ Take-off checks

Checks before take-off

Trims	Elevator neutral Rudder fully RIGHT
Throttle friction	Tight
Propeller pitch control	Fully forward
Pressure head heater	As required
Fuel:	
Main tanks	Selected
Fuel pressure light	Out
Priming pump	Screwed fully down
Contents	Sufficient
Overload tanks	OFF
Flaps	UP
Radiator flap	Open (lever fully forward)
Gyros	DI synchronised, uncaged Artificial horizon erect
Gauges	Temperatures and pressures
Hood	As required, bobbins engaged
Harness	Tight and locked

WARNING 1: Take-off must not be attempted if MAIN and RESERVE tanks are less than half full.

WARNING 2: RESERVE tank must always be selected for take-off whenever it contains more than the MAIN tank.

☐ Runway checks

Landing gear safety catch	To SELECT
DI	Check against runway heading
Temperatures and pressures	Within limits

☐ After take-off checks

Brakes	On the off
Landing gear	UP, 2 red lights
Boost	+4psi
rpm	2,400rpm
Landing gear/flap lever	Neutral
Hood	As required
Engine instruments	Temperatures and pressures
Fuel selector	As required
Radiator flap	As required

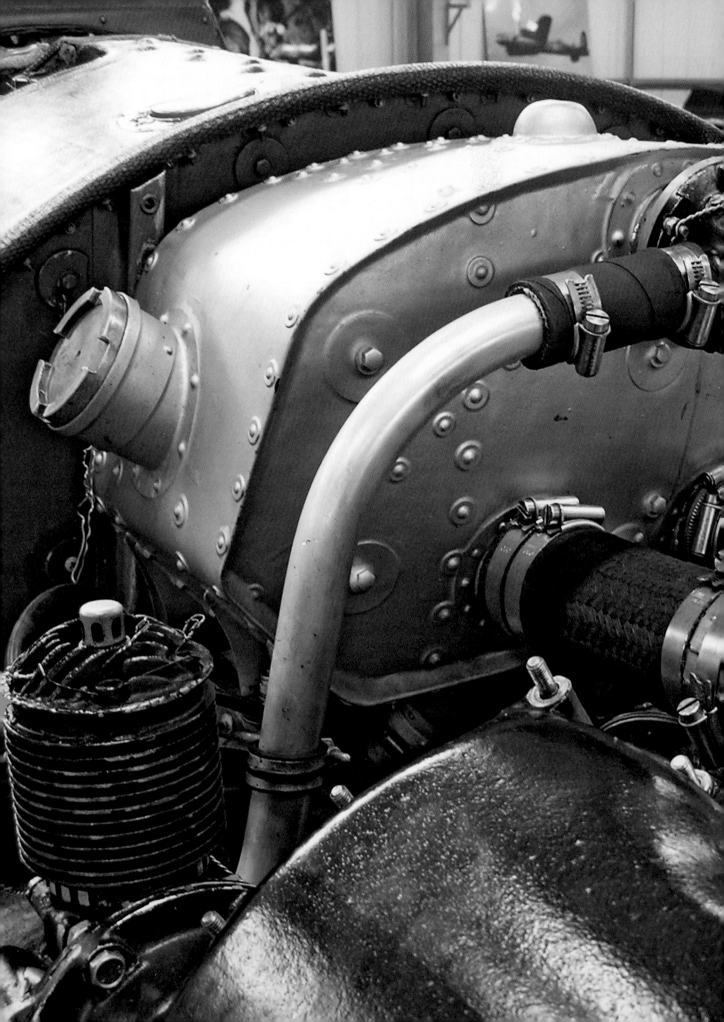

Chapter Seven

The Engineer's View

There is a dwindling number of individuals left in the world who worked on the Hurricane in its heyday. The skills that were commonplace during the Second World War are now increasingly being lost, leaving only a small number of skilled technicians whose profession it is to work on historic aircraft maintenance. Those who are familiar with modern-day aircraft are not necessarily able to cope with aspects of aircraft technology from six or more decades ago. This chapter gives an insight into the care, knowledge and skill needed to work with confidence on a Hurricane.

OPPOSITE **The coolant header tank for the Rolls-Royce Merlin engine.** *(Paul Blackah/Crown Copyright)*

Thoughts of a Hurricane ground engineer

Paul Blackah MBE

Paul Blackah is one of the team of skilled ground crew who work on the two Hurricanes of the Battle of Britain Memorial Flight, and is a co-author of this book and also the Lancaster Manual *and* Spitfire Manual. *Paul is highly respected among the historic aircraft community, having begun working on these fighters in 1982 when he became a member of the team who were restoring the Messerschmitt Bf109G-2, Black 6. He joined the BBMF in 1993 and has become one of the foremost authorities on these airframes. Paul received the MBE in the New Year's Honours List 2010, in recognition of his work in this field.*

As an engineer, the Hurricane is a relatively easy aircraft to work on. It has a lot of removable panels, that give you good access to all the major components and systems, however the fuselage has to be treated with care, because of its wooden and fabric covering. It is all too easy to slip with a screwdriver while undoing a fastener and then you have a hole in the fabric.

I'm often asked what are the major differences from an engineer's perspective between the Hurricane/Spitfire and the preserved, airworthy Messerschmitt Bf109G-2 Black 6, which I have also worked on. Each aircraft has its good and bad points; the biggest difference is that the Messerschmitt's main components are more easily accessible. The engine compartment can be accessed by undoing eight quick-release fasteners. The lower cowling then swings down and exposes the oil cooler and the underside of the engine. The two side cowlings of the Bf109 hinge upwards and are held in place with a bonnet stay. All this takes less than a minute to accomplish. Other parts of the aircraft can be accessed for inspection just as easily, as there are a number of panels with quick-release latches.

All the electrical components on the 109 are wired up with plugs and sockets, making disconnection fast and efficient compared to having to find a terminal block and undoing the individual wires to remove the item on a Hurricane or Spitfire.

The fluid and gas systems are colour coded in the 109, which makes pipework easy to identify.

The cockpit layout for the 109 pilot is more logical than the Spitfire and the Hurricane and some of the systems, such as the oil cooler control and radiator control, are automatic to reduce stress on the pilot. It is of note that the 109 has a cockpit floor, unlike the Spitfire and Hurricane, which has two running boards for the pilot's feet.

On the other hand, a Spitfire or Hurricane canopy does not weigh as much as the 109's, and allows better visibility for the pilot, and they are easier to open and close. The seat is also adjustable by the pilot, whereas the 109's seat has three positions, which have to be set before flight and cannot be readjusted while in-flight.

The Merlin appears to be a more reliable engine than the Daimler Benz of the 109; the Merlin servicing cycle is 500 hours between overhauls, compared to the Daimler Benz, which is 200 hours. The Daimler Benz engine has to have the block rings retightened every 12½ hours, which means the engine on a 109 needs more attention.

If I had to make a choice between the Hurricane, Spitfire and the Bf109G-2, then I would probably choose the 109, simply for ease of access from an engineer's view, however I enjoy working on all the aircraft despite, or perhaps regardless of, their individual quirks and foibles.

Once they are in the air it gives me a sense of pride and achievement that we are able to keep these rare historic aircraft flying as a memorial and tribute to those who once maintained and flew them.

Safety first

Even when it is on the ground, a Hurricane can be fatal if not treated with respect. It may appear obvious that a moving propeller can kill or injure you, however a static propeller should always be treated as 'live'. Even with the ignition in the OFF position, it may continue to rotate after being hand-turned, especially when the engine is hot.

Care should be taken when operating

the flying controls to ensure that there are no personnel or items of equipment in the immediate area.

Ear defenders are essential when the engine is running, as prolonged exposure to engine noise can cause partial deafness. Correct clothing should be worn at all times – no loose belts, ties or jewellery, as these may be caught in the machinery and cause injury or loss of limbs.

When replenishing the oil supplies, care must be taken to ensure that the container does actually contain the oil that you require. There are so many lubricants and fluids that are packaged in similar sized and coloured tins and mistakes could happen.

Finally, while entering a cockpit, pockets should be empty to prevent foreign object damage (FOD) occurring. Something as small as a coin could jam the controls, with possible fatal consequences if it happened in the air.

Tools and working facilities

For day-to-day management of the Hurricane, a good selection of BA, BSF and Whitworth spanners and sockets is essential. Pneumatic tools such as drills and riveting hammers are favoured, as are wire-locking pliers, files and the other more common tools in a standard kit.

The more specialised jobs, such as stripping down hydraulic components or an engine, require specific tools that will be listed in the relevant overhaul manuals. Some are difficult to obtain due to rarity and, in some cases, may have to be manufactured to order.

A supply of Irish linen and dope is advised, to allow for repairing any small tears or cuts in the fabric.

Recommended lubricants and fluids

Fuel	Avgas 100LL (low lead)/F18
Hydraulic oil	OX19
Coolant	AL3
Engine oil	W100/OM270
Lubricating oil	OX14 (used for bearing, hinge pins, chains, etc.)
Grease	XG287/G354 (used for bearings, linkages, etc.)
Gas	Nitrogen (for charging tyres and undercarriage oleos)

ABOVE **Tool cabinet used for servicing the aircraft. The tools are shadowed and tagged so that all tools in use can be accounted for.** *(Paul Blackah/Crown Copyright)*

Servicing the Hurricane

Just like a car, the Hurricane needs to be regularly serviced in order to maintain it in an airworthy condition. This applies to both the BBMF's aircraft and those that are privately owned. The BBMF follows its own strict schedule of inspections and we will take a closer look at the different types of servicing below.

Note: The BBMF's schedule and the private owner's schedule differ slightly from the Spitfire due to framework.

Before-flight servicing

A single technician, prior to the aircraft being required to fly, carries out this service and checks the following:

1. External check of the aircraft to make sure all panels are secure.
2. Checks the flying controls to ensure they move freely without restriction.
3. Checks the electrical systems, e.g. navigation lights, pressure head heater, battery voltage, etc.
4. Ensures that all the oil coolant, hydraulic and pneumatic systems are replenished.
5. Makes sure that the fuel tanks are full.
6. Checks tyres for the correct pressure.
7. Checks the parachute and tidies the harness straps.
8. Cleans the windscreen and canopy.

Once these tasks are completed, he signs Form F705, flight-servicing certificate, in the aircraft's Form F700. The pilot completes the relevant sections and the aircraft is ready for flight.

After-flight servicing

This is carried out once the aircraft has landed and shut down, which ensures that any problems identified are corrected before the aircraft flies again. It is carried out by a single technician.

1. Refuel the aircraft.
2. Clean the aircraft, including windscreen and canopy.
3. Carry out a visual inspection, looking for cracks, leaks, etc.
4. Tidy the parachute straps and harness straps.

Turn-around servicing

This is carried out if the aircraft is required to fly again within a few hours of landing, and is, basically, just to refuel, clean the windscreen and canopy, and have a quick visual check. Items such as coolant and oil are not checked, as they will be too hot.

Primary servicing

This is carried out at 28 hours' flying time or thereabouts. It consists of an inspection of the airframe and engine for general wear and tear and is undertaken by two or three technicians.

1. The engine and CSU filters are removed and checked for debris.
2. The engine oil has a spectromatic oil analysis programme (SOAP) sample taken to check for any metal particles, which may suggest that the engine components, such as the bearings and piston rings, may be wearing out.
3. Engine oil is changed.
4. Magnetos contact breaker points are checked to ensure they are set correctly.
5. The pneumatic system oil and water trap is drained.
6. Flying control hinge points and undercarriage pivot points are lubricated.

Annual servicing

The annual service is carried out at approximately 70 flying hours or one year,

whichever the aircraft reaches first. It takes about five months, using three or four technicians. The servicing begins with ground running the engine to check its performance and then the aircraft is jacked up and all panels removed. This servicing is carried out in greater depth than the primary servicing and covers all the same checks , including the following:

1. A detailed inspection is undertaken of the airframe, looking for signs of possible cracks, corrosion and loose rivets. Structurally significant items (SSIs), such as fuselage framework, engine bearer mounts and undercarriage mounts, are looked at closely using some non-destructive testing (NDT) techniques and visual aids, such as a 10X magnifier.
2. Flying control cables are removed and examined for wear and tear and fraying. If necessary they are replaced.
3. The engine rocker covers are removed and the cams and rocker arms are inspected for wear and tear.
4. Undercarriage oleos have their oil replaced.
5. Electrical wiring is inspected for wear and tear.
6. Any component the life of which has expired is replaced. Certain items on the aircraft are given a fixed period, or life, either in flying hours or by date. For example, a propeller has a life of 360 flying hours and the air cylinder has a life of five years.
7. On refit, all the systems are tested. This includes undercarriage retraction tests, checking the range of movements on all the flying controls and ground running the engine.
8. On completion of the annual servicing the aircraft is given a full air test. If this is satisfactory the aircraft is ready for duty.

Minor Servicing

The minor service is carried out at 210 flying hours or three years; it takes the same amount of time as an annual and requires the same manpower. More items are inspected in the minor than in the annual servicing. NDT is carried out on the undercarriage axles to check for cracking and a lot of the flight instruments are removed for bay service. After this servicing, the procedure is the same as for the annual.

RIGHT The engine is lifted clear. By using the gantry the men stop the engine from swinging whilst lifting. *(Paul Blackah/Crown Copyright)*

BELOW Once clear of the aircraft, the engine is lowered onto an engine stand. *(Paul Blackah/Crown Copyright)*

BOTTOM The engine on its stand. *(Paul Blackah/Crown Copyright)*

Major servicing

The major servicing is carried out at 420 flying hours or six years, whichever comes first. The aircraft is serviced by an outside contractor, such as ARCo (The Aircraft Restoration Company) at Duxford, and the work will include the following:

1. The aircraft metalwork will be stripped to bare metal to allow a closer inspection. Depending on the condition of the fabric on the fuselage, the decision may be made to strip the fabric down to expose the wooden framework.
2. The engine will be removed; the bearer will be X-rayed to check for internal corrosion or cracking.
3. All flying controls are removed and all fabric covering removed to inspect the control's framework.
4. All major components such as fuel tanks, oil cooler, radiator and the coolant header tank are removed, flushed and pressure tested.
5. The undercarriage and all hydraulic components are removed for bay servicing.
6. Pneumatic components are removed for bay servicing.
7. All electrical components such as generator, starting motor and instruments are removed for bay servicing.

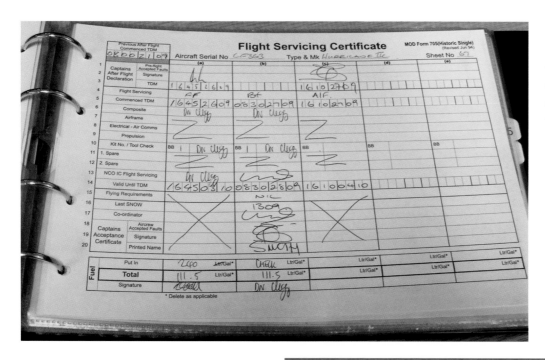

8. With all the components removed, a detailed inspection is carried out on the airframe and any problems addressed. Any out-of-life components are replaced at this point.

9. As with the other servicings, full functional testing is carried out after rebuild. The aircraft will be resprayed into new markings and then weighed to check its centre of gravity (CofG). A compass swing is carried out and the aircraft will then be given a full air test.

Keeping records

The RAF uses a Form F700 system for all its aircraft, historic or modern, to log the aircraft's flying hours and any faults. The log is kept as long as the aircraft is in service. For example, LF363 has a complete history dating back to 1943 when construction started, and operationally from 1944 when she was on No 309 Squadron. Log cards are kept for components such as the engine and propeller, which enable checks to be made on the item's history, such as where it was overhauled, which aircraft it was fitted to and any modifications that may have been carried out to it. Private owners run a similar system, where the aircraft and engine have their own respective logbooks.

Non-destructive testing (NDT)

Four methods of NDT are available: an X-ray check, an ultrasound check, a magnetic particle check and a dye penetrant check.

☐ **X-ray check** Used to examine parts of the Hurricane that cannot easily be accessed, such as the main spars and the engine bearer tubing. The X-ray check will usually show up any internal corrosion or cracking, though very careful examination of the results is necessary.

☐ **Ultrasound check** Uses sound waves to detect cracking around the bore of a hole. A probe is inserted into the hole, for example a spar hole, and a meter readout indicates if there are signs of damage in the vicinity of the hole.

☐ **Magnetic particle check** Used to look for cracks in ferrous metal components. The component is painted with a fluid containing iron fillings, and then an electric current is passed through it. The sample is then examined under ultraviolet light, which highlights any faults. Afterwards, the sample is demagnetised.

☐ **Dye penetrant check** Used when looking for cracks in ferrous and non-ferrous metal components. The component is painted with fluorescent purple dye, then cleaned and sprayed with a white developer. After a wait of about 40 minutes the component is examined and any cracks will be highlighted in purple.

Airworthy Hurricanes

RIGHT The Musée Royal de l'Armée et d'Histoire Militaire in Brussels, Belgium, has this Hurricane Mk IIc, LF658, on display. It is seen here in the early 1970s painted in spurious markings. *(Malcolm V. Lowe Collection)*

At the time of writing, there were just over a dozen airworthy or potentially airworthy Hurricanes at different locations worldwide – an exemplary total, which is far higher than that of, say, 20 years ago. This is in addition to a number of Hurricanes that exist in museums or in private collections as non-flying exhibits – although some of these are wrecks, and a small number are non-flying replicas built specially for the 1960's film *Battle of Britain*. It must be stressed that this number can go up or down, as several potentially airworthy museum exhibits or privately owned examples are allegedly on the long road to being made airworthy, including two very promising projects with Classic Aero Limited at Thruxton, Hampshire.

RIGHT The static display Hurricane Mk IIc, LF658, of the Musée Royal de l'Armée et d'Histoire Militaire in Brussels, Belgium, has been properly restored since the 1970s. It is authentically painted as a Mk IIc, LF345, flown by Belgian pilots on liaison duties in 1945–6 with the Allied Flight, Metropolitan Communications Squadron, based at RAF Hendon. *(via Didier Waelkens, IPMS Belgium)*

LEFT Hurricane
Mk I, R4118, G-HUPW,
above the clouds.

BELOW BE505 G-HHII,
Peter Teichman's
Mk IIb Hurricane,
complete with bomb
carriers. *(Richard Paver)*

RIGHT Probably the most famous Hurricane of them all is PZ865, the very last Hurricane to be built, during 1944. It flew for many years after the Second World War bearing the inscription beside the cockpit *'The Last of the Many'*. It is now proudly operated by the RAF's Battle of Britain Memorial Flight, and is looked after by co-author of this book, Paul Blackah. *(RAF Museum)*

The much-loved Hurricane *'The Last of the Many'* was well-known long before its current long-running service with the RAF's Battle of Britain Memorial Flight. It was on the British civil register in the 1950s as **G-AMAU** and was sometimes raced, wearing a smart blue overall finish trimmed in gold (or alternatively, for a time, blue trimmed in white). *(RAF Museum)*

Great Britain

Hurricane Mk I, R4118 (G-HUPW)
Genuine Battle of Britain veteran, ex-No 605 Squadron RAF. Peter Vacher, North Moreton Airfield, Oxfordshire.

Hurricane Mk IIb, 'BE505' (G-HHII)
Believed to be the last airworthy Hurribomber. The Hangar 11 Collection/Peter Teichman, North Weald, Essex.

Hurricane Mk IIc, LF363
Battle of Britain Memorial Flight, RAF Coningsby, Lincolnshire.

Hurricane Mk IIc PZ865
The last Hurricane completed. Battle of Britain Memorial Flight, RAF Coningsby, Lincolnshire.

Hurricane Mk XII, Z5140 (G-HURI)
Canadian-built Hurricane Mk XII painted to represent a Hurricane Mk IIb. Historic Aircraft Collection (Guy Black), Duxford, Cambridgeshire (on sale in January 2010).

Sea Hurricane Mk Ib Z7015 (G-BKTH)
Ex-Nos 759 and 880 Naval Air Squadrons, Fleet Air Arm. Shuttleworth Collection, Old Warden, Bedfordshire.

Canada

Hurricane Mk IV KZ321 (CF-TPM, previously G-HURY)

Believed to be the last surviving complete Mk IV in existence. Hawker Kingston-built (1942), ex-No 6 Squadron RAF in Italy. Vintage Wings of Canada Collection, Gatineau, Quebec.

Hurricane MkXII, 5481 (C-FDNL)
Russell Aviation Group, Niagara Falls, Ontario.

New Zealand

Hurricane Mk IIa, DR393 (ZK-TPL)
Originally a Mk I, P3351. Ex-RAF, ex-Soviet Air Force. Wreck restored as a Mk IIc in Britain during the 1990s after recovery from Russia. Later owned by the New Zealand Fighter Pilots' Museum, Wanaka, New Zealand.

United States

Hurricane Mk XII, 5667 (N2549)
The Fighter Factory, Virginia Beach, Virginia.

Hurricane Mk XII (N68RW)
Lone Star Flight Museum, Galveston, Texas. Damaged in ground collision with Spitfire and under repair.

Sea Hurricane MkX, AE977 (N33TF)
Chino Warbirds Collection, Chino, California.

Sea Hurricane Mk XII, BW881 (G-KAMM)
Flying Heritage Collection, Everett, Washington State. This aircraft is part of the collection of Paul Allen of Microsoft fame.

ABOVE Z7015, G-BKTH, Shuttleworth's rare airworthy Sea Hurricane.

Appendix II
Glossary

A&AEE	Aeroplane and Armament Experimental Establishment
AASF	Advanced Air Striking Force
ADF	automatic direction finder; a radio receiver that points to and shows direction to a selected receiver
ADLS	Air Despatch Letter Service
AFDU	Air Fighting Development Unit (RAF Wittering)
AI	Airborne Intercept or Interception (radar)
AP	Air Publication (official manual or other publication)
AP	armour-piercing (bomb or ammunition)
ARCo	The Aircraft Restoration Company
ASI	air speed indicator
BAe	British Aerospace
BBMF	Battle of Britain Memorial Flight
Bf	abbreviation for Messerschmitt aircraft; generally the Bf109 series was the last from this manufacturer to use this abbreviation, the company changing its name from BFW to Messerschmitt and so subsequently using 'Me'

BELOW Hurricanes over Lincolnshire on 14 May 2010. Front to back: LF363, R4118, Z5140 and PZ865.
(Mark Crosby)

BFW	Bayerische Flugzeugwerke AG, the original designer of the Bf109 and other types, such as the Bf110
CAM	Catapult Aircraft (or Armed) Merchantman
CCF	Canadian Car & Foundry Company Ltd
cg or CofG	centre of gravity
c/n	construction number
CFE	Central Fighter Establishment (RAF)
CSU	constant speed unit. Fitted to the engine, this unit automatically controls engine rpm and the propeller's pitch mechanism in conjunction, so that they operate at the best efficiency over a wide range of flight conditions. The pilot can select the engine rpm with a control lever in the cockpit, allowing a governor to automatically control the pitch of the propeller blades. This allows the aircraft to fly at the most efficient rating for the engine power selected and the speed of the aircraft. On the Hurricane, the Merlin III engine and Rotol constant speed propeller types were the start of this combination
DB	Daimler Benz (sometimes also written Daimler-Benz)
DI	directional indicator
F700	Form 700, an aircraft's technical log, containing records such as servicing and maintenance, faults that have been rectified, flying hours and landings
FOD	foreign object damage
Fw	Focke-Wulf Flugzeugbau GmbH
GC	Groupe de Chasse (Free French)
GmbH	Gesellschaft mit beschränkter Haftung (roughly equivalent to a British limited company)
GP	general purpose (bomb)

GPS	Global Positioning System
GSAP	Guards Ground Attack Regiment (Soviet Union)
HE	high explosive (bomb)
HF	high frequency (radio)
hp	horse power
HSA	Hawker Siddeley Aviation
HRL	Hawker Restorations Ltd
IAP	Fighter Regiment (Soviet Union)
IFF	identification friend/foe
IFR	Instrument Flight Rules
Ltd	limited company (UK)
Me	abbreviation for Messerschmitt aircraft; generally the Bf109 series was one of the last from this manufacturer to use this abbreviation, the company changing its name from BFW to Messerschmitt and so subsequently using 'Me' for types such as the Me209 and Me410.
MSFU	Merchant Ship Fighter Unit
MU	Maintenance Unit (RAF)
NDT	non-destructive testing
OC	Officer Commanding
OTU	Operational Training Unit (RAF)
psi	pounds per square inch (measurement of pressure)
RAAF	Royal Australian Air Force
RAE	Royal Aircraft Establishment, Farnborough
RAF	Royal Air Force
RCAF	Royal Canadian Air Force
RNZAF	Royal New Zealand Air Force
RP	rocket projectile
rpg	rounds per gun
rpm	revolutions per minute
SAAF	South African Air Force
s/n	serial number
SOAP	spectromatic oil analysis programme
SSI	structurally significant item
SWG	standard wire gauge
SU	Skinners Union Company
TacR	tactical (armed) reconnaissance
Trim Tab	a small additional control surface on the trailing edge of an aileron, rudder or elevator that can be ground-adjusted or (on some aircraft) adjusted in the air, which aids in fine-tuning the trim and stability of an aircraft at different weights or intended flight regimes
UHF	ultra-high frequency (radio), in the wavelengths 225–400MHz, mainly for military aircraft communications
UK	United Kingdom
US	United States
VDM	Vereinigte Deutsche Metallwerke AG, propeller manufacturer
VFR	Visual Flight Rules
VHF	very high frequency (radio), in the wavelengths 118–136MHz
VVS SF	Air Force of the Northern Fleet (Soviet Union)

Imperial and Metric Equivalents of Weapons Calibres and Weights

Imperial	Metric
0.303in	7.7mm
0.312in	7.92mm
0.512in	13mm
0.59in	15mm
0.787in	20mm
1.181in	30mm
1.57in	40mm
110lb	50 kg
250lb	113kg
500lb	227kg
551lb	250kg
1,102lb	500kg
33gal	150 litres
40gal	182 litres
66gal	300 litres
88gal	400 litres
90gal	409 litres
94gal	427 litres

Airframe Assemblies
Hangar 6S
Isle of Wight Airport
Sandown
Isle of Wight
PO36 OJP
Tel: 01983 408661
www.airframes.co.uk
Produces replacement airframe and wing components.

Anglia Radiators
Unit 4
Stanley Road
Cambridge CB5 8LB
Tel: 01223 314444
www.angliaradiators.co.uk
Builds replacement radiators and oil coolers.

ARCo (The Aircraft Restoration Company)
Building 425
Duxford Airfield
Duxford
Cambridgeshire
CB22 4QR
Tel: 01223 835313
www.arc-duxford.co.uk
Carries out maintenance on historic aircraft.

Classic Aero Engineering
Hangar 7
Thruxton Airport
Andover
Hampshire
SP11 8PW
Tel: 01264 772137
Restores Hurricane aircraft.

BELOW Hurricanes fly above Lincolnshire fields on 14 May 2010. *(Mark Crosby)*

Dunlop Aircraft Tyres
40 Fort Parkway
Erdington
Birmingham
West Midlands
B24 9HL
Tel: 0121 384 8800
www.dunlopaircrafttyres.com
Specialist manufacturer and retreader of aircraft
tyres.

Hanley Smith
7 South Road
Templefields
Harlow
Essex
CM20 2AP
Tel: 01279 414446
www.hanleysmith.co.uk
Overhauls undercarriage legs.

Hawker Restorations Limited
Moat Farm
Church Road
Milden
Ipswich
Suffolk
IP7 7AF
Tel: 01449 740544
www.hawker-restorations-ltd.co.uk
Restorers of Hurricanes.

Hoffmann-Propeller GmbH & Co KG
Kuepferlingstr. 9
D-83022 Rosenheim
Germany
Tel: 49 8031 18780
www.hoffmann-prop.com
Manufacture of wooden propeller blades and
overhaul of propeller hubs.

Retro Track and Air
Upthorpe Iron Works
Upthorpe Lane
Cam
Dursley
Gloucestershire
GL11 5HP
Tel: 01453 545360
www.retrotrackandair.com
Overhauls engines.

Skycraft
12 Silver Street
Litlington
Royston
Hertfordshire
SG8 0QE
01763 852150
Builds and refurbishes propellers.

Supermarine Aero Engineering
Mitchell Works
Steventon Place
Burslem
Stoke-on-Trent
Staffordshire ST6 4AS
Tel: 01782 811344
www.supermarine.net
Machine components.

Vintage Fabrics
Mitchell Hangar
Audley End Airfield
Saffron Waldon
Essex CB11 4LH
Tel: 01799 510756
www.vintagefabrics.co.uk
Fabric for flying control surfaces, and aircraft
spraying and artwork.

ABOVE The BBMF's
Hurricane Mk IIc,
LF363. *(Richard Paver)*

Index

Acquiring a Hurricane 132
Advanced Air Striking Force
(AASF) 15
Aerodynamic research 53
Aero Vintage 82
A&AEE 65
Boscombe Down 43, 45, 65, 137
Martlesham Heath 11, 13, 33, 65
Agarici, Horia 58
Aircraft carriers
HMS *Argus* 25-26
HMS *Nairana* 29
Air Dispatch Letter Service
(ADLS) 30-31
Air Ministry 10, 12, 66, 127
Specification 9
F.5/34 10-11
F.7/30 9
F36/34 11
Allen, Paul 169
Antonov G-11 and A-7 52
Armament 39, 44, 52-53, 61, 66,
112
bombs and carriers 70, 167
camera gun 68
cannon 20, 25, 43, 49, 70
20mm 24, 44, 49-50, 69, 95,
112, 121
40mm 45, 61
Hispano 44, 112
Oerlikon 70
ShVAK 61
Vickers 44
eight-gun 22, 25, 42-43, 46, 69
machine guns 12, 17, 43-44,
65-69
Browning 0.303in (BSA) 25,
40, 58, 66-68, 70, 83, 94
112, 133
Colt 66
ShKAS 52, 61
Vickers 66
twelve-gun 17, 28, 64, 68-69,
112
under-wing stores 44-45, 70
unguided rockets (RPs) 45, 61,
68, 70
upwards firing rockets 53
Armstrong Whitworth
Whitley 153
Arrester hook 46, 49-50
Auster 84
Austin Motor Co, Longbridge 17,
38, 66
Avions Fairey 57
Avro Lancaster 77, 80

BAC Lightning 147
Bader, Sqn Ldr Douglas 63, 72
BAe Hawk 144
Balkan Air Force 57
Ball, Flg Off G. E. 72

Barrick, Sgt John Frederick
'Tex' 72
Battle of Athens 74
Battle of Britain 8, 14, 16-18,
22-23, 32, 41, 43, 56, 61, 63-64,
67, 71-72, 128, 132-133, 135-
136-138, 144
Battle of Britain Memorial Flight
(BBMF) 8, 33, 79-81, 84-85,
95-96, 115, 121-128, 132, 138,
143-146-147, 150, 160-161,
168-169
Battle of France 15, 22, 32, 37, 41,
67, 71, 137
Bedford, Bill 128
Belgian Air Force 58
Belousov, Lt Col V. I. 73
Black, Guy 82, 135, 169
Blackah MBE, Paul 8, 160, 168
Blackburn
Roc 53
Skua 25
Bristol Blenheim 18-19
Brooklands 9-11, 56
Brussels aviation exhibition 1939 14
Bulman, Flt Lt P.W.S. 'George' 11,
151-152

Camm, Sir Sydney 9-10, 15, 38,
74, 81
Campaigns and theatres 125
Balkans 21, 73
Burma 21, 37, 55, 73, 133
'Channel Dash' 18
'Channel Stop' 18
Egypt 24
Far East 21-22, 42, 46, 70
Finland 133
France 21, 133
Greece 73-74
India 21, 37, 133
Italy 22-23, 169
Malta 22-24, 41, 133
Mediterranean 21, 23, 63
Middle East 21-23, 42, 54,
56, 61
North Africa 21-24, 25, 28, 37,
41-42, 44, 54-55, 61, 70,
72-73, 133
Norway 15, 25, 53, 133
Pacific 22
Russia (Soviet Union) 21, 29,
42, 59, 70-71
Sicily 22
Singapore 21
South Africa 54, 133
Sumatra 21
Canadian Car & Foundry Co. Ltd
17, 46, 64
Captured aircraft 63
Carey, Frank Reginald 73
CASA Heinkel He111 32

Catapult Aircraft Merchantmen
(CAM ships) 26-27, 47-49
SS *Empire Franklin* 27, 47-48
Chino Warbirds Collection,
California 169
Churchill, Winston 144
Civilian Repair Organisation 38
Classic Aero Ltd, Thruxton 166
Cockpit 36, 51, 112-114, 134,
137-138, 140, 144, 149, 155,
161
canopy 10, 12, 113, 138, 147,
149, 160
'dog kennel'/'doghouse'
assembly 81, 84, 138
emergency door 113
footstep 113-114, 147
gunsight and gun button 134,
138, 141
instruments and controls 114,
136, 140-141, 144, 147, 149,
155
lighting 103
luggage compartment 114
seat 113, 138
teardrop canopy 51-52
windscreen 20, 112-113, 138,
155
Colour schemes/camouflage and
markings 63, 85, 122, 125, 127-
128, 135, 145, 166, 168
Consolidated Catalina 137
Control column 108, 110, 138
spade grip 108, 140-141, 149
Coolant system 97-98, 119, 144,
163
header tank 82, 159
pump 117
radiator 98, 119
radiator fairing 7, 92, 98
radiator housing 12, 48, 74
tropical air (dust) filters 21, 23,
41, 45, 60, 62, 77
Cordescu, Petre 58
Curtiss
Kittyhawk 23
Tomahawk 23

Dahl, Plt Off Roald 74
David Rosenfield Ltd, Barton
aerodrome 38
de Havilland
Chipmunk 84, 147
Mosquito 20
Tiger Moth 84
Denny, Clive 84, 132
Dewoitine D.520 28
Dimensions and weights 91
Display flying 8, 144-151
Ditheridge 81
Dodds, Sgt Hamish 72
Dornier Do17P 15

Douglas Havoc 20
Drawings 132, 140
Dunn, Plt Off William Robert 'Bill'
72
Duxford 84, 135, 169
Dyer, Tony 137
Air Defence Collection 137

Eastleigh 11
Egyptian Air Force
2 Squadron 55
Electrics 102-103
generator drive 117
Engine 115-119
camshaft 116
controls 118-119
cowlings 115
crankcase and crankshaft 115
cylinders 115-116
lifting 164
pistons 116
reduction gear 116-117
starting 103, 119, 156-157
supercharger 116, 118-119
vacuum pump and CSU 117
valves 116
wheel case assembly 117
Engines
Allison 25
Bristol Hercules 53
Daimler Benz 74, 137, 160;
DB 601 57, 128;
DB 601A 53
Hispano-Suiza 56
Napier Dagger 53
Packard Merlin 18, 44, 77;
XX (20) 64; 28 46, 65, 77;
29 46, 65, 77
Rolls-Royce 10, 18, 56, 65, 77,
132
Eagle 10
Griffon 53
Kestrel (F.XI) 10, 12, 74
Merlin (PV.12) 10-11, 32, 42,
52-53, 57, 74-76, 137, 159-
160; 'C' 11, 75; II 15, 18, 39,
57, 75, 151; III 16, 18, 56, 58,
75-76; XX (20) 18, 42, 66, 75,
77, 115, 128; 25 115, 128-
129; 27 45, 70, 75; 29 65;
32 46; 225 115; 500 115
Evans, Plt Off D. 138
Everett, Robert 27
Exhaust system 36, 40, 115,
117, 134
Export orders 54
Belgium 57-58
Egypt
Finland 61
France 61
India 55
Persia 50-51, 61-62

Poland 56
Portugal 63, 138
Romania 58-59
Russia (Soviet Union) 51-52, 59, 61, 65, 73, 133
South Africa 54
Turkey 55-56
Yugoslavia 56

Fabric covering 12-13, 39-40, 56, 66-67, 79, 82-85, 87, 90, 109, 128, 132, 151, 160
Fairey
  Battle 15
  Fulmar 25, 49
  Swordfish 18
Female workers 38
F. Hills & Sons Ltd 53
Fiat
  CR.42 21
  G.50 21
Fighter Catapult Ships 26-27, 48
  HMS *Maplin* 27
Fighter Collection, The 81
Fighter Factory, Virginia 169
Films
  Angels One Five 33, 122, 138
  Battle of Britain 32-33, 125, 127, 137, 166
  Reach for the Sky 63, 122
  Test Pilot 33
Finnish Air Force 59, 61
Fleet Air Arm 25, 28, 48
  759 Squadron 169
  762 Squadron 28, 46
  768 Squadron 25-26
  800 Squadron 28
  804 Squadron 28
  806 Squadron 25
  835 Squadron 29
  880 Squadron 169
  894 Squadron 28
Flying controls 91, 93, 108-111, 145, 149, 161, 163
Flying Heritage Collection, Washington State 81, 169
Focke-Wulf
  Fw190 21
  Fw200 Condor 27
Foster, Wing Commander Bob 135
František, Sgt Josef 16, 71
French naval aviation 61
Fuel system 95-97, 105, 128, 149, 155
  carburettors 23, 41-42, 117-118, 128
  contents gauge 103
  fuel 75
  long-range tanks 45
  priming pump 119
  pump 117
  tanks 31, 37, 40-42, 68, 75, 96-97
  underwing tanks 31, 70
Fuselage 52, 84-85, 90-93, 140
  centre section 82, 90, 112
  engine mounting 90-91
  forward 41
  framework 81-82, 85, 87, 90, 124, 133
  keel 21, 25, 40

length 66
rear 12-13, 25, 40, 92
tail bay 92

Gable, Clark 33
Gillan, Sqn Ldr J.W. 151, 154-155
Gleed, Flt Lt I.R. 'Widge' 71
Gloster Aircraft Co. 17, 40, 47
  Brockworth (Hucclecote) factory 17
Gloster
  Gauntlet 153, 155
  Gladiator 9, 23, 73-74, 153
Great Patriotic War 51
Grey, Stephen 84
Grumman
  Hellcat 29
  Martlet (Wildcat) 29

Handley Page Harrow 39
Handling 36, 41, 136, 152-155
Hanger 11 Collection, North Weald 169
Hawker Aircraft Ltd 8-9, 17, 31, 36, 38, 74, 122, 126-127, 151
  Brooklands factory 17
  Canbury Park Road factory, Kingston upon Thames 8-9, 12, 17, 64, 169
  Dunsfold 127
  Langley factory 17, 37, 38, 50, 63, 74, 125
Hawker
  Demon 153, 155
  Fury (Hornet) 9-10, 12, 38, 56, 74, 87; Fury II 12
  Fury (Interceptor) Monoplane 11
  Hart 9, 127
  Henley 11
  Hunter 38, 123, 136
Hurricanes
  Mk I 13-18, 21-22, 24, 26, 30, 38-39-43, 46, 49, 56-57, 61, 63-64, 66-67, 71, 75-77, 112, 131-135, 141, 153, 155, 167, 169
  Mk Ib 60
  Mk II 17-18, 20, 24, 42, 44, 55, 58, 61, 70, 141
  Mk IIa 19, 22, 24, 30, 42, 49, 61, 69
  Mk IIb 17, 43, 49, 53, 57, 59-60, 70, 112, 122, 167, 169
  Mk IIc 8, 17, 19-20, 22, 24, 28, 31, 35, 37, 42-45, 51, 56, 61-63, 66, 69-70, 115, 122, 125, 166, 169
  Mk IId 23, 44-45, 70-71
  Mk IIe 43-44
  Mk III 44, 70
  Mk IV 29, 44-46, 61, 70, 75, 122, 169
  Mk V 29, 45-46
  Mk X 18, 30, 46, 64-65
  Mk XI 54, 65
  Mk XIb 52
  Mk XII 31, 64-65, 84, 135, 143, 169
  Mk XIIa 46, 65, 169
  PR Mk II 24
  biplane ('slip-wing') 53

floatplane conversion 53
'Hurribomber' 21, 23, 43-44, 70, 169
prototypes 7, 10-13, 33, 36, 42, 46, 48, 75-76
three-seat non-flying 52
Tropical (Trop) 41, 55-56, 62
two-seat 50-52, 61-62
Nimrod 9
Sea Fury 38, 127
Sea Hurricane 25, 27-29, 37, 39, 46-47, 65, 138
'Hurricat' 26-27, 48, 59
Mk Ia 47-48
Mk Ib 25-26, 28, 46, 48-49, 169
Mk Ic 49
Mk IIc 29, 50
Mk X 169
Mk XII 169
Mk XIIa 50
Mk XIIb 28
Tempest 51
Typhoon 31, 38, 46, 53
P.1127/Kestrel/Harrier 126-127
Hawker Restorations Ltd 80, 133
Hawker Siddeley Group 17, 128
Heated pressure head 103
Heinkel (see also CASA)
  He111 16
  He115 15
H.G. Hawker Engineering Ltd 8-9
Hillson
  F.H. 40 53
  Praga 53
Hispano HA-1112-MIL Buchón 32
Historic Aircraft Collection, Duxford 135, 169
Historic Flying Ltd 124-125
Hydraulic system 77, 104-105, 140, 147

Ignition system 118
IAR 80 59
IFF system 103
Ilyushin Il-2 'Shturmovik' 61
Indian Air Force 55
  1 Squadron 55
  2 Squadron 55
  4 Squadron 55
  6 Squadron 55
Insurance 132
Irish Air Corps
  1 Squadron 61
Italian Air Force 63
IWM 138

Japanese Air Force
  64th Sentai 63
Junkers
  Ju87 'Stuka' 16
  Ju88 16
  Ju290 29

Kain, Flg Off Edgar James 'Cobber' 71
King Peter II of Yugoslavia 57
King's Cup Air Race 1950 127
Kuttelwascher, Flt Lt Karel 21, 122, 145
Kuznetsov, Maj Gen A.A. 60

Landing 20, 136, 150-153
Landing/identification/navigation lights and switches 7, 102-103, 118-119, 147
Lone Star Flight Museum, Texas 169
Lubricants 161
Luftwaffe 15, 18-19, 32-33, 37, 39, 59, 73

Mahaddie, Gp Capt Hamish 32
Mainplane (wings) 67-68, 94-95, 124, 133
  all-metal/metal-covered 12, 40, 44, 56, 67-68, 83
  centre section 94
  gun-bay 13, 40, 55, 83, 96
  laminar-flow wing 53
  outer wing 12-13, 37, 40, 44, 56, 83, 94-95, 103
  universal wing 29, 45, 68
  wing ribs 83
Maker's plate 138
Malta Convoy 'Pedestal' 29
Margaret, HRH Princess 127
McKnight, Plt Off W.L. 72
Merchant Ship Fighter Unit (MSFU) 27
Messerschmitt
  Bf109 16, 36-37, 59, 74, 76, 87, 133, 141
  Bf109E 16, 21, 25, 41, 53, 59, 71, 128, 138
  Bf109F 21
  Bf109G 32, 160
  Bf110 41, 74
Metropolitan Communications Squadron 58, 166
Miles
  Magister 57
  Master 50
Mitchell, R. J. 10
Morane Saulnier MS.406 37
Mould, Plt Off P.W.O. 'Boy' 15
Munich Crisis 64
Musée Royal de l'Armée et d'Histoire Militaire, Brussels 166

Nakajima Ki-43 'Oscar' 55
Newark Air Museum 141
New Zealand Fighter Pilots' Museum 169
Nicholson VC, James 16
Non-destructive testing (NDT) 162, 165
North American
  Harvard 133
  B-25 Mitchell 32
  P-51 Mustang 31, 77
    Allison-engined 25, 122
    Merlin-engined 18, 122
North Moreton Airfield 169

Oil system 98-100, 115, 161
Operation 'Barbarossa', Russia 58
Operation 'Dynamo', Dunkirk 15
Operation 'Torch', North Africa 28-29

Operations
    air ambulance 52
    anti-tank 61, 70
    artillery spotting 52, 122
    bomber escort 18
    chase plane 126-127
    convoy protection 27, 29, 59
    'Circus' missions 18
    fast communications/liaison 31,
        58, 62, 127, 166
    fighter-bomber 29, 55, 65, 70
    glider tugs 52
    ground-attack 17-18, 20-21, 24,
        29, 31, 45-46, 53, 61, 68, 70
    ground instructional
        airframes 40, 58
    'hack' transport 23, 127
    intruder air-to-ground 17, 68
    'Kipper' patrol fisheries
        protection 18
    meteorological flying 31
    night fighting 19-20, 24, 31, 61
    night intruder 18, 20-21
    racing 127, 168
    radar calibration 31
    'Ramrod' missions 18
    reconnaissance 21, 24, 31, 52,
        55, 61, 122
    'Rhubarbs' 18
    'Roadstead' anti-shipping 18
    'Rodeo' attacks 18
    ship-borne fighter 25-27, 47-48,
        59
    tactical reconnaissance
        (TacR) 25, 70
    training 25-26, 29, 31, 41,
        51, 62
Orde, Cuthbert 71

Panavia Tornado 147
Pattle, Sqn Ldr Marmaduke
    Thomas St John 73-74
Personal Plane Services,
    Booker 137
Phoney War 15, 37, 41, 71
Pilot's Notes 45, 66
Pinner, Sqn Ldr Al 134
Pneumatics 105-106
Polikarpov I-16 58
Pomut, Constantin 58
Production 17
    figure 37-38
    licence 39, 54
        Austin 17, 38
        Gloster 40
    overseas
        Belgium 15, 17, 39, 54, 57-58,
            71
        Canada 17-18, 26, 28, 30-31,
            37, 41, 44, 46-50, 52, 54,
            61, 63-65, 77, 85, 135, 143,
            169
        Yugoslavia 15, 17, 39, 54, 56-57
Propellers 16, 66, 75, 100-102,
    132, 160
    control 118
    de Havilland three-bladed
        metal 40, 76
    four-bladed 46
    Hamilton Standard 54, 64-65,
        76-77

Hoffmann 132
Hydulignum wood 102
Jabo wood blades 40, 67, 77,
    102
Rotol three-bladed, variable
    pitch 14, 40, 58, 76-77, 100
Sitka spruce or Douglas fir
    blades 102
Watts two-bladed wooden 14, 36,
    39-40, 57-58, 75-76, 151, 154

RAAF
    3 Squadron 54
Radar 20
Radio equipment 40-41, 48, 103,
    149
    mast 7, 10, 40
RAF bases
    Acklington 14
    Aston Down 31
    Biggin Hill 125
    Charmy Down 35
    Colerne 70
    Coltishall 70, 128
    Coningsby 33, 80, 121, 125, 169
    Croydon 133
    Digby 31
    Drem 122
    Duxford 32
    El Adem, Libya 21
    Hal Far, Malta 22
    Hendon 58, 166
    Hullavington 41
    Maison Blanche, Algeria 28
    Middle Wallop 122
    North Coates 15
    Northolt 14-15, 19, 30, 39, 71,
        76, 151-153, 155
    North Weald 41, 72, 169
    Odiham 122
    Ouston 122
    Speke 27
    Tangmere 9, 43, 66, 68
    Waterbeach 122
    Wittering 125
    Wyton 31
RAF Coastal Command 27, 69
RAF Desert Air Force 23
RAF Empire Central Flying
    School 41
RAF Fighter Command 15-16, 18
RAF Historic Aircraft Flight 125, 128
RAF squadrons and units
    1 Squadron 15, 21
    3 Squadron 24, 70
    6 Squadron 31, 70, 169
    17 Squadron 72
    26 Squadron 31, 122
    33 Squadron 73
    41 Squadron 144
    43 Squadron 9, 20, 28
    46 Squadron 15
    56 Squadron 41, 123
    63 Squadron 122
    71 (Eagle) Squadron 18, 72
    73 Squadron 15, 21, 71
    80 Squadron 73
    81 Squadron 59
    87 Squadron 19, 35, 69
    94 Squadron 22
    111 Squadron 14-15, 19, 39,

151-155
    134 Squadron 59-60
    164 Squadron 70
    214 Squadron 39
    229 Squadron 24
    242 Squadron 72
    249 Squadron 16, 18
    257 Squadron 18, 70, 72
    260 Squadron 22
    261 Squadron 23
    267 Squadron 73
    274 Squadron 72
    303 (Polish) Squadron 16, 71
    309 (Polish) Squadron 31, 122,
        165
    351 (Yugoslav) Squadron 57
    352 (Yugoslav) Squadron 57
    402 (Canadian) Squadron 43
    450 (Australian) Squadron 54
    451 (Australian) Squadron 54
    486 (New Zealand) Squadron 54
    488 (New Zealand) Squadron 54
    527 Squadron 31
    601 Squadron 17, 66, 68
    605 Squadron 133, 169
    607 (County of Durham)
        Squadron 138
    1688 Bomber Defence Training
        Flight 31
    5 MU 122
    5 OTU 31
    55 OTU 30
    61 OTU 122
    71 OTU 57
    151 Wing 59-61
RCAF 65
    1 Squadron 64
Records (forms, logbooks etc) 127,
    165
Republic P-47 Thunderbolt 72
Retro Track and Air 132
Romanian Air Force
    Escadrila 53 58
Rowley, Sqn Ldr Clive 147
Royal Aircraft Establishment
    Farnborough 53
Royal Navy – see Fleet Air Arm
Running costs 132
Russell Aviation Group,
    Ontario 169

Safety 160-161
SBAC display, Hatfield
    1937 36
Schneider Trophy races 10, 74
SEPECAT Jaguar 144
Servicing 161-165
Shuttleworth Collection 138, 169
Skycraft Ltd 132
Smallwood, Sqn Ldr Dennis G.
    19, 35
Sopwith Aviation Co. 8
    Camel 8-9
    Pup 9
    Triplane 9
Sopwith, Thomas 9, 17, 81
South African Air Force (SAAF)
    24, 54
Soviet Air Force 60-61, 169
    17 GSAP 73
    760 IAP 61

Spare parts 132
Specialised services 132
Specifications 66
    Hurricane Mk I 65; Mk IIc 65
    Rolls-Royce Merlin 25
        engine 129
Static restoration project 137-141

Tail unit 10, 93
    fin 82, 84, 93
    leg 107
    rudder 21, 108-111, 141
    tailplane 82, 84, 93
Take-off 148, 152
Taxiing 148, 151-152
Teichman, Peter 167, 169
Tools and working facilities 161
Townsend, Gp Capt
    Peter 127
Tuck, Sqn Ldr Robert Roland
    Stanford 70, 72
Tupolev SB 58, 60
Turbinlite experiment 20, 31

Undercarriage 20, 25-26, 36-37,
    82, 106-107, 133, 150
    brakes 107-108, 141, 148
    indicator lights 103
    main wheel 107
    main wheel covers 10
    retraction mechanism 37,
        104-107
    skis 54
    tailwheel 137, 150
    tyres 36, 91, 107
        Dunlop 132
US Army Air Force 62
    Bovingdon air base 63
    Eighth Army Air Force 62-63
    Twelfth Army Air Force 63
    4th Fighter Group 18
    406th Fighter Group 72
USAF Museum, Dayton 85

Vacher, Peter 80, 100, 131-133,
    169
Verma, Flg Off J.C. 55
Vichy French air force 28
Vickers Wellington 14
Vickers Supermarine 9-11
    Seafire 25, 28-29
    Spitfire 8, 10, 14-17, 20, 23,
        25, 31-32, 36-37, 39, 41, 51,
        53, 67, 72, 74, 80, 87, 123,
        128, 131, 133, 135, 144-145,
        160
Victoria Cross 16
Vintage Fabrics 84, 132
Vintage Wings of Canada
    Collection 169
Vought Corsair 29

War in the Air, The, television
    series 125
Westland
    Lysander 57
    Whirlwind 138
Wings – see Mainplane
Winter War 61

Yugoslav Air Force 57